Eros and Economy

Eros and Economy: Jung, Deleuze, sexual difference explores the possibility that social relations between things, partially inscribed in their aesthetics, offer important insights into collective political-economic relations of domination and desire. Drawing on the analytical psychology of Carl Jung and the philosophy of Gilles Deleuze, this book focuses on the idea that desire or libido, overlaid by sexual difference, is a driving force behind the material manifestations of cultural production in practices as diverse as art or economy. Re-reading the history of capitalism and aesthetics with an awareness of the forces of sexual difference reveals not just their integral role in the development of capitalist markets, but a new understanding of our political-economic relations as humans.

The appearance of the energies of sexual difference is highlighted in a number of different historical periods and political economies, from the Rococo period of pre-revolutionary France, to the aesthetics and economics of Keynesian Bloomsbury, to our contemporary Postmodern sensibility. With these examples, Jenkins demonstrates that the very constitution of capitalist markets is affected by the interaction of these forces; and she argues that a conscious appreciation and negotiation of them is integral to an immanent, democratic understanding of power.

With its unique application of Jungian theory, this book provides important new insights into debates surrounding art, aesthetics, and identity politics, as well as into the quest for autonomous, democratic institutions of politics and economics. As such, this book will appeal to researchers, academics, and postgraduate students in the fields of Jung, psychoanalysis, political economy, cultural studies, and gender studies, as well as those interested in the field of cultural economy.

Barbara Jenkins is Associate Professor at Wilfrid Laurier University, Canada. She teaches in the areas of political economy of communication and culture, visual culture, and the political economy of art and architecture. Her research interests include political economy, visual culture, cultural policy, and psychoanalytic theory. She is the author of *The Paradox of Continental Production*.

Research in Analytical Psychology and Jungian Studies Series

Series Advisor: Andrew Samuels, Professor of Analytical Psychology, Essex University, UK.

The *Research in Analytical Psychology and Jungian Studies* series features research-focused volumes involving qualitative and quantitative research, historical/archival research, theoretical developments, heuristic research, grounded theory, narrative approaches, collaborative research, practitioner-led research, and self-study. The series also includes focused works by clinical practitioners, and provides new research-informed explorations of the work of C. G. Jung that will appeal to researchers, academics, and scholars alike.

Books in this series:

Jung and Levinas
An ethics of mediation
Frances Gray

Symptom, Symbol, and the Other of Language
A Jungian interpretation of the linguistic turn
Bret Alderman

Post-Jungian Psychology and the Short Stories of Ray Bradbury and Kurt Vonnegut
Golden apples of the monkey house
Steve Gronert Ellerhoff

Eros and Economy
Jung, Deleuze, sexual difference
Barbara Jenkins

Towards a Jungian Theory of the Ego
Karen Evers-Fahey

Eros and Economy

Jung, Deleuze, sexual difference

Barbara Jenkins

LONDON AND NEW YORK

First published 2017
by Routledge
2 Park Square, Milton Park, Abingdon, Oxon OX14 4RN

and by Routledge
711 Third Avenue, New York, NY 10017

*Routledge is an imprint of the Taylor & Francis Group,
an informa business*

© 2017 Barbara Jenkins

The right of Barbara Jenkins to be identified as author of this work has been asserted by her in accordance with sections 77 and 78 of the Copyright, Designs and Patents Act 1988.

All rights reserved. No part of this book may be reprinted or reproduced or utilised in any form or by any electronic, mechanical, or other means, now known or hereafter invented, including photocopying and recording, or in any information storage or retrieval system, without permission in writing from the publishers.

Trademark notice: Product or corporate names may be trademarks or registered trademarks, and are used only for identification and explanation without intent to infringe.

British Library Cataloguing in Publication Data
A catalogue record for this book is available from the British Library

Library of Congress Cataloging-in-Publication Data
Names: Jenkins, Barbara, 1959– author.
Title: Eros and economy : Jung, Deleuze, sexual difference / Barbara Jenkins.
Description: 1 Edition. | New York : Routledge, 2016. | Includes bibliographical references and index.
Identifiers: LCCN 2016002259 (print) | LCCN 2016015858 (ebook) |
    ISBN 9781138929838 (hardback) | ISBN 9781315680910 (ebk) |
    ISBN 9781315680910 (ebook)
Subjects: LCSH: Jungian psychology. | Psychology—Social aspects.
Classification: LCC BF173.J85 J46 2016 (print) | LCC BF173.J85 (ebook) |
    DDC 302—dc23
LC record available at https://lccn.loc.gov/2016002259

ISBN: 978-1-138-92983-8 (hbk)
ISBN: 978-1-315-68091-0 (ebk)

Typeset in Sabon
by Apex CoVantage, LLC

For my mother

Contents

List of figures	viii
Acknowledgements	ix

PART I
Theory   I

1	Toward a political economy of the unconscious	3
2	The compensatory unconscious	24
3	Venus ♀: toward a biopolitics of the unconscious	69
4	Containment/transformation: *Eros* as interval	97

PART II
Genealogies   129

5	Channelling the feminine: Rococo	131
6	Erotic economics	160
7	Life in the rhizome	182
8	Finding Ariadne	203

Index	213

Figures

1.1	Leon Bakst Costume Sketch from the ballet *Narcissus*, 1911	11
2.1	The Hermetic Androgyne, late 17th century miniature from a German manuscript	36
3.1	Diego Velázquez, *The Toilet of Venus* ('The Rokeby Venus'), 1647–51, National Gallery, London	70
4.1	Leonardo da Vinci, *St. Anne, the Virgin Mary, and the Christ Child*, 1452–1519, Musée de Louvre, Paris	122
5.1	Jean Honoré Fragonard, *The Swing*, 1767	139
5.2	Dragon detail from a chest of drawers designed by Antoine-Robert Gaudreaus, 1739	141
5.3	François Boucher, *Madame de Pompadour*, 1759	144
5.4	Jacques Louis David, *The Oath of the Horatii*, 1789, Musée du Louvre, Paris	147
5.5	*Encyclopedie du Siècle: L'Exposition de Paris*, 1900	154

Acknowledgements

I am lucky to work in a dynamic department of communication studies with especially generous colleagues who have contributed extensively to this project. I am particularly grateful to Paul Heyer and Greig de Peuter, who read and commented on all, or significant proportions of, this book. Thanks also to members of the department research group who also provided important insights (especially Alex Boutros, Jeremy Hunsinger, Anne-Marie Kinahan, Jade Miller, Judith Nicholson, Ian Roderick, and Ghislain Thibault) and to Jonathan Finn for being such a fantastic department chair. Wilfrid Laurier University has also been supportive of this study, which largely was completed during a one-semester sabbatical. I would also like to thank several anonymous reviewers who made invaluable suggestions at the formative stages of this book, as well as many commentators who brought valuable insights during conference presentations. Finally, I express my gratitude to the team at Routledge who so efficiently guided this book from review to publication, especially series editor Andrew Samuels and Clare Ashworth, Emily Bedford, Kate Fornadel, Heidi Lee, and Thomas Storr.

Many graduate students, friends, and family members had an important influence on my thinking for this book, mostly in their tolerance for a project that seemed a little 'out there' to them. Special thanks go to Patricia Goff, Art and Natalie Green, Judith Harris (for her encyclopaedic knowledge of Jung), Ken and Carmen Jenkins, Dave and Sharon Jenkins, Carla Johnston, Cynthia Venables, Nancy McDonald, Jill and Dennis McKeown, Diane Sewell, and Steve Weed. To my daughter Maya – special recognition for filling our house with joyous music and making the sometimes arduous task of writing so much more pleasant.

Parts of Chapters 6 and 7 were previously published as 'Erotic Economics' in the *Journal of Cultural Economy*, vol. 6, no. 2, 2013.

Part I

Theory

Chapter 1

Toward a political economy of the unconscious

According to Zizek, it was Marx who identified the first social 'symptom'. His concept of commodity fetishism, or the displacement of social relations between people onto social relations between things, constituted the first hysterical symptom of capitalism. The commodity, Marx claimed, is actually 'a very queer thing, abounding in metaphysical subtleties and theological niceties' (Marx 1949, p. 41). When someone makes something for her or his own use, the labour involved in its manufacture is clear. But when it becomes integrated into a system of mass production and consumption, the link to the labourer who made the commodity is severed, along with the knowledge of the social relationships inherent to it. The (exploited) labour that manufactured the commodity becomes obscured, and what is really a relation of trade between people becomes 'the fantastic form of a relation between things' (p. 43). Unlike feudal subjects, where relations between people are mystified by concepts such as the divine right of kings and religious belief, the supposedly emancipated citizens of capitalism let things or commodities 'believe' for them. '[I]t is as if all their beliefs, superstitions and metaphysical mystifications . . . are embodied in the "social relations between things"' (Zizek 1989, p. 31).

The central premise of this book is that social relations between things, partially inscribed in their aesthetics, offer important insights into collective political-economic relations of domination and desire. This point, of course, is not new. The political and economic relevance of aesthetics has been emphasized in the work of Adorno and Horkheimer (2002), Baudrillard (2004), Benjamin (2007), Bourdieu (1984), Harvey (1990), Jameson (1995), and Rancière (2004) among others. The novelty of my claim is that these aesthetics reveal not just the mystifications inherent to class relations, but also the 'hysterical' repression of relations of sexual difference. Re-reading the history of capitalism and aesthetics with an awareness of the forces of sexual difference reveals not just their integral role in the development of capitalist markets, but a new understanding of our political-economic relations as humans.

Understanding this relation requires an act of imagination, a willingness to see things differently. For unlike the exploitive relations between capital and labour Marx describes, the forces of sexual difference I will be discussing are unconscious. To be sure, these forces have material consequences and are intimately involved with the touchable matter of bodies and manufactured goods. By and large, however, they are unseen forces of the psyche that travel across and through not just bodies but material objects. My hope and contention is that once revealed, these previously mystified relations of sexual difference will help us understand some of the dis-ease or discontent we citizens of global capitalism currently endure. For if we can go so far as to imagine this possibility, then perhaps we can move onto the question they imply: what happens if we become conscious of them? Because in practice, this repression is rather one sided, with the feminine aspects of sexual difference far more blocked or occluded than masculine ones. For this reason, my focus here will be on evoking what these feminine energies might reveal.

One of the first of many steps necessary to a more democratic future is the recognition of the immanent power of the subject (Deleuze and Guattari 1983 & 1987; Hardt and Negri 2000, 2005 & 2009; Purcell 2013). But when the very notion of what it *feels* like to be a politically included subject is denied to a majority of the population (de Beauvoir 1974; Irigaray 1985), her ability to speak or be recognized in the realm of the 'sensible' diminished (Rancière 2004), the democratic process is radically imperfect. Psychoanalytic theory has done little to address this situation, effectively defining woman in terms of the status quo – either as 'lack' relative to the regulatory signifier of the Phallus (à la Lacan), or reducing her subjectivity to the phenomenon of penis envy (as in Freud).

A first step forward to addressing this 'lack' of feminine subjectivity is to approach the study of the unconscious in a way that provides for positive forces or energies of sexual difference, specifically, transpersonal, libidinal forces bearing the energies of sexual difference. These forces become manifest in the realm of representation in multiple practices of sexuality, identity, language, aesthetic expression, and, last but not least, political economy. My Jungian approach also insists, however, that the energies of the feminine are key to an understanding of the subjectivities of all persons, not just those who identify as women. Indeed, most of the stories I will tell involve men 'channelling' these feminine energies, and explicitly recognizing that they are doing so. This contra-sexual negotiation of identity will be central to the overall argument I make here.

Explaining these energies of sexual difference involves going beyond the politics of representation to focus on forces, whether we consider them ontological, pre-ontological, or *a priori*, that drive our desire. In this respect, my account relies heavily on the ideas of Deleuze, especially his work with Guattari, which describe forces of libidinal energy flowing across and through molecular bodies. The crux of my argument, however, lies in the contention that this libidinal energy is overlaid with the forces of sexual difference. Here the work of Jung and his concepts of the archetypal masculine as *Logos/Sol* and the archetypal feminine as *Eros/Luna* become central to my imagination of these libidinal flows. I argue that adding the perspective of *Eros* or love to understandings of economy and democracy strengthens and broadens classical liberal portrayals of democracy and economics as primarily rational, contractual arrangements. As Negri (2013, p. 98) notes in a remark that I will develop in Chapter 3, 'Democracy is an act of love'.

I invoke Jung because the notion of a transpersonal, recurring energy based on sexual difference bears affinities to his notion of the archetypal masculine and feminine, but Jung's work should also be considered in the context of other vitalist (Lash 2006) analyses. It is curious that the progenitor of the 'collective unconscious' has not figured prominently in the contemporary revival of a fascination with transpersonal flows of energy that appear to affect 'both one and many' (Blackman 2008, p. 24), but as Pint points out, the fact that almost everyone in the social sciences has forgotten about Jung can be an advantage (Pint 2011, p. 48). Unlike Freud or Lacan, the application of Jung's ideas is relatively unmapped territory in cultural studies and political economy, providing a fresh perspective on well-worn debates over foundationalism, essentialism, and sexual difference. A nascent 'Jungian turn' in Deleuzean and cultural studies (Hauke 2000; Kazarian 2010; Kerslake 2007; Pint 2011) suggests it may be time for a Jungian complement to the views of those similarly concerned with transpersonal connections, usually based on the ideas of thinkers such as James, Whitehead, or Tarde (Blackman 2007 & 2008; Connolly 2011; Despret 2004; Stengers 2011). My focus will be on tracing what Zizek claims is a direct lineage from Jung to Deleuze (Zizek 2004, p. 663).

There is no denying that Jung uses his conception of the archetypal feminine and masculine in a highly sexist way at times. Like any male philosopher prior to the Postmodern period, his work bears the marks of blindness to his own patriarchal privilege. Frankly, this is the least of the things he has been accused of. As Shamdasani (2003, p. 1) notes, Jung has simultaneously been regarded as 'Occultist, Scientist, Prophet, Charlatan, Philosopher, Racist, Guru, Anti-Semite, Liberator of Women, Misogynist, Freudian Apostate, Gnostic, Post-Modernist, Polygamist, Healer, Poet, Con-Artist, Psychiatrist and Anti-Psychiatrist'. At the risk of adding yet another label to this list, I would argue that Jung might also be considered what Connolly (2011) calls a 'connectionist': 'someone who presents a world in the making in an evolving universe that is open to an uncertain degree' (p. 35).

6 Theory

From this perspective, I view Jung's work less from a psychological perspective and more in terms of its contributions to philosophy. As Bergson once noted, 'I have great respect for the work of Jung, which isn't only interesting for the psychologist and psychopathologist, but also for the philosopher! It is here that psychoanalysis has found its philosophy' (quoted in Shamdasani 2003, p. 107).

On the surface, Jung's ideas on sexual difference constitute precisely the kind of discourse that feminists aim to deconstruct: a man telling women what the feminine is, often in ways that map the characteristics of his own projections of the 'feminine' onto the bodies of women. Yet Jung's work also focuses on transformation. His insistence on the process of individuation as a 'coming-to-be' of the self resonates with the emphasis in Nietzsche, Bergson, Deleuze, or Grosz on 'becoming', or the self as event. More importantly, Jung and Jungians have undertaken a genealogical and archaeological analysis of the symbolic feminine that is one of the most systematic and inventive archives in existence.

Jung acknowledged the deleterious effects of the repression of the symbolic feminine long before French feminism did; his work is permeated with an unrelenting appreciation of and advocacy for the integration of the divine feminine, not just in analytical psychology but in the everyday life of the spiritual, social, and political. In his view, this was not a feminist mission, but necessary for the psychic health of society as a whole. Despite his extreme ambivalence toward organized religion, he considered Pius XII's proclamation of the dogma of the Assumption of the Virgin Mary on November 1, 1950 to be one of the most important religious developments for 400 years (Jung 1973a, p. 567) in its acknowledgment of a least some role for the feminine in the divine symbolic. His colleague Erich Neumann similarly decried the predominance of a one-sided patriarchal consciousness. 'This modern consciousness', he maintained, 'is threatening the existence of Western mankind, for the one-sidedness of masculine development has led to a hypertrophy of consciousness at the expense of the whole man [*sic*]' (Neumann 1974, p. 57).

Looking at political-economic relations in this manner involves different conceptions of ideology, philosophy, and art. Returning to Zizek (1989, p. 30), I agree with his Lacanian influenced definition of ideology not as a Marxist false consciousness or illusion, but as an unconscious fantasy that structures social reality. From this perspective, ideology and the philosophies that accompany it are, in part, 'already staged' by our unconscious desires. From Zizek's Lacanian perspective, such desires must remain unknown – both philosophy and ideology are defined by their blindness to desire – the unnameable 'kernel of enjoyment' or *jouissance* whose lack or void the social symptom of ideology rotates around.

It is here that I part company with Zizek's Lacanian approach. His argument that unconscious desires must remain unknowable is belied by the revelation of unconscious forces that become especially apparent in artistic and economic production and discourse. Persistent references to the sexualized nature of aesthetic and economic production are not just 'symptoms' played out in the realm of signification, but the manifestation of libidinal energies that express themselves in terms we recognize as sexual difference. Recognizing them is key not only to an understanding of individual subjectivity, but a collective consciousness of the extent to which the forces of sexual difference both inhere to, and interfere with, the immanent sources of political power.

Understanding aesthetics and economy this way means going into the unconscious and engaging with 'unknowable' forces, something that Lacan expressly warned against and which, Zizek (2004, p. 661) laments, both Jung and Deleuze insisted upon. This, as Jung and Deleuze and Guattari knew, is a dangerous undertaking. Psychologically, it risks the radical 'destratification' of identity, a potentially explosive enterprise. On a theoretical level, it means wading into the equally volatile debates surrounding essentialism, foundationalism, and social constructionism. One of the thorniest issues a contra-sexual exploration of identity raises is how a feminine energy can be applied to all persons, yet still remain politically relevant to the collectivity of singularities we call women.

My approach to this issue involves some delicate perceptual manoeuvres that in many ways defy typical practices of knowledge and understanding. I view feminine energies as being associated with, but not equivalent to, the bodies of women. Understanding the feminine this way involves thinking of it in terms that Jung and Deleuze considered to be symbolic. Jung, for example, considered the psychic energy he called the archetypal feminine to be an unknowable or unrepresentable thing that could only be understood through projection. The images he associated with his concept of *anima* might present themselves in the figure of a woman because that image comes closest to explaining what they mean. This does not mean that such energies are the *same thing* as woman. In his words, 'When projected, the anima always has a feminine form with definite characteristics. This empirical finding does not mean that the archetype is constituted like that *in itself*' (Jung 1980, pp. 69–70).

In contrast to Freud, who focused on the unconscious repression of energies, Jung viewed the images that appear in dreams, reveries, and fantasies as attempts by the unconscious to express something 'as best it can' (Jung 1973b, pp. 161–2). To do so, the unconscious draws from the assortment of images and signifiers frequently used to communicate in the realm of representation, including cultural manifestations such as language and art.

These words and images only approximate what the unconscious is trying to communicate; they are not coterminous with it. This, in part, explains how Jung could argue that all human psyches possessed both a masculine and feminine aspect. Feminine energies are somehow *related to*, but not the *same as*, the singularities we refer to as women.

Nonetheless, Jung did argue that these feminine energies had a specific content to them. He referred to the archetypal feminine as *Eros* or *Luna*, and the archetypal masculine as *Logos* or *Sol*. Despite his own admonitions not to apply these concepts literally, Jung frequently used them in an essentializing, stereotypical way that is not in alignment with contemporary understandings of sexual difference. In spite of this, I argue that his conceptualization of these energies is still valid – it is his essentialist application of these terms to the human body that is objectionable. The importance of negotiating the complex relationship between sexual difference and the body becomes particularly clear when examining Deleuze and Guattari's conception of *anima*: becoming-woman, a molecular energy that is key to transformation and becoming for both men and women. This molecular conception of the transformative energies of becoming-woman will be central to my understanding of the functioning of feminine energies throughout the book. In contrast to Jung's issues with essentialism, however, it is precisely their attempt to withdraw this feminine energy from the bodies of women that creates problems. If becoming-woman is not the same as woman, then what relevance does she have for women?

My solution to this conundrum, I believe, is already inherent to the theories of both Jung and Deleuze. For Jung, it means taking seriously his idea that the archetypal energies of sexual difference are related to, but not the same as, the bodies they inhabit; for Deleuze, it means de-emphasizing the molecular nature of this energy to focus on its more embodied forms. Both of these moves are compatible with the revolutionary ideas of these two thinkers, and also help to make them more relevant to contemporary political, cultural, and economic realities. What this effectively involves is pulling the association of the archetypal feminine away from the bodies of women into a psychic-material space that Jung described as the subtle body, and Deleuze and Guattari called the *intermezzo*. This in-between space, comprising both body and mind, is a transformative place of imagination and becoming where the symbolic meaning of archetypal energies (for Jung) or virtual Ideas (for Deleuze) become transformed phenomenologically into embodied practice.

For this practice to be meaningful, I argue, it is important to 'imagine' what the energies of the feminine look and feel like. In this respect, I accept Jung's association of the feminine with *Eros/Luna*, but add to this a less emphasized aspect of his understanding of *anima* as butterfly or surface. To avoid stereotypical politics, however, it is also important to emphasize the transferability of these energies. This transferability applies not just to the human psyche, but to things. Indeed, it is the manifestation of such energies in designed objects and art that appears to be so transformative in political terms. If one can hold this delicate manoeuvre and understand these energies as somehow connected to women since they manifest themselves in her image, while still acknowledging their transferability, the political consequences can be transformative. Indeed, I will argue that this link explains why time periods where aesthetics that are considered to be 'feminine' are embraced and appreciated have yielded some of the most important advances in democracy for women. In Part Two of this book, I examine examples of four such aesthetics: the Rococo, *Art Nouveau*, the Bloomsbury aesthetic, and the art and architecture of our contemporary Postmodern period. In Chapter 6, I will further implicate feminine energies in the development of capitalist markets.

These examples highlight another key point: when we take conceptions of what are generally considered purely sexual energies and pull them away from the body, their political implications become even more evident. This practice, inherent to Jung's conception of libido and Deleuze's understanding of desire, means rejecting the Freudian understanding of desire as purely sexual. If we can similarly pull this understanding of libido/desire away from the bodies of humans and into the *intermezzo* of the subtle body, the highly political implications of the energies of sexual difference become apparent.

I argue that all of the time periods I examine are marked by such a politics of the subtle body/*intermezzo*, enabling a biopolitical renegotiation of subjectivity marked by a fluidity of identity. And the celebration of, and contradictions inherent to, this negotiation of identity become manifest in the aesthetic forms of art and architecture of the time. I borrow the term biopolitics from Hardt and Negri's (2000, 2005 & 2009) understanding of the politics involved in the construction of alternative subjectivities. Influenced by the ideas of Foucault and Deleuze, Hardt and Negri argue that such a renegotiation of subjectivity is integral to any sort of genuine political change. The fluidity of subjectivities involved in such a biopolitical event is always 'queer', a subversive shattering of identities and norms (Hardt and Negri 2009, pp. 62–3). Like the approach I am advocating, Hardt and Negri use the term queer in this context not just as a form of sexual politics, but as a metaphor for the sliding-sideways and fluidity of subjectivities necessary for change. I will qualify this comment to argue that the biopolitical event involved in negotiating the energies of sexual difference might be more accurately called 'hermaphroditic' in terms of its ability to retain the characteristics of these forces, while simultaneously morphing them into the eddying of energies Deleuze and Guattari referred to as the plateau.

Aesthetics, political economy, sexual difference

The idea that art and architecture can manifest unconscious psychological discomfort, as I noted above, is already commonplace in much political economic theorization. What is less emphasized, in fact rarely mentioned, is the role of the energies of sexual difference in this aesthetico-politics. And yet, this connection is consistently there for all to see. I will argue that it is possible to tell an entirely different story about aesthetics and politics, narrated from the perspective of sexual difference. Consider Wollen's examination of Orientalism in early 20th century France. He identified two opposing aesthetic movements representing fundamentally different interpretations of Modern art, fashion, and architecture. On the one hand were the Orientalists, celebrating colour, ornamentation, pleasure, the feminine, and the body. Opposing them were the Minimalists, advocating functionalism, rationality, morality, masculinity, and the machine. Wollen described these opposing movements as a 'cascade of oppositions', a series of antimonies that interact and overlap: 'Engineer/leisure class, reality principle/pleasure principle, production/consumption, active/passive, masculine/feminine, machine/body, west/east . . . these pairs are not homologous . . . |but each| suggests another, step by step' (Wollen 1993, p. 16).

Wollen argues that fashion designer Paul Poiret, artist and theatre designer Léon Bakst, and painter Henri Matisse were the great colourists of the early 20th century. They were decorative artists, a pejorative term in the world of modern art criticism dominated by Clement Greenberg, where the decorative was considered 'feminine'. Against the Eiffel Tower aesthetic of the masculine, modern engineer, they ornamented, coloured, and decorated using a frankly curvaceous style. They decorated not just the stage or canvasses, but also women's bodies. Figure 1.1, one of Bakst's designs for the ballet *Narcissus*, is emblematic of this celebration of the female form.

In the years around 1910, Poiret, Matisse, and Bakst were much more famous than Picasso or other artists. With the 1920s, however, came the great masculine renunciation. At this time, the predominance of an aesthetic described as masculine spread from male to female wardrobes, as well as through the design and art worlds. Praised in the work of Loos and Veblen, the masculine was exemplified by the well-designed men's suit. In contrast to the high heels and ribbons of ladies' wear, the great masculine renunciation involved minimalism, functionalism, and straight lines. The feminine body itself had to be repressed to become 'raide': 'taut, stiff, and tight' (Wollen 1993, p. 20). Designers such as Coco Chanel explicitly borrowed from men's fashion to create a fashion aesthetic that dramatically broke with previous trends. Modernism in its

Figure 1.1 Leon Bakst Costume Sketch from the ballet *Narcissus*, 1911
Photo credit: Erich Lessing/Art Resource, NY

minimalist form reigned victorious. Already in 1915, one year into World War I, Poiret's work was denounced as 'munichois' and boche. The Munich taste and this feminine aesthetic were considered one and the same: the enemy. By 1929, he had closed his fashion house.

Wollen's account is fascinating because it immediately prompts the question: what kind of performance is being enacted here? It seems like an unconscious erotic, feminine energy had swept across Europe, centred in France (although this trend was evident across the continent, especially in Germany), combining with racial fantasies in its Orientalist manifestation

(Pham 2013), then trickling down not just into the decoration of women's bodies but into artistic production as well. There also seems to be a link between these aesthetic trends and capitalism, namely in the context of the production/consumption contrast. And then it is repressed, quickly and apparently decisively. I say 'apparently' because this feminine energy can never be completely repressed – it is an integral aspect of being. One could argue, in fact, that its reappearance during the Modern period Wollen describes is a purposeful reincarnation of a similar feminine energy that surfaced in the Rococo period prior to the French Revolution (described in Chapter 5), and that will appear once again like a repressed memory in the culture of the Postmodern period (outlined in Chapter 7).

What Wollen describes as the great masculine renunciation is more generally associated with a reforming aesthetic discourse known as Good Design (Jenkins 2006). The Good Design aesthetic is frequently associated with the minimalist approach to the design of both buildings and industrial products of the Modern movement, emphasizing clean lines and eschewing ornamentation. In his study of British design discourses between the 16th and 20th centuries, Lubbock (1995) argues that the idea of Good Design predated the Modern movement by centuries, acting as a disciplinary force on both design producers and consumers. From the start, the Good Design discourse had a distinctly gendered tone. Ornamentation and decoration was considered 'feminine', while the unadorned design techniques favoured by this discourse were 'masculine'. Plato, for example, argued that the arts should be controlled by law in order to prevent corrupt and effeminate forms, such as Ionic columns, from affecting the self-control of citizens (p. 169).

Hence it is not surprising that in telling this tale, Wollen developed his gendered cascade of oppositions, the opposing sides of a developing Modern aesthetic. Later, Reed added another set of oppositions to Wollen's list in his history of the Bloomsbury Group: heroism/housework. Reed's (2004) study of Bloomsbury will be outlined in greater detail in Chapter 6, but briefly, he tracks the preoccupation with the home evident in the work of both the men and women of the Bloomsbury Group, as well as the innovative design, decorating and sexual/living arrangements they pioneered. In contrast to the heroic images of modernity associated with the lean curtain walls or radical revisions of the urban fabric advocated by the Bauhaus or Le Corbusier, the 'Bloomsberries' focused much of their creative energy on the relatively more mundane level of the home.

In the end, those advocating the first half of each of Wollen's oppositions triumphed in the struggle to define Modernity. According to both Wollen and Reed, however, this does not mean that the opposing movement was not present and relevant as an alternative representation of Modernity. It simply indicates that in the battle to define a Modernist discourse for the art history books, minimalism and functionalism prevailed. Similarly, although their work was often rejected as kitsch in the face of the more dominant strain of Modernism he describes as Heroism, Reed argues that the anti-heroic housework of Bloomsbury was nonetheless an important element of the Modern aesthetic (Reed 2004).

This aesthetic dynamic presents an alternative story to the political economy accounts mentioned above. Its gendered perspective on aesthetics indicates that this is another highly politicized aspect of aesthetics that intertwines with this political economy perspective, one that is related to sexual politics. 'Intertwining' is actually not a good way of describing this phenomenon, because in this case some kind of gendered relationship seems to be *propelling* aesthetic and political changes. But how does one describe this relationship? It is too simplistic to project the aesthetic conceptions of 'masculine' or 'feminine' design onto the bodies of men and women because in most of the examples provided by Wollen and Reed, it is men who are creating in this feminine style. It is also too facile to relate this feminine aesthetic to a purely sexualized version of desire. Although there is definitely an element of sexual eroticism to it, it is much broader than this. In any case, the collective nature of this attraction does not lend itself to such a Freudian analysis. Could everyone creating in the feminine style Wollen describes be experiencing the same sort of sexual repression?

It is as if there is an attraction to a different sort of creative energy that eschews, to borrow Reed's term, the heroic version of creativity typically equated with (male) artistic genius. Just as exuberant and transformative, this feminine creative energy evokes sensuous pleasure as opposed to avant-garde bravado; it is decidedly and purposefully anti-heroic. Its serpentine curves suggest a 'containing' energy that, to use Hogarth's (1973) terms, acts as a lure to the eye to hold together the swarming elements of these highly decorative surfaces. In fact, in many ways it appears to be an aesthetics of surface.

In other words, what seems to be interacting here is a set of forces, two 'intensities' or aspects of desire that move together in a manner that goes far beyond the semiotic descriptions provided in political economy. These forces, which appear to be ontological, or at least *a priori,* seem almost to be in movement – pushing each other along – although in Wollen's story, one of these aesthetics (the masculine one) appears to repress the other – or overpower it in the realm of representation.

Viewed from my Jungian/Deleuzean perspective, Wollen and Reed under-estimate the power of the opposition between these opposing aesthetics they identify. A tension between antinomies similar to what they describe has counterposed and intertwined to exert an influence that extends far beyond the turn-of-the-century Modernism to which they apply it. It is a cosmic intra-action that transcends the Modern movement, overlapping and enjoining the traditional 'stages' of art and architecture developed in art history discourses. In the stories I will tell, it overflows the boundaries of Modernism, spilling forward from the Rococo period and tumbling with equal urgency into the cataract of Postmodern debate. When we focus on this dialectic, differentiations between periods of aesthetics and capitalism become meaningful only insofar as the changing synthesis of these oppositions brings different manifestations of art and economy. The central interaction remains the same: that of a libidinal interaction of sexual difference flowing across bodies, art, and practices of production and consumption. This, in essence, is the thesis that motivates this book.

Further, these aesthetics trends have a collective impact and appear to have political implications. As I will show in the chapters that follow, the periods associated with such feminine aesthetics have witnessed some of the most remarkable progress in women's rights and the fight for the acknowledgement of women's subjectivity. In the Baroque/Rococo period there is the rise of women in royal courts, private *salons*, and eventually in terms of constitutional political rights. The *Art Nouveau* period of the late 19th century coincided with the rise of the suffragist movement, and finally the feminist movement of the 1960s and 1970s can be associated with Postmodernism. These changes occurred despite the fact that in many of the stories I will tell here, including Wollen's, this feminine energy is being 'channelled' by men.

These considerations dislodge aesthetics that are discursively categorized as masculine and feminine from the bodies that they are associated with, challenging many presumptions inherent to social constructionist perspectives. For example, one could analyze Wollen's story in Foucauldian terms by focusing on these aesthetic forces as discourses that stratify and hierarchize human relations, exemplified by the eventual patriarchal repression of any aesthetic manifestation described as feminine. For Foucault (1980 & 1995), the value-laden discourses that create categories such as gender norms are socially constructed via regulatory practices exercised through organizations such as medical institutions, legal apparatuses, religious discourses, family practices – or more generally through forms of knowledge, as in the case of theories of aesthetics. These constructions become intelligible through the cultural matrix that such institutions create, giving the impression that what are actually socially constructed representations of the body, sex, and gender are ontologically given truths.

Exposing these discourses involves performing what Foucault called a genealogical critique. Rather than looking for some 'real' or alternative truth that particular social constructions might be repressing, a genealogical approach asks what the political reasons for representing things as 'true' might be. In other words, a genealogical critique asks *why* such constructions are formulated and in whose interest they might be. My historically specific analyses of aesthetic-political constructions of the Rococo in Chapter 5, the development of capitalist markets in Chapter 6, and contemporary cultural economy in Chapter 7 are examples of genealogical critiques that expose how sexual difference infiltrates discourses of political economy and aesthetics.

These genealogies will reveal, however, that a constructionist focus on discourse analysis cannot sufficiently explain what is happening here. I will argue that the forces Wollen describes cannot be accurately described purely in social constructivist terms. Although they definitely become entangled in the political relationships of the realm of representation, the forces of sexual difference I will describe cannot be contained there. The realm of representation – of language and aesthetics and politics – might be described as the space where these forces are imagined and converted into material manifestations. In my account, although these libidinal energies may be expressed, or become 'known' via images or signifiers, they exist prior to the phenomenon of representation. This means accepting an ontological, or at minimum, *a priori*, understanding of the energies of the feminine and masculine, as opposed to focusing solely on their social construction.

This view is compatible with Foucault's ideas, if one focuses more on his understanding of power, as opposed to his conception of discourse. For Foucault, power emanates spontaneously from multiple, dispersed sources. Social constructionist applications of Foucault's ideas typically focus primarily on his concept of discourse, using it to effectively deny that anything resembling an *a priori* understanding of gender, sexuality, aesthetics, or politics is possible. But Foucault's views on power reveal more immanent sources of energy that seem to emanate from both bodies and collectivities, suggesting that understanding such forces cannot focus purely on the discursive construction of knowledge and power. In his terms,

> power must be understood in the first instance as the multiplicity of force relations immanent in the sphere in which they operate and which constitute their own organization; as the process which, through ceaseless struggles and confrontations, transforms, strengthens, or reverses them; as the support which these force relations find in one another, thus forming a chain or system, or on the contrary, the disjunctions and contradictions which isolate them from one another; and lastly, as the strategies in which they take effect, whose general design or institutional crystallization is embodied in the state apparatus, in the formulation of law, in the various social hegemonies.
>
> (Foucault 1980, p. 92–3)

This immanent view of power aligns with the theories of Jung, Deleuze, and Grosz that I will draw on throughout this book. Theories that focus on the creation of meaning in the realm of representation are excellent at understanding the *logos*, or what Deleuze and Guattari call the stratification, of forces once they enter a particular politico-aesthetic *assemblage* – a term the latter use to describe the complex relations between flows of feeling, belief, and technology that become agglomerated in various times and spaces. They effectively deny, however, the possibility of knowing the nature of the immanent sources of power that are 'represented'.

The work of Jung and Deleuze moves beyond the discussions of what I will call the 'realm of representation' of knowledge, language, and politics to include forces from what Deleuze would call the 'outside' that, as Grosz puts it in her description of sexual difference, 'preexist the entities they produce' (2005, p. 174). In her view, discussions focusing solely on the politics of representation flatten and reduce the complexity of culture. From this perspective, understanding the aesthetic forces Wollen describes involves looking at forces *outside* the cultural, not inside it (Grosz 2005, p. 48).

This does not mean denying the importance of social discourses; indeed, this approach is invaluable in exposing the transformation of immanent power into highly stereotypical assumptions. Social constructivist (and deconstructionist) accounts expose the binaries Wollen uncovers as hierarchical relationships where one side of the binary – generally the white male side – inevitably dominates. Indeed, that is precisely what seems to be playing out in Wollen's example – where the feminine, Orientalist 'other' is repressed by a rational, masculine subject, which in turn becomes the norm against which all else is judged. This approach suggests that doing away with such binaries might be the solution to the problem. Yet this is a necessary, but not sufficient explanation of what is happening here.

What if we re-imagine Wollen's antinomies as ontological forces that form dualisms where one aspect does not dominate the other, but is the underlying expression of the other – where neither term could exist outside of the binary? This, I believe, is a more accurate depiction of the Jungian conception of the opposition/binary. As Grosz points out, Deleuze also made use of such a conception of dualisms, not in a hierarchical sense but as an expression of a single force (Grosz 2011, p. 50). I also want to emphasize Deleuze's invocation of the Stoics' use of paradox in understanding such dualisms. In this respect, apparent oppositions such as the masculine and feminine may have an ontological existence, but rather than conceiving such concepts in terms of depth (meaning) and surface (representation) they can be perceived as moving laterally, on the surface, sliding across each other to become, at times, both at once.

As I will describe in greater detail in my discussion of contemporary aesthetico-economy in Chapter 7, such moments, which Deleuze describes as becomings or 'events', present dualisms that are paradoxically *neither one nor the other, but rather their common result*' (Deleuze 1990, p. 8, his emphasis). This interpretation does not posit a representation or simulacrum as detached from a deeper meaning and rising to the surface. On the contrary, the 'depth' rises to the surface and the image, which then becomes what Jung and Deleuze considered a symbol, combines both surface and depth in its resonating meaning. For both Jung and Deleuze, the hermaphrodite was such a symbol. It does not involve the dissolution or absorption of differences; indeed, such oppositions seem to be integral to the paradox of the event. Instead, it is both at once.

All of this begs the question of what impact the forces of sexual difference have on politics and economics. Answering this question involves following a serpentine line that meanders through the remaining chapters of this book, but I will summarize some of my key points here. My analysis is divided into two parts, with Part I focusing primarily on theoretical and methodological issues, and Part II looking at historical genealogies intended to illustrate these theoretical points. Those interested in Jungian or Deleuzean philosophy will primarily be interested in Part I. Those more concerned with the empirical application of these ideas can read my theoretical arguments in Chapter 2, then move directly to the genealogies in Part II.

Chapter 2 is a discussion of the philosophy of Jung and Deleuze, emphasizing the similarities in their understandings of the unconscious and symbolic knowledge. It is here that I first review Jungian definitions of the archetypal feminine and masculine as *Eros/Luna* and *Logos/Sol,* as well as Deleuze and Guattari's conception of the transformative, molecular force of becoming-woman. My methodological approach is not without its controversies, and I attempt to address these issues in this chapter. For those immersed in feminist philosophy, for example, simply using the term 'sexual difference', let alone associating the feminine with a concept like *Eros,* can be a highly contentious act. Charges of essentialism are inevitable in such an approach, but it is important to note that Jung's archetypal feminine is not coterminous with 'woman', nor is it relevant solely to the female psyche. This move by Jung potentially liberates this feminine essence from a strictly biological approach, differentiating it to the extent that there is an interval between the symbol and the individual psyche.

My emphasis on sexual difference is counter to accounts such as Butler's, for example, which view Irigaray's emphasis on sexual difference as a presumed heteronormativity. Although I appreciate Butler's focus on performativity, I draw from theories such as Grosz's that conceive of such energies as 'that which discourse and representation cannot contain and politics cannot direct: sexual difference as force; and force itself as divided, differentiated, sexualized' (Grosz 2005, p. 172). The importance of Grosz's thinking will resonate throughout this book. While acknowledging the importance of Butler's emphasis on the performance of identity and her attention to the socially constructed aspect of gender and sex, I argue that her understanding of sexual difference as a purely posited construction creates a false dichotomy between being and the realm of representation or signification. On the other hand, her understanding of performativity, combined with a Foucauldian understanding of discourse, is integral to showing how the forces of sexual difference play out in aesthetic fantasies in the realm of representation.

Jung's essentialist conceptions of sexual difference may appear anachronistic in the context of contemporary feminist philosophy, but I believe there is much to be gained from his cosmic approach to these terms. If we stick to what Rowland (2002) refers to as the 'deconstructionist' Jung, we find a world where body, mind, and the cosmos intertwine in a fascinating and evocative way. As I will show, Jung anticipated and influenced many of Deleuze's ideas. His notion of the subtle body, for example, where body and mind merge, is analogous to Deleuze and Guattari's 'body without organs' and offers important insights into the mind/body problem, not to mention his influence on Deleuze's understanding of the compensatory nature of the unconscious, and the role of the symbol.

In Chapter 3 I address the connection between aesthetics and politics more directly, and link it to theories of the collective manifestation of psychological complexes. Both Jung and Freud viewed such collective complexes with considerable concern, arguing that they brought people down to their lowest common denominator. Jung's description of the mythological revival of Wotan in fascist Germany was written the same year that Walter Benjamin (2007) famously described the aestheticization of politics he saw evident in fascism. In both accounts, one sees the dark side of the collective unconscious manifested largely in aesthetic terms.

In contrast to this is Rancière's more hopeful account of the transformative potential of aesthetics. I agree with Rancière's critique that aesthetics should not be uniquely 'understood as the perverse commandeering of politics by a will to art' as Benjamin argued, but as a Kantian 'system of a priori forms determining what presents itself to sense experience' (Rancière 2004, p. 13). In support of Rancière's argument that aesthetics presents to us a 'distribution of the sensible' – an understanding of who and what is eligible to be included in politics – I will highlight the relationship between aesthetic trends and political transformations. Integrating sexual difference into Rancière's account, however, both challenges his periodization of aesthetic regimes, and provides explanations for them. Reading sexual difference into aesthetic fantasies, however contentious this may be, reveals the highly gendered nature of aesthetic and political transformation. It also shows that Rancière was too cavalier in completely rejecting Benjamin's concerns. I review Zizek's, Jung's, and Polanyi's conceptions of the relations between politics and the collective complex, showing the parallels and differences between them. In the end, however, it is Hardt and Negri's concept of biopolitics and the search for alternative forms of political organization apart from the social contract that I find most compelling for my argument, provided that it is overlaid with an understanding of the energies of sexual difference.

This analysis of the collective aspects of aesthetics is followed by a more in-depth elaboration of the nature of feminine energy as containment/transformation in Chapter 4. I examine the neurological nature of the mind/body relation with reference to the work of Jungian analyst Jean Knox, relating this to Neumann's distinction between the elemental/containing aspects of the feminine and its transformative effects. I read this double-sided understanding of the feminine as containment/transformation into the myth of Demeter/Persephone/Kore, also showing its implications for Deleuze and Guattari's molecular becoming-woman/girl. In the process, I develop the concept of the 'interval' of love that becomes central to much of the analysis in the chapters that follow, and to my interpretation of Negri's that 'democracy is an act of love'. I argue that the negotiated peace amongst masculine and feminine gods enacted primarily by Demeter metaphorically conveys the democratic power of love.

In the second half of the book I undertake more historical genealogical studies intended to illustrate some of the theoretical points discussed above. I begin in the late 17th and early 18th century, with a discussion of the Rococo in Chapter 5. Generally dismissed as kitsch, overwrought, and effeminate, I argue that the Rococo period should be considered a biopolitical event that allowed significant opportunities for women to engage in the public realm. Conversely, the heavy repression of the Rococo's feminine aesthetic in the second half of the 18th century was accompanied by the retraction of many of the rights accorded to women in the early days of the French Revolution.

That capitalist markets are conceived of in aesthetic, gendered terms will also become clear. I will explore the possibility that capitalism itself is the product of forces of sexual difference in chapter 6, pointing to the political implications of the gendering of capitalist markets, and the changes that examining them from the perspective of sexual difference can bring. It is in this context that the importance of *Eros* – defined in a Jungian sense as an aspect of the archetypal feminine referring to sensuous pleasure and relatedness between people – becomes apparent as a transformative, libidinal energy. In my examination of Keynesian economics, however, the *Luna-esque* nature of the feminine also becomes apparent, as Keynes's emphasis on the 'in-between' and contingent moments of economic activity becomes clear.

I end my discussion with an analysis of the sensibilities of Postmodern aesthetics and political economy in Chapter 7, with a particular emphasis on the return of the politics of surface that were also evident in the Rococo period. It is here that Hillman's emphasis on Jung's conception of *anima* as a butterfly skimming the surface of the field becomes important, but Deleuze's understanding of the simultaneity of becoming also takes centre stage in my account. While accepting Deleuze's philosophy of surface, however, I also point to the dark side of the feminine evident in the contemporary cultural economy, where Hogarth's Rococo, meandering serpentine line becomes usurped into the *Logos* of algorithmic identity.

Throughout, I embrace Jung's conception of the archetypal feminine as an 'essence' in the sense of something that is 'beyond knowing', but can be a force for change and movement (Schor and Weed 1994, p. xiv). I also consider the term feminine as 'essential' in Spivak's understanding of the word – as an acknowledgement of its usefulness and importance, at the same time acknowledging its danger (Spivak 1994, p. 157). As Butler notes, essence can be understood both as something that does not 'appear' and as a term that is necessary, essential – without which we cannot do (Cheah et al 1998, p. 22).

Even those who defend the feminine as an essence in these senses of the word are reluctant to view it as a category with specific characteristics, something that Jung did and that I will defend throughout this study. It is true that what Jung described as the essence of the feminine is often conveyed in stereotypes, but as Gray (2008, p. 146) notes with reference to Putnam's ideas on essentialism, there is no meaning without stereotype. I use these essences in the spirit of what Spivak calls 'building for difference' (Spivak 1994, p. 157), examining expressions of the feminine and treating the energy of the feminine in a contingent, conditional manner. As Spivak notes, something might be essence, it might not, but the very act of re-reading through the essence in this way can lead to discovery. Using the idea of a feminine essence as critique, you can 'miraculate' as you speak – create a new something, a new way of seeing that was not there before. As she notes, Derrida used this as a technique – taking something familiar with such literal seriousness that it transforms itself, an approach that bears similarities to Irigaray's technique of mimesis. In Spivak's view, this is not necessarily a strategy, which comes across as too deliberate. The critique invoked by an attention to feminine energies should not be an exposure of error, but an acknowledgement of the usefulness of this concept (Spivak 1994, p. 157).

I evoke the role of *Eros* contingently, in both economic and aesthetic contexts, treating this purported feminine energy not in Derrida's terms of *'s'il y en a'* (if there is any), but *'comme si c'était'* – as if it were. I undertake this study as an act of imagination, a conditional probing of the feminine *comme si c'était*, to evoke her energy, her impact on the human psyche and her material manifestation as projected in politics, economy, and art.

Bibliography

Adorno, T. and Horkheimer, M. (2002) *Dialectic of Enlightenment,* Stanford University Press, Stanford, CA.

Baudrillard, J. (2004) *Simulacra and Simulation,* trans. Sheila Faria Glaser, The University of Michigan Press, Ann Arbor.

de Beauvoir, S. (1974) *The Second Sex,* Alfred A. Knopf, New York.

Benjamin, W. (2007) 'The Work of Art in the Age of Mechanical Reproduction', in *Illuminations,* ed. Hannah Arendt, trans. Harry Zohn, Schocken Books, New York, pp. 217–251.

Blackman, L. (2007) 'Reinventing Psycholocial Matters: The Importance of the Suggestive Realm of Tarde's Ontology', *Economy and Society,* vol. 36, no. 5, pp. 574–596.

Blackman, L. (2008) 'Affect, Relationality and the 'Problem of Personality', *Theory, Culture and Society,* vol. 25, no. 1, pp. 23–47.

Bourdieu, P. (1984) *Distinction: A Social Critique of the Judgement of Taste,* Harvard University Press, Cambridge, MA.

Cheah, P., Grosz, E., Butler, J. and Cornell, D. (1998) 'The Future of Sexual Difference: An Interview with Judith Butler and Drucilla Cornell', *Diacritics,* vol. 28, no. 1, pp. 19–42.

Connolly, W. (2011) *A World of Becoming,* Durham University Press, Durham, NC.

Deleuze, G. (1990) *The Logic of Sense,* trans. Mark Lester, Columbia University Press, New York.

Deleuze, G. and Guattari, F. (1983) *Anti-Oedipus: Capitalism and Schizophrenia,* University of Minnesota Press, Minneapolis.

Deleuze, G. and Guattari, F. (1987) *A Thousand Plateaus: Capitalism and Schizophrenia,* University of Minnesota Press, Minneapolis and London.

Despret, V. (2004) 'The Body We Care for: Figure of Anthropo-zoo-genesis', *Body and Society,* vol. 10, nos. 2–3, pp. 111–124.

Foucault, M. (1980) *The History of Sexuality,* vol. 1, Vintage Books, New York.

Foucault, M. (1995) *Discipline and Punish: The Birth of the Prison,* 2nd ed., Vintage Books, New York.

Gray, F. (2008) *Jung, Irigaray, Individuation: Philosophy, Analytical Psychology, and the Question of the Feminine,* Routledge, London and New York.

Grosz, E. (2005) *Time Travels: Feminism, Nature, Power,* Duke University Press, Durham, NC.

Grosz, E. (2011) *Becoming Undone: Darwinian Reflections on Life, Politics, and Art,* Duke University Press, Durham, NC.

Hardt, M. and Negri, A. (2000) *Empire*, Harvard University Press, Cambridge, MA.

Hardt, M. and Negri, A. (2005) *Multitude: War and Democracy in the Age of Empire*, Penguin Books, New York.

Hardt, M. and Negri, A. (2009) *Commonwealth*, The Belknap Press of Harvard University Press, Cambridge, MA.

Harvey, D. (1990) *The Condition of Postmodernity*, Blackwell, Cambridge, MA and Oxford.

Hauke, C. (2000) *Jung and the Postmodern: The Interpretation of Realities*, Routledge, London and Philadelphia.

Hogarth, W. (1973) *The Analysis of Beauty*, Garland Publishing, Inc., New York.

Irigaray, L. (1985) *Speculum of the Other Woman*, trans. Gillian C. Gill. Cornell University Press, Ithaca.

Jameson, F. (1995) *Postmodernism: Or, the Cultural Logic of Late Capitalism*, Duke University Press, Durham, NC.

Jenkins, B. (2006) 'The Dialectics of Design', *Space and Culture*, vol. 9, no. 2, pp. 195–209.

Jung, C. G. (1973a) 'Letter to Victor White, Nov. 25, 1950', in *C.G. Jung Letters*, ed. Gerhard Adler, in collaboration with Aniela Jaffe, trans. R. F. C. Hull, Bollingen Series XCV: 1, Princeton University Press, Princeton, NJ, p. 567.

Jung, C. G. (1973b) *Memories, Dreams, Reflections*, Pantheon Books, New York.

Jung, C. G. (1980) *Collected Works*, vol. 9, no. 1, Bollingen Series, Princeton University Press, Princeton, NJ.

Kazarian, E. (2010) 'The Revolutionary Unconscious: Deleuze and Masoch', *SubStance*, vol. 39, no. 2, pp. 91–106.

Kerslake, C. (2007) *Deleuze and the Unconscious*, Continuum, London and New York.

Lash, S. (2006) 'Life (Vitalism)', *Theory, Culture and Society*, vol. 23, nos. 2–3, pp. 323–349.

Lubbock, J. (1995) *The Tyranny of Taste: The Politics of Architecture and Design in Britain 1550–1960*, Yale University Press, New Haven, CT.

Marx, K. (1949) *Capital*, vol. 1, George Allen & Unwin Ltd, London.

Negri, A. (2013) *Spinoza for our Time*, trans. William McCuaig, Columbia University Press, New York.

Neumann, E. (1974) *The Great Mother: An Analysis of the Archetype*, trans. Ralph Manheim, Bollingen Series, Princeton University Press, Princeton, NJ.

Pham, M. (2013) 'Paul Poiret's Magical Techno-Oriental Fashions (1911): Race, Clothing, and Virtuality in the Machine Age', *Configurations*, vol. 21, no. 1, pp. 1–26.

Pint, K. (2011) 'Doubling Back: Psychoanalytical Literary Theory and the Perverse Return to Jungian Space', *S: Journal of the Jan van Eyck Circle for Lancanian Ideology Critique*, vol. 4, pp. 47–55.

Purcell, M. (2013) *The Down-Deep Delight of Democracy*, Wiley-Blackwell, Malden, MA and West Sussex, UK.

Rancière, J. (2004) *The Politics of Aesthetics: The Distribution of the Sensible*, trans. Gabriel Rockhill, Continuum, London and New York.

Reed, C. (2004) *Bloomsbury Rooms: Modernism, Subculture, and Domesticity*, Yale University Press, New Haven and London.

Rowland, S. (2002) *Jung: A Feminist Revision*, Polity, Cambridge, UK.

Schor, N. and Weed, E. (1994) *The Essential Difference*, Indiana University Press, Bloomington and Indianapolis.

Shamdasani, S. (2003) *Jung and the Making of Modern Psychology: The Dreams of a Science*, Cambridge University Press, Cambridge, UK.

Spivak, G. (1994) 'In a Word, Interview', in *The Essential Difference*, eds. N. Schor and E. Weed, Indiana University Press, Bloomington and Indianapolis, pp. 151–182.

Stengers, I. (2011) *Thinking with Whitehead*, Harvard University Press, Cambridge, MA.

Wollen, P. (1993) 'Out of the Past: Fashion/Orientalism/the Body', in *Raiding the Icebox: Reflections on Twentieth Century Culture*, Indiana University Press, Bloomington and Indianapolis, pp. 1–34.

Zizek, S. (1989) *The Sublime Object of Ideology*, Verso, London and New York.

Zizek, S. (2004) 'Notes on a Debate "From Within the People" ', *Criticism*, vol. 26, no. 4, pp. 661–666.

Chapter 2

The compensatory unconscious

This chapter develops my conception of a libidinal energy layered by sexual difference flowing through bodies, art, and practices of production and consumption. This energy is often expressed in aesthetic terms, but it also becomes manifest in practices of politics and economics. It is both immanent to the individual *and* creates connections between individuals. This approach goes beyond the focus on representation often evident in feminist and political economy approaches to combine it with a more ontological approach to understanding sexual difference, emphasizing its political and economic relevance beyond questions of sexuality. Drawing first on the thoughts of Jung and Deleuze, then relating their ideas to feminist debates exemplified by the ideas of Butler and Grosz, I explore the involvement of feminine energies – symbolized in Jungian terms as *Eros/Luna* – in the lived practices of art and economy. Expanding on Kerslake's (2007, p. 69) claim that Deleuze 'was, at least one point in his career, a Jungian', I will explore these connections with a special emphasis on Deleuze and Guattari's understanding of a molecular feminine energy, also using Grosz's work to analyze the connections between sexual difference, aesthetics, and political change.

I make a case for considering an archetypal feminine energy as a force that is different from, but related to, the actual bodies of women. The energies of sexual difference, including those considered 'feminine', are affective forces that flow across and through all bodies, influencing not just aesthetic, but political sensibilities. Viewed in this manner, it becomes clear that such forces of sexual difference have an influence beyond considerations of gender identity and sexuality. They can be viewed as aspects of what Hardt and Negri (2009) call biopolitics – the explorations of alternative subjectivities necessary for material, political change.

Addressing these issues will involve a long segue through the work of Jung, Deleuze, and also feminist theorists such as Butler and Grosz; so to map my path in advance, I will draw on Jung's description of the archetypal energies of the masculine and feminine, filtered through the philosophy of

Gilles Deleuze as a first cut at understanding this phenomenon. This involves taking a 'molecular' view of the energies of sexual difference in which they flow across, and settle in-between, the cuts and distinctions we make on bodies, space, and time. Manifested culturally in art, economics, and politics, these unconscious forces reveal the complexity of the binaries identified by both Wollen and Reed in Chapter 1. They also reveal the shortcomings of viewing the energies of sexual differences purely in sexual terms. In what follows, I will examine Jung's and Deleuze's ideas of what these immanent, symbolic forces might look like. Understanding their ideas regarding sexual difference involves looking at their conception of the unconscious, their emphasis on the importance of the symbol, and the molecular nature of the sources of sexual difference.

Jung, Deleuze, and the unconscious

> Life has always seemed to me like a plant that lives on its rhizome. Its true life is invisible, hidden in the rhizome. The part that appears above ground lasts only a single summer. Then it withers away – an ephemeral apparition. When we think of the unending growth and decay of life and civilizations, we cannot escape the impression of absolute nullity. Yet I have never lost a sense of something that lives and endures underneath the eternal flux. What we see is the blossom, which passes. The rhizome remains.
>
> (Jung 1973b, p. 4.)

Although Deleuze and Guattari can claim squatters' rights to the metaphor of the rhizome, it was, as others have pointed out, a concept they borrowed from Jung (Kerslake 2007; Zizek 2004). 'There is a direct lineage from Jung to *Anti-Oedipus*', notes Zizek (2004, p. 663) disparagingly, an observation reinforced by numerous other parallels in the voluminous pages of both authors' work. Deleuze's emphasis on the transformative impact of the symbol, his version of *anima* (becoming-woman) and especially his conception of the unconscious bear numerous affinities to Jungian 'analytical psychology' (as opposed to Freudian 'psychoanalysis'). Many other similarities derive from Jung's overt (1967 & 1977) and Deleuze's more obscured engagement with esotericism (Ramey 2012).

Deleuze and Guattari's approach, known as schizoanalysis, attempts to explode the Freudian Oedipal triangle, rejecting the Freudian and Lacanian view of desire as 'lack' or the craving for something or someone that one does not possess and cannot ever fully comprehend. Instead, libidinal flows of desire are conceived positively as a productive force. Flows of erotic energy, or 'desiring-machines', pass across and through 'Bodies without

Organs' (BwOs) 'permeated by unformed, unstable matters, by flows in all directions, by free intensities or nomadic singularities, by mad or transitory particles' (Deleuze and Guattari 1987, p. 40). There they intersect with other energies, such as 'becoming-animal' or 'becoming-woman' in ways that have a direct impact on the individual psyche, as well as economic and social production. The body as an organic entity is replaced with a more permeable and flattened surface that energies of different speeds and intensities flow across.

All of this takes place in the space of the rhizome, a decentralized space characterized by multiple, non-hierarchical connections. The rhizome is not composed of units but 'directions in motion' that can take the form of confining lines of stratification, or in the case of transformation, deterritorializing 'lines of flight' and new becomings. Strata are acts of capture; they are like 'black holes' or occlusions striving to seize whatever comes within their reach (p. 40). 'Becoming' intensities are molecular, composed of particles that are always in a relation of movement or rest. To use an example that will be important to my argument, their concept of becoming-woman is a 'microfemininity' – a molecular conception of the transformative aspects of woman (p. 275). Any attempt to make the dispersed molecular a whole or stable identity is 'molar', in this case, the concept of molar woman or a woman defined by her organs and bodily form. This differentiation between the molecular and the molar will be key to my critique of both Deleuze's and Jung's conception of sexual difference, analyzed below.

Deleuze and Guattari describe the relationship between the molecular and molar using the metaphor of a crystal that, as I will show, was also used by Jung to describe the manifestation of the archetype as an image. Deleuze and Guattari contend that 'content (form and substance) is molecular, and expression (form and substance) is molar'. As in the process of crystallization, 'the molar can be said to express microscopic molecular interactions (the crystal is the macroscopic expression of a microscopic structure . . .)' (p. 57).

This 'energic' interpretation of being is in part drawn from the work of Henri Bergson, who also influenced Jung. Jung's break with Freud primarily centred on their differences over the role of sex in the unconscious. In a 1912 presentation to the New York Academy of Medicine, he announced his intent to liberate psychoanalytic theory from 'the purely sexual standpoint', comparing his notion of libido to the idea of 'vital energy', a direct reference to Bergson's *élan vital* (Shamdasani 2003, p. 103). Although it includes sexual desire, Jung's notion of libido also refers to desire in its broadest sense – anything that provokes interest or psychic energy. In this sense, Deleuze and Guattari's argument that desire should be described as 'intensities' is very close to Jung's, especially their many references to desire that are not explicitly sexual (Kerslake 2007, p. 74).

This conception of libido is key to Jung's understanding of how desire might manifest itself in forms other than sexual activity, such as culture or economy – an argument that will be central to this book. It is a mistake, Jung argued, to believe that if a person lets go of expending energy on a certain sexual symptom, the energy will re-emerge as a sexual symptom elsewhere. It may take the form of a spiritual or material expenditure of energy instead. Jung (1960, p. 41) referred to this conversion of energy as the 'canalization of libido' – the transformation of one form of psychic energy into another, in the same way a steam engine converts heat into steam and then motion.

For Jung, it was the transformation of this libidinal energy that was responsible for cultural manifestations such as work or art. When left to move naturally, he argued, this energy is transformed along the line of its natural gradient, similar to the way water flows going down a slope. This flow produces natural phenomena, according to Jung, but not 'work', which is a cultural phenomenon. 'Culture provides the machine whereby the natural gradient is exploited for the performance of work' (p. 41). The living body converts the libidinal energies it uses into other, equivalent manifestations – not just work, but also artistic creations such as paintings, designs, and literature.

This understanding of libidinal energy is also evident in the work of Deleuze and Guattari (1983 & 1987), who similarly viewed art and economy as a 'territorialization' of libidinal forces. For both Jung and Deleuze, artistic activity can be a non-representational mode of cognition that allows the presentation of unknowable things; a method whereby suprasensible clues to the destination of individuation may be intuited and expressed. Deleuze (2000, p. 42) quotes Proust's notion that, 'Only by art can we emerge from ourselves, can we know what . . . would have remained as unknown to us as those that might be on the moon'. In a passage with decidedly alchemical overtones, he argues 'Art is a veritable transmutation of substance. By it, substance is spiritualized and physical surroundings dematerialized in order to refract essence, that is, the quality of an original world' (p. 47). For Jung, opening oneself up to unconscious energies involved a 'letting go of oneself' that could be achieved not just through dreaming, reverie, and fantasy, but also through art, drawing, sculpture, and writing (Jung 1967, p. 17).

This emphasis on art as a presentation, rather than a re-presentation, of unknowable things is related to Jung's understanding of the symbol, another area where he diverges from Freud and converges with Deleuze. There are times, Jung acknowledged, when Freud's approach of interpreting a dream image as a signifier or symptom of aspects of a patient's repressed sexuality is appropriate. He considered such approaches, where the supposedly 'symbolic' expression represents a known (but perhaps repressed) thing, to be 'semiotic'. Jung objected to Freud's approach, however, because he *only* considered the semiotic interpretation of symbols, and as such, he wasn't really considering 'symbols' at all, but signifiers. 'The true symbol', Jung argued 'differs essentially from this [semantic form], and should be understood as an expression of an intuitive idea that cannot yet be formulated in any other or better way' (quoted in Kerslake 2007, p. 107). It is not necessarily a symptom that refers to a once conscious element that has been repressed, nor an un-expressible lack or void, but a positive force that cannot directly be brought to consciousness because it is 'irrepresentable'.

For Jung, symbols are manifestations of the unconscious as it attempts to communicate with us in a compensatory way. The unconscious usually does this by pointing up 'problems' – issues that we cannot be aware of because they are irrepresentable. Kerslake (2007, p. 97) describes Jung's concept of the problem as something that 'breaks through first as a problem *for* conscious representation, and then *as* a problem that points to something neglected in the very conceptual hierarchy itself'. Intuitively acknowledging this unconscious prodding actually modifies consciousness, and is the key to the transformative process Jung referred to as individuation.

This understanding of the symbol, in turn, emerged from a very different conception of the unconscious than Freud's. As Jung described it, the Freudian unconscious consisted of personal elements that had once been conscious (and therefore were capable of consciousness) but had been repressed because of their morally incompatible nature. They could therefore be 'recovered' by looking for associations through dreams and other techniques, and once again be made available to the conscious mind (Jung 1960, p. 179). In contrast, Jung viewed the unconscious as a living, moving, communicative thing. In his account of his break with Freud in his memoire, he says,

> I was never able to agree with Freud that the dream is a 'façade' behind which its meaning lies hidden – a meaning already known but maliciously, so to speak, withheld from consciousness. To me dreams are a part of nature, which harbours no intention to deceive, but expresses something as best it can, just as a plant grows or an animal seeks its food as best it can.
>
> (Jung 1973, pp. 161–2)

Jung (1960, p. 185) laid out his idea of the unconscious in a sort of James + Freud + Jung formula, including everything in James's understanding of the 'fringe of consciousness', Freud's repressed elements discussed above, and Jung's own conception of what he called 'psychoid' functions: elements 'that are not capable of consciousness and of whose existence we have only indirect knowledge'. It is these unknowable, psychoid elements that possess the

The compensatory unconscious 29

dynamic, irrepresentable, and compensatory aspects of Jung's notion of the unconscious.

From time to time the unconscious brings to the surface symbols that should be built into conscious life, thereby eliminating conflicts between the unconscious and the conscious and making the individual more psychologically whole. Jung acknowledged that this was the basis of Freud's psychoanalysis, but argued that the unconscious consists of far more than 'infantile and morally inferior contents' (Jung 1958, p. 551). Although everyone has their 'lumber-room full of dirty secrets', these are not so much unconscious as forgotten and hidden or repressed. For him, '[t]he unconscious is the matrix of all metaphysical statements, of all mythology, of all philosophy (so far as this is not merely critical), and of all expressions of life that are based on psychological premises' (p. 552). While consciousness splits concepts up into units and fragments to allow human comprehension, the Jungian unconscious is total and undivided.

This is why when a symbol breaks through from the unconscious, it has such an overpowering effect. 'It is the unexpected, all-embracing, completely illuminating answer, which works all the more as illumination and revelation since the conscious mind has got itself wedged into a hopeless blind alley' (p. 552). Jung compares this to the Buddhist spiritual goal of 'satori'. The Zen experience of satori comes upon one unawares, and one has the feeling of 'touching upon a true secret' (p. 541). In this respect, he argues, it is more akin to the experiences of mystics like Meister Eckhart or Hildegarde of Bingen. It is experienced like a 'break-through' by a consciousness that was once limited to the ego-form, which then expands with an insight into a self of which the ego is only a part – a sort of 'supersession' of the ego by the self (p. 543). A new state of consciousness ensues: '*It is not that something different is seen, but that one sees differently.* It is as though the spatial act of seeing were changed by a new dimension' (his emphasis, p. 546). Along with this new consciousness comes a sense of detachment from complexes and a new understanding of their sources.

There are distinct parallels in Deleuze to Jung's conception of the unconscious and his understanding of the symbol. Similar to Jung's critique of the Freudian unconscious as 'malicious', Deleuze remarked in conversation with Parnet that in Freudian psychology, 'The unconscious is understood as negative, it's the enemy' (Deleuze and Parnet 2007, p. 77). Kerslake (2007) shows that Deleuze's conception of the unconscious was directly influenced by Jung, arguing that Deleuze's Kantian inspired notion of the 'Idea' configures his conception of the 'virtual' in a manner similar to Jung's understanding of the unconscious.

Borrowed from Bergson, Deleuze's concept of the virtual is composed of differential Ideas or 'multiplicities' that are not unconscious in the

Freudian sense that they lie outside of consciousness and can only be known by their representation, but because 'we cannot be *conscious of them* in the way we are conscious of empirical things or representational states of mind' (Deleuze quoted in Kerslake 2007, p. 112). Ideas provide a sort of virtual 'structure' that underlies the conception of actual things. They pose or constitute 'problems' that, if left solely to understanding would 'remain entangled in its separate and divided procedures, a prisoner of partial empirical enquiries' (Deleuze 2004a, p. 214). They present, rather than *re*-present, the unconscious. In his essay on Sacher-Masoch, a young Deleuze (2004b, p. 128) explicitly noted his preference for the Jungian view of the unconscious. As Zizek points out, in Deleuze and Guattari's desire to 'go to the end' and deal more directly with the texture of the Lacanian Real, they 'do to Lacan what Carl Gustav Jung did to Freud' (Zizek 2004, p. 662).

As Kerslake notes, Deleuze's symbol, like Jung's, is not a direct representation or a 'signifier' tied to a 'signified'. In Deleuze's evocative terms, it is

> an intensive compound that vibrates and expands, that has no meaning, but makes us whirl about until we harness the maximum of possible forces in every direction, each of which receives a new meaning by entering into relations with the others.
>
> (quoted in Kerslake 2007, p. 124)

In words that echo the Jungian perspective, Deleuze speaks to the importance of the symbol as a way forward, lamenting the demise of the symbolic dimension in contemporary philosophy. Ramey notes that the symbolic is so important for Deleuze that he links the will and force of action and decision to symbolic intensity, rather than to rational deliberation. Says Deleuze,

> The symbol is a maelstrom, it makes us whirl about until it produces the intense state out of which the solution, the decision, emerges. The symbol is the process of action and decision; in this sense, it is linked to the oracle that furnished it with these whirling images. For this is how we make a true decision: we turn into ourselves, upon ourselves, ever more rapidly, until a center is formed and we know what to do.
>
> (Deleuze cited in Ramey 2012, p. 107)

Thus the symbol, especially in the context of thought and art, changes or transforms the material world. This explains Deleuze's belief that such symbolic knowledge makes possible 'a kind of cognition that can, through a sort of intuitive leap, develop an image capable of effectively altering reality in conformity with itself' (Ramey 2012, p. 96). This concept is key to my understanding of the politically transformative aspects of both art and the unconscious.

Understanding how this leap might occur can be deduced from Jung's analogy to satori. As in the Zen adept's experience of satori, the process starts when the symbol breaks through, coming upon the individual unawares and allowing her/him to see things in a different light. In effect, the symbolic image enters the individual's imaginary, which in turn affects the individual's sense of 'reality'. As Jung explains, the imagination then becomes real:

> Every psychic process is an image and an 'imagining,' otherwise no consciousness could exist and the occurrence would lack phenomenality. Imagination itself is a psychic process, for which reason it is completely irrelevant whether the enlightenment [satori] be called 'real' or 'imaginary.' The person who has the enlightenment, or alleges that he has it, thinks at all events that he is enlightened. What others think about it decides nothing whatever for him in regard to his experience. Even if he were lying this lie would still be a psychic fact.
>
> (Jung 1964, p. 544)

The individual then starts to let this new imaginary sense 'live' him or her, developing these imaginary images by 'letting themselves go to them, or what in Taoism is known as 'wu wei' (Jung 1967, pp. 16–17). As noted above, Jung argued that a good way to encourage this letting go was engaging in art or visualization, enabling these images to become assimilated into the individual psyche. Once these images are accepted, he argued, one sees an enlarging and enriching of the personality (p. 18).

But where does this new thing, this symbol come from? Jung argued that it came from 'obscure possibilities inside or outside' the individual (p. 15). This vague comment insinuates a permeable individual where the relationship between inside and outside is blurred. Understanding this necessarily involves an examination of his approach to the relationship between the universal and the particular.

Individuation: the relation of the particular to the universal

As noted above, for Jung symbols are manifestations of the unconscious as it attempts to communicate with us in a compensatory way. The unconscious usually does this by pointing up 'problems' – issues that we cannot consciously continence or be aware of, often because they are un-representable.

Intuitively acknowledging this unconscious prodding is the key to the transformative process Jung referred to as individuation.

Stein describes individuation as a 'life-line' that is constantly fluid and shifting. Although Jung accepted Freud's emphasis on the importance of the influence of family, past trauma, and phylogenetic memory for the psyche, he argued that the unconscious is forward looking, hinting at what may be unfolding and where the libido is headed. Despite this 'prospective orientation' of the psyche, it is not teleological in the sense of describing a pre-ordained fate, but rather 'anticipates possible futures' (Stein 2005, p. 10). A successful individuation process brings awareness of unconscious aspects, allowing a union of unconscious and conscious contents that results in Jung's concept of the 'transcendent function': a 'third thing' that is the culmination of a dialogue between the conscious and unconscious aspects of the psyche (p. 11).

This process of awareness contributes to the development of the 'self', not to be confused, Jung emphasized, with the ego or ego-consciousness. As Jung insisted,

> the self comprises infinitely more than a mere ego, as the symbolism has shown from of old. It is as much one's self, and all other selves, as the ego. Individuation does not shut one out from the world, but gathers the world to oneself.
>
> (Jung 1960, p. 432)

Instead, Jung proposed a decentring of ego-consciousness, portraying it as surrounded by a 'multitude of little luminosities', or the archetypes (pp. 190–1).

Jung's notion of individuation is the antithesis of classical liberal conceptions of the individual, which insinuate an enclosed, rational decision maker who interacts with others as if they were atoms bouncing off one another. Rather, the Jungian individuation process involves the discovery that the individual is embedded in a collective psyche or unconscious and interacts with it in a manner that is mutually constitutive. In Taylor's terms, Jung's porous individual is open to a pre-modern 'enchanted' universe (Taylor 2007, p. 300). As Hillman noted, in the Jungian view we live *in* psyche, it does not only reside within us. The soul *within* is a microcosm of the soul *without*, or in alchemical terms, 'as above, so below'. Jungian psychology is an immanent spirituality where the gods live in the solar plexus (Jung 1967, p. 37). Says Hillman:

> A self-knowledge that rests within a cosmology which declares the mineral, vegetable, and animal world beyond the human person to be

impersonal and inanimate is not only inadequate. It is also delusional . . .
From Plato through the alchemists on whom Jung leans, and for Jung
himself, it was not the personal anima alone that counted but also the
anima mundi [World Soul].

(Hillman 1985, p. 109)

This notion of the permeable nature of the boundary between the inside and
outside of the body also resonates with those who insist upon the vitality
of the non-human world in which humans operate (Bennett 2010; Blackman 2008; Despret 2004; Latour 2004). Not only is there a sense of decentring the place of humans in the universe here (Deleuze and Guattari 1987,
p. 235), but also a notion that Barad (2006) refers to as 'entanglement': the
mutual constitution of human, animal, and material object.

Jung's conception of the individual as a microcosm of the macrocosm,
or the *anima mundi,* is echoed in Deleuze's hermetic understanding of the
relationship of the individual to the world. For Deleuze:

It is at the very moment when the living being persists stubbornly in
its individuality that it affirms itself as universal. At the moment when
the living being closed in upon itself, defining the universality of life as
an outside, it did not see that it had, in fact, interiorized that universal: realized the universal on its own account, and defined itself as a
microcosm.

(quoted in Ramey 2012, p. 100)

Like Jung's conception of individuation, there is a teleology to the Berg-
son/Deleuzean conception of the unconscious; a notion that it motivates
or moves us ever forward toward an end, even if that end is never made
explicit. The notion of 'becoming' so integral to Deleuze's work runs parallel
to Jung's process of individuation. In this respect, Jung's individuation process is similar to Deleuze's notion of 'grasping ourselves as events', which,
as Ramey notes, is derived from an hermetic, alchemical understanding of
seeing ourselves as 'each in all and all in each' (p. 148). At this point, the
mutual immersion of both Jung and Deleuze in esoteric imagery becomes
compelling.

Esotericism, the archetypes, and sexual difference

The western esoteric tradition is defined more fully in Faivre and Needleman (1992, p. 51), but may be partially described as a form of herme-
neutics through which the individual uses symbol, myth, and experience

to endure a personal struggle of elucidation (xii). The three 'sciences' of Western esotericism are alchemy, astrology, and magic (in the Renaissance sense of the science of numbers), but it also includes a number of other streams such as Kabbalah, Hermeticism, German *Naturphilosophie*, and Rosicrucianism (xiv). Jung's esotericism centred on both Eastern and Western alchemy (Jung 1967 & 1977), while Deleuze's was more focused on Alexandrian hermeticism, especially as interpreted by Malfatti (Kerslake 2007 & 2008; Ramey 2012).

Jung partly developed his conception of archetypal symbols intuitively, deriving his definitions from his experiences with his own and his patients' dreams, fantasies, and active imaginations. However, the ancient, cosmopolitan art of alchemy had a special influence on his work. The alchemical connection began when he increasingly noticed the parallels between the symbolism of his patients' dreams and the cryptic visual language of alchemy. It is here, too, that we can begin to understand Jung's elaboration of the archetypal symbols of the masculine and feminine that I will further develop below.

Like the alchemical adepts, Jung believed that by immersing oneself in a lifelong process of experimentation (the process of individuation), and after a series of conjunctions or *coniunctio* between oppositions within the psyche, the individual could experience an enlightened state symbolized by the alchemical hermaphrodite. This enlightened state symbolized by the *coniunctio* bears many similarities with Jung's understanding of the assimilation of unconscious symbols outlined above, and will be key to my description of his idea of the subtle body below. A key aspect of the *coniunctio* is the adage 'as above, so below', which von Franz described as making the body incorporeal and the spirit concrete: 'The body, the material thing, becomes spiritualized and the spirit in turn becomes concrete' (von Franz 1980, p. 258). Note the almost exact parallel to Deleuze's description of art above.

The purpose of alchemy was to combine and alter opposing substances in order to bring them to a transcendent third, or higher state. Jung believed, however, that although the alchemical adepts spent considerable time in their laboratories manipulating actual substances, their purposes were not just material, but psychological and spiritual. The consummate example of Taylor's porous individuals, the adepts perceived a direct connection between the matter that they manipulated and themselves. As they united and altered the metals they melted and re-solidified in a new form, they believed they were changing themselves. Indeed, this repeated process of experimentation and change was the basis of the accumulation of alchemical knowledge and wisdom, and was considered a sacred act. The clear connection between the chemical unions enacted in the laboratory and the development of the practitioner's psyche prompted Jung to view alchemy as a metaphor for the process of individuation, or individual growth, with the *lapis* or philosopher's stone representing the Self.

Since one of the goals of alchemy was eternal rebirth, the idea was to return to the primal matter, or *prima materia,* through a process called putrefaction. Matter had to be broken down or putrefied in order to grow again, much as putrefied dung serves as a fertilizer, in order to be reworked into another form. Out of this abject chaos and filth, this 'putrefied dung-hill', comes the *lapis* – the philosopher's stone. The stone is to be found 'in filth' so despicable that it is thrown out into the streets and trodden upon by people (Fabricius 1976, p. 21). Here we see a focus on the importance of the abject that is also central to the work of Kristeva (2002).

The alchemical experiments were to be performed repeatedly, each time bringing the adept, and the materials he/she was manipulating, to a new level of re-birth. In this process of experimentation, a series of substances that are considered to oppose each other are brought together. These opposites may either confront each other in enmity or be drawn to each other in love; in both cases they come together in a union known as the *coniunctio.* The most common alchemical opposites are: moist/dry, cold/warm, lower/upper, spirit/body, heaven/earth, fire/water, bright/dark, active/passive, volatile/solid, precious or costly / cheap or common, good/evil, open/hidden, West/East, living/dead, masculine/feminine, Sol/Luna (Jung 1977, p. 3).

Jung's list of oppositions bears an uncanny resemblance to those outlined in Wollen's account of French Orientalism in Chapter 1. Given that such binaries are now often dismissed as the basis for the hierarchical denigration of the implicitly inferior term, recall that for both Jung and Deleuze these antinomies are not what Derrida would call 'violent hierarchies'. If one term dominates the other, it is a temporary phenomenon. Although it may be true that one side may temporarily dominate the other, this situation cannot last. As I will explain in Chapter 3, Jung subscribed to the idea of an *enantiodromia* between opposites so that when one becomes too dominant, the other automatically begins to increase its influence in response. In other words, one term *grows out of* the other. Each opposition is the underlying expression of the other; neither term could exist outside of the binary.

As noted above, one of the goals of the adept was to combine or unite different substances in a 'chymical marriage' known as the *coniunctio.* The highest form of the *coniunctio* is the *hierosgamos* or the sacred wedding, which has a lineage as a sacred experience common to ancient matriarchal religions that has since been rejected by patriarchal religions such as Christianity, Judaism, or Islam (Schwartz-Salant 1995, p. 8). Sometimes the *coniunctio* is symbolized by a king and queen, other times it is represented by the

Figure 2.1 The Hermetic Androgyne, late 17th century miniature from a German manuscript
Photo Credit: HIP/Art Resource, NY

sun and moon or *Sol* and *Luna*. One of the highest forms of the *coniunctio* is represented by the image of the hermaphrodite (Figure 2.1).

Although this mixing of the masculine and feminine may appear to have a hetero-normative bias, or an emphasis on bisexuality, it is important to remember that this process is *symbolic*, not literal. It is true that these terms were often interpreted literally; women frequently appear in hermetic texts as the alchemist's *soror mystica* (mystical sister), for example, who was considered essential to the alchemical process. Sometimes the *coniunctio* literally was practiced as a form of sacred sexual intercourse. Other times, however, the *soror mystica* is interpreted as the feminine *anima* or soul of the male alchemist, with whom he must interact as he works through his alchemical *opus*. As will become clearer below, it is important in Jung and in alchemy generally not to associate the 'feminine' directly with 'woman', since there is a feminine and masculine aspect to every person.

Jung's explanation of an illustration similar to Figure 2.1, but from the European alchemical text *Rosarium Philosophorum* of 1550, illustrates the fallacy of assuming that references to the feminine refer to women or the masculine to men in alchemical texts. Although it might seem obvious that the king represents a man in this illustration and the queen a woman, Jung argues that the opposite is actually the case and there is a 'counter-crossing' of the sexes. Thus, he claims that the queen represents a transference or projection of the male alchemist's *anima* or soul onto the form of a woman, and the king is the transference of the *soror's animus* or masculine aspect onto the figure of a man. The complexities of the concepts of 'masculine' and 'feminine' are underlined in this image of the hermaphrodite, which can be interpreted as a simple relationship between a man and a woman; as a relationship between a man and his *anima* and a woman with her *animus;* the relationship of the projected *anima* to the projected *animus*, or the relationship of the woman's *animus* to her human alchemical male lab partner and vice versa (Jung 1954, p. 221).

Jung's captivation with the hermetic arts is paralleled in Deleuze's attention to the hermaphrodite, which according to Kerslake derives primarily from his involvement with the theosophy of Malfatti (Kerslake 2007, pp. 133–7 & 2008). Ramey (2012) argues that almost all of Deleuze's later works grew out of a fascination with such esoteric symbols. As a symbol, Kerslake notes, Deleuze's hermaphrodite is a condensation of many oppositions and energies that when 'exploded' reveals a cosmic openness uncontained by the literal translations of masculine and feminine. Emphatically, it should not be equated with a sign of a compulsory hetero- or bi-sexuality, indeed sexuality is only a metaphor here (Samuels 1985, p. 212). It is generally agreed that Jung saw sexuality as something that was to be handled on a contingent, individual basis (Hauke 2000; Rowland 2002).

In the true androgyne there is a 'plateauing' of body and spirit in what Jung called the subtle body that is similar to the 'spirit being transformed into matter, and matter being transformed into spirit' of tantric yoga (Woodman 1982, p. 92). That this tantric, alchemical process may be performed either psychically or physically (relationally within or relationally without) detaches it from practices of sexuality and makes it available to anyone, regardless of their sexual preferences, including celibacy. As Kerslake points out, with this doubling of the masculine and feminine within a couple, the psychic aspect of sexual relationships can take many forms. A heterosexual relationship can be psychically homosexual because a man and a woman are attracted to each other's masculine aspects. Conversely, homosexual relationships can be psychically heterosexual in situations where the feminine aspect of a woman in a lesbian relationship is attracted to her partner's masculine aspect, or two homosexual men could be having a psychic lesbian relationship if they are attracted to each other's feminine side. Once the symbol of the hermaphrodite is understood and unleashed, the human becomes the 'libidinal microcosm' of Deleuze and Guattari's BwO (Kerslake 2007, p. 137).

Although Jung's adoption of alchemical terms is in part responsible for his dismissal in academic circles, Deleuze's more metaphorical use of esotericism shows that it can be used not solely as some mysterious, alternative form of spirituality, but as philosophy. Although Deleuze eventually evacuated most direct references to esoteric philosophy from his work, both Kerslake (2007) and Ramey (2012) show that esoteric concepts and principles animate much of his philosophy. Throughout this book, I will use the concepts of the hermaphrodite and the *coniunctio* in metaphorical terms to explain biopolitical events of coming together, or what Berardi (2009) calls 'conjunction'.

The significance of Jung's immersion in alchemy resonates in his conception of the archetypes. Although Jung frequently referred to the unconscious as being 'structured' by archetypes, his use of the word structure should be interpreted loosely. He defined the archetypes in terms derived from alchemy: as multiple *scintillae* or 'seeds of light broadcast in the chaos' (Jung 1960, p. 190). They are numinous sparks, or germinal luminosities that shine forth from the darkness of the unconscious (p. 192).

In a somewhat paradoxical discussion under the heading 'The Unconscious as a Multiple Consciousness', Jung maintains that these numinous sparks or symbols are also luminous sites of consciousness, sparks of light that when meditated upon provide profound insight. Although the uniqueness of these symbols can only be approximated and never fully be brought into reality, they remain the absolute basis of all consciousness (Jung 1980, p. 173). Becoming conscious of the symbols of the archetypes cannot just mean intellectually grasping their significance. The subject, according to Jung, must be *affected* by the process: 'It is through the "affect" that the subject becomes involved and so comes to feel the whole weight of reality' (Jung 1959, p. 33). As noted above, this understanding of the affective weight of the archetype is also apparent in Deleuze's conception of the symbol.

The compensatory unconscious 39

Implied in this notion of the archetype is the idea that they are collective. Jung postulated two kinds of products of the unconscious: 1. fantasies and dreams relating to personal experience; and 2. fantasies and dreams that appear to have no connection to personal experience, and thus appear to be related to the collective elements of the human psyche in general. These elements frequently appear in the form of stories, for example, such as myths or fairy tales, or shapes and images that are replicated across cultures. While some of the commonalities in images and symbols across cultures in widely dispersed parts of the world can be explained by migration, he argued, they cannot all be. Jung concluded there must be a 'collective psychic substratum' that he called the collective unconscious (Jung 1980, p. 155). Symbols from this collective substratum arise in a reduced state of consciousness he equated to Janet's *abaissement du niveau mental*: the space of dreams, fantasies, and reveries.

Since the archetype itself is unknowable and irrepresentable, we never really know precisely what constitutes its 'meaning'. Our only clues are the metaphoric symbols or images that appear in dreams, daydreams, or fantasies, which might be described as culturally and individually inflected projections of the archetype. Jung cautioned against attempts to pin down any single meaning to an archetypal symbol or image:

> The ground principles, the *archai*, of the unconscious are undescribable because of their wealth of reference . . . The discriminating intellect naturally keeps on trying to establish their singleness of meaning and thus misses the essential point; for what we can above all establish as the one thing consistent with their nature is their manifold meaning, their almost limitless wealth of reference, which makes any unilateral formulation impossible.
>
> (Jung 1980, p. 38)

Jung frequently described his approach as phenomenological – the only way to understand an archetype was to observe it in practice, as symbolized in an individual's dream or fantasy and in the context of their actual lives. Expanding upon such symbols outside of their context in order to abstract their 'real essence' made them cloudy and indistinct, he argued. In order to understand the archetype as a living thing, 'we must let it remain an organic thing in all its complexity and not try to examine the anatomy of its corpse in the manner of the scientist, or the archaeology of its ruins in the manner of the historian' (p. 182).

Given its irrepresentable quality, the only way the conscious mind can access an archetype is through projection. To use an example that will be important to my analysis below, the archetypal feminine may manifest itself as the image of a woman because 'woman' as we conceive of her is the closest the unconscious can come to communicating its meaning. That does not mean, as Jung pointed out, that the archetype we describe as feminine *is* 'woman'. In his words, 'When projected, the anima always has a feminine form with definite characteristics. This empirical finding does not mean that the archetype is constituted like that *in itself*' (pp. 69–70, his emphasis).

Hence, when the archetype manifests itself in an image, it should be treated as Grosz or Deleuze would describe a piece of art, or as Kristeva thinks of poetry: as a living communication of desire, force, and matter that must be meditated on or interacted with in a state of reverie, and from which a meaning can only be intuited rather than intellectually arrived at. This conception derives from what Jung considered the most transformative experience of his life when, during a period of mental fragility after his split with Freud in 1913–1914, he meticulously painted, drew, and interacted with the various dream images and fantasies featured in the recently published *Red Book* (Jung 2009).

Equally importantly, unconscious symbols must be considered in a contingent manner. As noted above, Jung argued that symbolic images are not semiotic signs attached to only one meaning, and emphasized that their manifestations in images and words are merely *projections*. In this respect, Jung's symbol operates in a way similar to Zizek's (1989) Lacanian concept of the *point de capiton* or fixed signifier, a term that will be more fully defined in Chapter 3. It is not attached to any definite meaning, but the meaning becomes contingently affixed to it in a compensatory way. Jung argues that:

> It is commonly supposed that [unconscious] meaning[s] have only one meaning and are marked with an unalterable plus or minus sign. In my humble opinion, this view is too naïve. The psyche is a self- regulating system that maintains its equilibrium just as the body does. Every process that goes too far immediately and inevitably calls forth compensations, and without these there would be neither a normal metabolism nor a normal psyche . . . When we set out to interpret a dream, it is always helpful to ask: What conscious attitude does it compensate?
>
> (Jung 1954, p. 153)

This means symbols must be regarded contingently in the context of the dreamer's philosophical, religious, and moral convictions as well as other aspects of their immediate conscious attitude. 'It is far wiser,' he notes, 'not to regard dream-symbols semiotically, i.e., as signs or symptoms of a fixed character, but as true symbols, i.e. as expression of a content not yet consciously recognized or conceptually formulated' (p. 156). Even those symbols with a relatively fixed content should not be treated as if they can be known or formulated as a concept.

As an example, he looks at phallic symbols, a symbol relevant to Lacanian understandings of the unconscious. Zizek (1989, p. 176) has attributed to Jung a statement making a direct analogy between the Phallus and a penis, but Jung's actual analysis specifically denies this. Instead, he uses a more anthropological approach, referring to the various understandings of the Phallus as healing, fertility, potency, or creative mana that have many mythological equivalents (including menstrual blood) (Jung 1954, p. 157). Yet even in cases such as this where the meaning of symbols is relatively fixed, there is no *a priori* certainty that it should be interpreted in a specific way. Instead, it must be interpreted contingently in the context of the dreamer's situation, their beliefs, relationships, and how such a symbol might resonate with meaning in the specific context of their life, in order to discern its compensatory nature for their individual psyche.

Where do the archetypal symbols come from and how do they enter the individual's psyche? In line with my description above of the individual's immersion within psyche, Jung affirmed Kerényi's view that the symbol is nothing other than the world itself speaking, hence its collective nature. 'The more archaic and "deeper," that is the more *physiological,* the symbol is, the more collective and universal, the more "material" it is' (Jung 1980, p. 173). As it approaches individual consciousness it loses its universal character, running the risk of becoming a mere allegory that is 'exposed to all sorts of attempts at rationalistic and therefore inadequate explanation' (p. 173).

Although Jung explicitly acknowledged that the psycho-physical relation is poorly understood (Jung 1960, p. 7), he ultimately provided a description of the archetypes that relied heavily on an amorphous blending of body and mind. Jung believed that unity between body and mind was central to a sound relationship between self and the world. As Barbara Hannah, an analyst trained by Jung once said, 'You can be anything but you must stay in your body' (cited in Harris 2001, p. 19).

Although he acknowledged that a split between mind and matter was necessary for consciousness, he believed that the post-Cartesian emphasis on this separation destabilized the mind/body relationship, resulting in alienation and a general sense of meaninglessness. Instead, Jung argued that body and psyche were probably two aspects of the same thing. This said, there is considerable ambivalence in his descriptions of whether the archetype is inherited in some sort of genetic way or whether it might be related to bodily instinct (Samuels 1985, pp. 23–30), so what follows is only a general outline of this complex phenomenon.

Jung argued that the psyche is layered in the sense that it manifests itself through individual consciousness, but descends deeper and deeper into a collective unknown. 'It is impossible to say where the archetype comes from,' he notes, 'because there is no Archimedean point outside the *a priori* conditions it represents' (Jung 1980, p. 69, fn 27). 'Lower down' symbols become increasingly collective and universal until they are extinguished in the chemical substances that make up the body's materiality; the body's carbon is the same chemical substance carbon that is found everywhere in nature, he notes. He conjectures that the body is the 'stuff of the world' in which fantasies become visible. Without the body, these fantasies could not become visible at all, remaining, in words similarly invoked by Deleuze and Guattari several decades later, 'a sort of crystalline lattice in a solution where the crystallization process had not yet started' (Jung 1980, p. 173). Symbols rise from the depths of the body, which expresses their materiality as much as psychic consciousness of them does.

The archetype thus serves as a 'bridge' mediating between the deep layers of the unconscious, through the body to the conscious mind, connecting the present day to its primeval roots (p. 174). Although Jung's description of this process references depth and height and indicates a vertical relationship, his idea of a continuum between body and spirit should not be construed as hierarchical but horizontal. Jung believed that understanding matter and spirit as two different aspects of one and the same thing in part explained psychosomatic illness. If there is a problem, the body will experience symptoms until the psyche is strong enough to carry the conflict on its own (Harris 2001, pp. 19–21). Referencing his theory of synchronicity and his work with the Nobel laureate physicist Wolfgang Pauli, he noted that

> The non-psychic can behave like the psychic, and vice versa, without there being any causal connection between them. Our present knowledge does not allow us to do much more than compare the relation of the psychic to the material world with two cones, whose apices [apexes], meeting in a point without extension – a real zero-point – touch and do not touch.
>
> (Jung 1960, p. 215)

Drawing on alchemy and philosophies such as Tao, Tantra, Yoga, and Buddhism, he referred to the point where the psyche and soma 'touch but do not touch' as the 'subtle body', where the mind and body mutually influence each other.

Deleuze's conception of the tripartite nature of ontological difference both differs from, and owes a legacy to, Jung's conception of the mind/body relation. Jung's phenomenological explanation of the bodily absorption of symbolic knowledge has parallels to Deleuze's understanding of the relation between the Virtual, the Intensive, and the Actual. In Protevi's (2010) reading of Deleuze's conception of ontological difference, differential Ideas, multiplicities or 'pre-individual' singularities from the *virtual*, effectively 'structure' or induce *intensive* morphogenetic processes that work phenomenologically through the body to produce individuated, *actual* effects. As in Jung's description of the embodiment of the archetypes, Deleuze's Ideas or multiplicities are 'pre-individual singularities' that work through the body to create 'impersonal individuations' or intensive morphogentic processes that in turn produce actual system states (p. 422). In both Jung's and Deleuze's explanations, there is an understanding that unconscious knowledge, if effectively assimilated, can have significant material effects.

As in Jung's description of the transformation inherent to satori, there is an important phenomenological element in Deleuze's schema. One has to 'walk the thought' or enact it for it to become transformative. Like Jung's archetypes, Deleuze's Ideas are 'nothing' before they emerge as an actual pattern. For both Jung and Deleuze, the 'middle' component between archetype/Idea and output is an embodied, phenomenological enactment where the world is revealed between subject and thing. The major difference, of course, is that while Jung divided or stratified ideas into archetypal categories that he named and extensively described, Deleuze's Ideas are not defined categories, but rather operate on the basis of pure difference. These Ideas are constantly mutating on the basis of feedback loops or what Protevi refers to as 'counter-effectuations'. Once an Idea becomes 'intensive' in terms of being enacted through the body it in turn affects the 'affordances' of Ideas. Hence the structure of Ideas is temporary, not fixed, and in constant mutation.

This feedback mechanism is, I believe, compatible with, but less emphasized in, Jung's thinking. Jung emphasizes the need for a contingent interpretation of archetypal knowledge, and implicitly acknowledges in his understanding of individuation that the way archetypal knowledge is received will change as the individual passes through various *coniunctio* over time. But can Jungian theory acknowledge that these *coniunctio* will in turn have an impact on the collective unconscious? It is still possible to accept that these unconscious forces have a formative influence on culture and politics, while acknowledging that there is what I will describe in Chapter 3 as an 'intra-action' or mutually constitutive entanglement between them. What I am referring to here is a relation between the realm of representation and the cosmos/unconscious, similar to Jung's conception of the relation between mind and body inherent to the subtle body.

In my case study of the Rococo and *Art Nouveau* in Chapter 5, for example, I argue that although feminine energies were brutally repressed during the French Revolution, a *coniunctio* between the energies of sexual difference took place during the Rococo period that changed the way that feminine energies were received in the future. In Chapter 6, I show how the conscious acceptance of feminine energies at critical points in history resulted in completely novel economic arrangements. Does this intra-action mean that the 'eternal' forces of the unconscious are merely being received differently in the Actual or realm of representation due to changes in consciousness, or does it mean the unconscious is also being transformed, growing and transmuting in conjunction with changes in the realm of representation?

It is possible that physical actions can feed back to change the nature of the energy itself or the power of unconscious energies relative to each other. In other words, it is possible that consciously playing with the energies of sexual difference in the realm of art, language, and politics can have an effect on the nature of the unconscious itself. This relation is not unidirectional in either way, but rather simultaneously and mutually constitutive or what Barad (2006) would call intra-active. This way of thinking is also compatible with Knox's ideas outlined in Chapter 4. If the archetypes are 'reliably repeated early developmental achievements' (Knox 2003, p. 60) configured in the neural pathways of the brain, and if these neural pathways can in turn be altered by physical behaviour or beliefs, then this feedback loop between behaviour and the unconscious, or in Deleuze's terms the Actual and the Virtual, is confirmed. As I will argue further in Chapter 3, a greater openness to the possibility of the mutation of archetypal energies such as the masculine and feminine is necessary for the sort of fully contingent analysis Jung called for.

These differences and similarities between Jung's and Deleuze's approaches are particularly apparent in their conceptions of sexual difference. Jung defined the notion of the archetype in terms that correspond to Deleuze and Guattari's notion of the molecular, or at minimum, some stage in between the molar and molecular. In his actual use of the archetype, however, his ideas sometimes transform from what Pint (2011, p. 53) refers to as a Nietzschean line of flight away from Freud into a reterritorialization governed by the Platonic quest for transcendental truth. Frequently, his insistence on a 'molecular' version of the archetypes inexplicably becomes fixated on the 'molar' aspects of the archetype's manifestation. This is particularly true in his application of the archetypal masculine and feminine.

Like Freud, Jung believed that all humans possessed a bisexual psyche. For Jung, this union went back to primeval times, where differences and contrasts were either barely separated or completely merged (think of Plato's hermaphroditic beings in *Symposium)*. With the development of consciousness these opposites became more separate, however, and the hermaphroditic rebus has resonated across time as a 'uniting symbol' of the creative union of opposites. As noted above, for Jung it was a symbol of psychic wholeness, a union of the conscious and unconscious personality. The masculine and feminine unite in the human psyche as they do genetically in the human body:

> Just as every individual derives from the masculine and feminine genes, and the sex is determined by the predominance of the corresponding genes, so in the psyche it is only the conscious mind, in a man, that has the masculine sign, while the unconscious is by nature feminine. The reverse is true in the case of a woman.
>
> (Jung 1980, p. 175)

In *Anti-Oedipus*, Deleuze and Guattari present a discussion of the bisexual psyche that is almost identical to Jung's interpretation, with the exception that these two aspects of the psyche appear to be non-communicating within the individual:

> everyone is bisexual, everyone has two sexes, but partitioned, noncommunicating; the man is merely the one in whom the male part, and the woman the one in whom the female part, dominates statistically. So that at the level of elementary combinations, at least two men and two women must be made to intervene to constitute the multiplicity in which transverse communications are established connections of partial objects and flows: the male part of a man can communicate with the female part of a woman, but also with the male part of a woman, or with the female part of another man, or yet again with the male part of the other man, etc.
>
> (Deleuze and Guattari 1983, pp. 69–70)

For Jung, while the conscious aspect of the mind corresponds to one's biological sex, the contra-sexual aspect of the Self is always unconscious. In other words, as opposed to the Freudian emphasis on *sex* as the prime motivator in the human psyche, one of Jung's and Deleuze and Guattari's key motors is *sexual difference*. And this sexual difference, to borrow Grosz's (2011, p. 107) description of Irigaray's use of the term, 'is universal, an ontological condition of life on earth rather than a performatively produced artifact'.

Jung, however, reverted to an essentialist understanding of the bisexual psyche that has caused much consternation in post-Jungian circles. He referred to the contra-sexual feminine aspect of a man's psyche as the *anima*. The *anima* may appear in dreams in either a positive sense, such as a high priestess, or negatively, perhaps as a witch or femme fatale. Von Franz notes that men sometimes project aspects of their *anima* onto a particular woman.

A man might fall helplessly in love with a woman because he is projecting aspects of his *anima* onto her. The negative *anima* in a man is moody, irritable, or makes constant devaluing comments. The *anima* also has a transformative, positive function, however, in that she can act as a mediator or guide to a man's inner values, bringing him to a more profound depth. A man can develop his positive anima by taking seriously the feelings, moods, expectations, and fantasies sent by his anima and fixing them in the form of writing, painting, music, or various forms of art. The terms feminine and *anima* were not coterminous for Jung, however. He argued that there are feminine symbols with especially numinous qualities (like mother symbols) that are particularly important for both women and men that would not be included in the contra-sexual *anima*.

Especially in his early work, Jung saw the feminine encapsulated in the term *Eros*, or psychic relatedness. At times, he associated the feminine more generally with psyche. Jung's notion of *Eros* as relationship is much closer to the Platonic sense of this term outlined in the *Symposium*, and is not restricted to sexuality or sexual desire. When Socrates visits the wise woman Diotima to discover the true meaning of *Eros*, she explains to him that true *Eros* leads one to see the beloved as just one example of a more universal, archetypal beauty. When someone appreciates one person's body, she explains, they realize that beauty in one body is related to that in others. This leads to the realization that erotic intensity for one body is petty. The lover will thus begin to seek beauty more broadly in 'pursuits and laws', then the sciences, then nature,

> and looking at the beautiful, which is now so vast, no longer be content like a lackey with the beauty in one, of a boy, of some human being, or of one practice; . . . but with a permanent turn to the vast open sea of the beautiful, behold it and give birth . . . to many beautiful and magnificent speeches and thoughts.
>
> (Plato 2001, p. 41)

Jung's interpretation of the symbolic feminine as *Eros* was in part derived from a reading of his own and his patients' dreams, but he developed these concepts in the context of a genealogical study of the cross-cultural and cross-temporal symbolic portrayals of women. Given that some of the most prominent physical aspects of women are that they give birth to children and have wombs and breasts, it is not surprising that these physical facts are drawn on when trying to symbolize an energic force or power that affectively *feels* similar to mothering.

Jung saw a wisdom in *Eros* equal to the objectivity and morality inherent to the archetypal masculine, which he characterized as *Logos*. The *animus* is the masculine side of the female psyche, which Jung defined as discrimination, judgment, and insight (Jung 1977, p. 179). Like the *anima*, the animus has its positive and negative aspects, taking forms as disparate as the hero or the cold-blooded Bluebeard. The negative animus in a woman is cold, brutal, or obstinate. An overwhelming negative animus in a woman's psyche can lead to passivity and paralysis. The positive animus, on the other hand bears the qualities of initiative, creativity, spirituality, courage, and objectivity. In its highest stage, the *animus* is the mediator of a religious experience that brings a woman's life new meaning (von Franz 1964, pp. 198–207).

In his later work, Jung (1977, p. 179) said he preferred the alchemical terms *Sol* and *Luna* (sun and moon) rather than *Logos* and *Eros* to characterize the masculine and feminine, which he saw as 'intellectually formulated intuitive equivalents' of the former (p. 179). While *Sol* emits the bright light that allows for clear discernment and judgment, *Luna* is the 'universal receptacle of all things' (p. 176). Her lower luminosity, rather than discerning differences, often overlooks them, a key to her dominant *Eros*. Jung follows this observation with a highly stereotypical example that links this capacity to overlook differences to women's superior role in managing the family. I would restate this by saying that *Luna's* ability to reside in between points of difference is another (devalued) aspect of knowledge that, when considered in tandem with the rational discerning of difference inherent to *Logos*, is integral to the way humans perceive and function on a daily basis. This emphasis on the feminine as *Luna* might also explain Jung's comments that characterize the psyche more generally as feminine. The dispersed, hazy light of the moon is an apt metaphor for the non-rational nature of psychic knowledge, which must be felt as much as seen.

We might try to understand this by considering Bergson's explanation of the dualisms underlying consciousness. For Bergson, perception in part occurs when individuals make artificial 'cuts' to the flow of duration. But being, he argued, cannot be comprised merely of separate states placed side by side. It is more like a 'gentle slope' of discrete events that exist only through the intervals linking them. Like beads on a necklace, they must be joined by the thread of psychical life (Bergson 2007, p. 2). Bergson's metaphor of cuts and intervals parallels Jung's notions of a masculine, discerning *Logos* and feminine, relational *Eros*. For both Bergson and Jung, these dualisms are opposing, but also mutually constitutive or simultaneous, comprising two very different conceptions of both being and perception.

I will add a less emphasized aspect of Jung's understanding of the feminine to these portrayals of *Eros* or *Luna*: *anima* as butterfly. Hillman (1985) cites many references by Jung to *anima* as butterfly and I will argue that this is a parallel to Deleuze's concept of a philosophy of surface. Hillman argues that *anima* as butterfly 'flutters over the field of events' (p. 25) appearing to be skimming the surface, but in fact revealing a new conception of depth. As Hillman points out, the butterfly's hovering flight reveals a consciousness 'that does not soar but stays attached . . . Like the butterfly, anima-consciousness moves through phases, bearing a process, a history. It is egg, worm, cocoon, bright wing – and not only successively but all at once' (p. 25). This version of *anima* hints at a novel conception of both space and time – of simultaneity and the paradoxical depth of surface that bears many similarities to Deleuze's (1990) philosophy of surface outlined in *The Logic of Sense.*

I will explain this concept in greater detail in Chapter 7, drawing on this image of *anima* to develop the dimension of sexual difference inherent to Deleuze's (1990, p. 9) emphasis on the paradoxes and new understandings of depth inherent to a philosophy of surface, in which an 'old depth having been spread out became width', allowing for a 'becoming unlimited that is maintained entirely within this inverted width'. On this surface, things slide sideways, often in both directions at once, rather than move up and down; there is a simultaneity and fluidity here that defies traditional conceptions of time and space. Deleuze explains this phenomenon using examples from Lewis Carroll's *Alice in Wonderland,* arguing that although this paradox of depth is actually drawn from Stoic philosophy, it took a girl to discover it in Modern times. The connection that both Jung and Deleuze make between the feminine and this new conception of depth will reappear in my discussions of Demeter and Persephone in Chapter 4, in the swarming curves of the Rococo in Chapter 5, and in my analysis of the Postmodern sensibility in Chapter 7. Although both Jung and Deleuze make a connection between this sensibility of surface and the feminine, it is never clear, in my view, whether this emphasis on surface is related to the feminine itself, or if it is an effect manifested when the energies of sexual difference eddy or plateau.

I also pay attention to Neumann's discussion of the elemental and transformative aspects of the feminine. Erich Neumann (1974) went beyond his friend and mentor to exhaustively categorize these manifestations of the symbolic feminine in his book *The Great Mother.* In this encyclopaedic survey of the symbols of the feminine, Neumann categorizes them as positive (light) or negative (dark) and elementary (fixed) or transformative (fluid), with a variety of permutations between these limits. A positive elemental feminine might symbolize the feelings of a successful 'containment' experience and evoke feelings such as contentment, safety, relatedness, or even sensual pleasure in terms of the tactile pleasures of being gently held and nurtured or breast-fed. Negative elemental symbols, on the other hand, indicate sensations of being devoured or trapped. Positive images of the transformative feminine can be associated with wisdom or spiritual ideals, while negative ones can indicate madness or even death (Carey Ford 2004, p. 99).

Importantly, Neumann emphasized that the elemental and the transformative were two sides of the same coin, or two aspects of the same phenomenon. One rarely finds signs of one sort of this feminine energy apart from the other.

For Jung, addressing both the masculine and feminine aspects of the psyche was not just important to the individuation process, but in a collective sense as well. He despaired for the one-sided masculine emphasis of contemporary patriarchy and religion, but viewed patriarchy not as a stable situation, but part of the larger phenomenon of a term I will describe in Chapter 3 as the *enantiodromia*. In his view, this situation was destined to change.

Jung's elaboration of the bisexual psyche, despite its emphasis on transformation, has essentialist, foundationalist undertones. Curiously, Jung's essentialism seems to betray his own warnings not to rationally define the archetypes, especially when he projects archetypal characteristics onto the bodies of women and men. Although Jung argued that there were aspects of the masculine and feminine in both men and women, he clearly stated that women are more feminine than masculine, unless they have a problematic over-identification with the animus, with the opposite true of men. This infers that there are 'normal' ways of being a woman or man and that not acting this way may indicate a neurosis. The assumption of contra-sexuality in the psyche also suggests a demarcated psychic duality, which infers that the path for transformation for a woman is through her masculine animus, while a man must channel his anima to individuate.

No one has been more critical of this aspect of his thought than post-Jungians. In a particularly strenuous objection to Jung's notion of the contra-sexual psyche, Jungian analyst McKenzie (2006) notes:

> Jung's anima/animus (A/A) thinking leads us into a trap of linear orderliness, fixed identities, androgynous symmetries, and archetypes that are differentially inherited, based on sexual anatomy, a breach in the universality of the collective unconscious. His gender theory does however allow for both genders to reside in an individual but posits a slow and sex-appropriate emergence of the contra-sexual from the unconscious. Jung's A/A cannot account for the transgendered experience with its reversal of starting points and fluidity of sexual attractions. Jung's A/A is a terrible fit for our time. We live in an era of emergent, not fixed realities, and are beginning to value the overt display of masculinity and femininity in both sexes.
>
> (McKenzie 2006, p. 407)

McKenzie's rejection of the association of fixed definitions of the masculine and feminine with body morphology is indicative of a broader critique of sexual difference whose most prominent proponent is Judith Butler. Butler does not deny the possibility of an ontological nature of the body, but claims it is impossible to know what it is because it is 'never simply a function of material differences which are not in some way both marked and formed by discursive practices' (Butler 2011, p. 1). Although our desire to know the body impels us toward attempts to understand it, the actual ontological nature of the body is 'foreclosed' to us by our inability to understand it outside of the political and cultural assumptions inherent to language; for this reason, it remains always on the 'outside'. To fill this persistent gap, we continually 'posit' what the sexed body is – but our only means of doing this is through culturally inflected systems of language. This process of positing obviously opens the door to highly political assumptions about the nature of sexed bodies that are in fact historically and socially constructed.

These social constructions of the appropriate or 'natural' roles of masculinity or femininity, including the very notion that there can only be binary forms of sexed bodies, become posited or naturalized as ontological truths. These posited 'ontologies' are reinforced by the repeated ritualization or performance of culturally inflected understandings of sex and gender which, although imaginary, become reality, as in Jung's phenomenology of the imagination noted above. Butler thus denies that bodily sex can be a natural foundation upon which culturally influenced notions of gender are based. What we consider to be the 'ontological' basis of sex itself is a discursive creation, reinforced by the repeated performance of discursively created understandings of sex. In effect, she is denying the possibility of knowing any foundational essence of sexual difference because our only way of knowing is through our constructed, inflected, and imperfect modes of language. Thus, she claims that the sexed body 'has no ontological status apart from the various acts which constitute its reality' (Butler 1999, p. 136).

Although she does not deny the impact of material aspects of the body such as hormones, age, illness, etc., she argues that even these ostensibly biological 'facts' are actually affirmed by the 'interpretive matrices' that condition and enable them. She thus argues that we should view matter as a 'process of materialization that stabilizes over time to produce the effect of boundary, fixity and surface we call matter' (Butler 2011, p. 9). Sex is not pre-given but becomes naturalized by reiterative or ritual practice (p. 10). She therefore rejects the emphasis on sexual difference that is evident in the work of feminists such as Irigaray, viewing it as evidence of heteronormative bias.

Butler's argument deserves serious consideration in terms of its relevance to Jungian understandings of the symbol. From this perspective, it is not possible to be 'pre-cultural' as Jung claimed his archetypes were, nor to talk about ontological forces or energies as Deleuze and Guattari and Grosz do.

How can we separate the characteristics Jung attributes to the symbolic feminine from both his own and more collective political-cultural constructions of women? As he himself noted, 'most of what men say about feminine eroticism, and particularly about the emotional life of women, is derived from their own anima projections and distorted accordingly' (Jung 1981, p. 198). So why should we take any man's (or woman's, for that matter) understanding of something called the archetypal feminine seriously?

Butler's critique must be constantly borne in mind when discussing understandings of sexual difference, but she goes too far in her distinction between ontology and representation. How can she 'know' that one cannot 'know' a fundamental essence of sex? We can certainly empirically ascertain that these essences become discursively stereotyped and politicized in the realm of representation, but can we really prove that this is the only way they can be experienced? Should we be jettisoning what might be ontological expressions simply because we know they have the potential to be manipulated as culturally inflected representations? Jung's and Deleuze's claims that such knowledge is effectively unrepresentable and transmitted primarily via affect suggests that in doing so, we might also be disregarding important sources of meaning and transformation.

Butler's approach places a firm boundary between the ontological body and the way it is signified in the realm of representation. Colebrook (2000, p. 83) argues that Butler's 'insistence of sex as an *effect of representation*' (her emphasis) enacts a strict boundary between nature or sex and its representation (language or gender). In effect, she refuses to engage with the question of precisely what it is that gender re-presents, which ultimately results in defining the ontological nature of the body in opposition to its signification (p. 84). As noted above, Jung explicitly purged this boundary in his concept of the subtle body, where mind and body 'touch but do not touch', as did Deleuze in his conception of the relation between the Idea/intensive/actual. This is a practice I will continue throughout this book, stressing the mutual constitution of the body/matter and the psychic, or the ontological and the realm of representation.

Butler's critique contains many important insights that are highly relevant to the Jungian approach. It seems clear, however, that the only thing we can say with certainty about the debate between approaches that insist on sexual difference, and views such as Butler's which deny its existence, is that we cannot *know* in any rational way which perspective is 'true'. This said, jettisoning ontological or pre-ontological assumptions risks precluding potential forces for change. Symbols make themselves known through projection, using the culturally inflected language and images of the contemporary realm of signification – but that does not mean we should dismiss them as inherently conservative. On the contrary, if properly understood, they can be the basis for a creative re-imagining of the forces of sexual difference in the space of the subtle body, a practice that can be contingently based on changing individual and collective experience. This process, as I will elaborate further in Chapter 3, is what Hardt and Negri call biopolitics.

For example, in her critique of the foundational status of the Oedipal myth in Lacanian psychoanalysis Butler categorically rejects the usefulness of the notion of sexual difference. She argues that the Oedipal story with its triangular family relationships gives sexual difference a structural status that makes it more foundational than other differences (Butler 2000, p. 143). Is it really foundational, she asks, or is it only posited as such? Do we want to affirm this foundational status, she wonders 'Or do we want to question whether any ideality that pertains to sexual difference is ever not constituted by actively reproduced gender norms that pass their ideality off as essential to a pre-social and ineffable sexual difference?' (p. 144). Her rhetorical question presupposes her answer. In her view, sexual difference should be 'rigorously opposed by anyone who wants to guard against a theory that would prescribe in advance what kinds of sexual arrangements will and will not be permitted in intelligible culture' (p. 148).

Butler makes a valid point regarding the heteronormativity of the Oedipal myth, but her use of this point to reject sexual difference has been opposed by those who find potential for new forms of subjectivity in Irigaray's concept of sexual difference. In a comment similar to Jung's critique of Freud's semiotic approach to the symbol above, Grosz (2011, p. 85) criticizes the deconstructive approaches of Postmodern feminists for veiling the Real, calling for its reconceptualization in terms that function both beyond and within representation. The idea that something is ontological or *a priori* does not mean that its meaning is written in stone or incapable of morphing into new manifestations and understandings over time.

A good example of this is the use of the concept of *hierosgamos* or 'marriage' in alchemy. Not long ago, this conception would have been evidence of alchemy's presumptive heterosexuality – now, in the context of same-sex marriage, it cannot be. One could argue that this example shows, in line with Butler's argument, how changes in the representation of marriage in the realm of signification can lead to a different 'positing' of the supposedly 'natural' understanding of marriage as heterosexual. From the perspective of Grosz's emphasis on the ontological nature of sexual difference, however, it shows the potential for evolution in the understanding of ontological forces of sexual difference, and the necessity for understanding their meaning contingently and symbolically, as Jung argued, and not semiotically. This latter perspective shows the interaction between ontological forces and their representation, emphasizing their co-constitution, rather than assuming a unidirectional positing from the realm of signification to the ontological.

The compensatory unconscious 53

Throughout this book I will be discussing the entangled relationship between symbolic knowledge, the body, and what I will call the realm of representation.[1] This approach offers an alternative way to develop a methodology of contingency for understanding sexual difference – viewing essential forces as flowing into the realm of signification in ways that 'refract' off the politics in play there. It means that political change comes not only from showing the discursive construction of being in the realm of representation or signification (Butler's approach), but also from feeling the resonance of the ontological forces that might instigate such changes. For both Jung and Deleuze, such an 'aesthetic' understanding of ontological forces can have transformational results, in effect changing the individual's entire perspective on their involvement in the realm of representation surrounding them.

Applying this approach to the forces of sexual difference means working in both the realms of representation and the ontological world of what Jung called the unconscious and Deleuze and Guattari called the rhizome, playing with the representation of energies in a way that transforms our understanding of them. Such a strategy invokes Irigaray's focus on the future anterior – what will have been. It is short-sighted to reject the potential of symbolic forces simply because of the politicized nature of their meaning in the realm of signification. Perhaps we cannot 'know', but we can dream, fantasize, imagine.

Understanding this relationship involves an affective relationship to both the realms of the ontological symbolic and the realm of signification, sorting out this question in a more negotiated way, rather than categorically asserting that the complications of language and epistemology make 'knowing' the ontological impossible. This involves a different kind of epistemological approach to analyzing the image. From the perspective of rational ways of knowing, for example, Butler's ideas pose a valid question in terms of how one is supposed to distinguish between the *a priori* values of the symbol and their posited projection in the realm of signification. Jung's claim that some images may be semiotic, while others are symbolic raises a similar question: how do we 'know' how to make this distinction? Answering this question involves deconstructing the concept of 'knowing' itself.

For both Jung and Deleuze, a numinous, symbolic message is felt, rather than rationally known. Recall that for Jung, it is through the affect that one acknowledges the symbol, a point that was also true for Deleuze. As Braidotti notes, for Deleuze the truth value of thoughts and ideas are determined not by their propositional content, but by the intensity of their affective force (Braidotti 1994, p. 113). One *feels* when something has symbolic value, which in turn explains its transformative properties.

This does not mean ignoring the realm of signification and the politics and representations that constitute it. Understanding how to interpret these feelings involves a deep meditative relationship with the energies they are related to. In this respect, the feminist tactic of saying that there is sexual difference, but not defining what form such differences may take, or the post-Jungian approach of simply regarding it as 'other' often will not suffice if one is to have a satisfying assimilation of these energies. Also, if one accepts the Jungian/Deleuzean idea that these energies might be compensatory, how can we know what we are compensating for if we do not try to evoke some notion of what they might mean?

This problem becomes evident in Deleuze and Guattari's concept of *anima*: becoming-woman. The molecular notion of becoming-woman is key to Deleuze and Guattari's (1987) notion of transformation; indeed, they claim that 'All becomings begin with and pass through becoming-woman' (p. 277). This is so because it is the girl (who is literally a 'becoming-woman') who is first disciplined into behaving according to the discourses of history, or to use their example, is told 'you're not a little girl anymore, stop behaving like . . .' The boy is subsequently disciplined by reference to the girl as the object of desire, through which a dominant history becomes imposed on him, too (p. 276). Their molecular girl lives in the *intermezzo* – opposing herself to the molar forms of man, woman, or child.

But Deleuze and Guattari's emphasis on becoming-woman is also related to woman's status as 'minoritarian'. The 'majoritarian' view assumes the pre-given rights of man in the universe. In contrast, women, children, plants, animals, and molecules are minoritarian. 'It is perhaps the special situation of women in relation to the man-standard that accounts for the fact that becomings, being minoritarian, always pass through a becoming-woman' (p. 291). Parallel to Jung's conception of the role of *anima* in the male psyche, they argue that woman's status as 'other' to man means that she is the root to transformation, since any becoming-minoritarian necessarily 'rends him from his major identity' (p. 291). In this respect, it necessarily affects woman as much as majoritarian man (p. 291).

As Flieger (2000) points out, becoming-woman is Deleuze's version of the more familiar post-structuralist critique of binary oppositions and hierarchies that assume an average white, male, rational, European subject. For Deleuze and Guattari, 'There is no becoming man because man is the molar entity par excellence, whereas becomings are molecular' (Deleuze and Guattari 1987, p. 292). From this perspective, becoming woman is a deterritorialization, a decentring of the subject (Flieger 2000, pp. 45–6). In this respect, 'Becoming woman is a way of understanding transformative possibilities – the ways in which identity might escape from the codes which constitute the subject' (Driscoll 2000, p. 75).

Deleuze and Guattari (1987) warn, however, that becoming-woman risks stratification and becoming molar as a 'macropolitics' of the feminine.

While they acknowledge the need for women to conduct a molar politics to win back their own organism, they caution that women's politics should be conceived in a molecular fashion 'that slips into molar confrontations, and passes under or through them' (p. 276). By this, they mean that although women may use the minoritarian energies of becoming-woman to draw attention to their claims, the creation of a concrete or molar political movement that assumes the coincidence between these molecular energies and a group of people called women risks stifling becoming-woman's transformative potential.

Many feminists have made similar arguments, pointing to the exclusionary effects of assuming that women as a group have similar goals and viewpoints regardless of race, class, or sexual preference. However, for others this emphasis on the molecular constitution of becoming woman, combined with the tendency to separate this energy from the actual bodies of women, has been a focus of critique. The central concern is that this approach denies sex-specific forms of agency that are important for struggles to redefine female subjectivity (Grosz 1994, pp. 162–3). As Braidotti notes,

> Deleuze's work displays a great empathy with the feminist assumption that sexual difference is the primary axis of differentiation and therefore must be given priority. On the other hand, he also displays the tendency to dilute metaphysical difference into a multiple and undifferentiated becoming.
>
> (Braidotti 2003, p. 47)

In her view, this presupposes a subjective symmetry between the sexes, as if there is an understanding of feminine subjectivity equivalent to the hegemonic masculine one. As she points out, however, deconstructing a subjectivity that one has not been fully granted control over is premature. 'In order to announce the death of the subject, one must first have gained the right to speak as one', (Braidotti 2003, p. 51). Jardine voices similar concerns, describing Deleuze and Guattari's work as 'fervently worshipped' by male students and curiously out of sync with the concerns of feminism (Jardine 1985).

Grosz (1994, p. 184) notes that while becoming woman appears to be a necessary force of transformation, it is not clear what she symbolizes for women or men. How does this becoming relate to 'being'? Haraway is much blunter in her critique of Deleuze and Guattari's molecular more generally, noting 'I am not sure I can find in philosophy a clearer display of misogyny, fear of aging, incuriosity about animals, and horror of the ordinariness of flesh, here covered by the alibi of an anti-Oedipal and anti-capitalist project' (Haraway 2008, p. 3).

Deleuze and Guattari's resistance to relating becoming-woman to the 'molar', flesh-and-blood bodies of women lies at the centre of these critiques. Finding a balance between their more molecular approach and Jung's more molar one is key to developing a dynamic notion of the symbolic, transformative feminine. In other words, is it possible to understand an embodied essence of something we call the 'feminine', but avoid being essentialist?

Working through Jung's and Deleuze's views in combination with what Colebrook refers to as a 'dynamic embodiment' approach of Australian feminists such as Grosz, Gatens, and Lloyd can provide some insight into this problem. This approach focuses on the specificity of men's and women's bodies, arguing that physical differences mean different lived experiences for the bodies and minds that inhabit them. From this perspective, the body can be described as a force that both limits and mobilizes its representational becoming (Grosz 1994, p. 84).

For Grosz, Gatens, and Colebrook, the experience of the lived body will differ according to sex, but there is nothing permanently 'given' in this process. In Colebrook's words,

> Masculinity and Femininity are *more* than mental or cultural representations; but at the same time they cannot be appealed to as self-present substances or essences given once and for all through certain attributes and qualities. Rather, we might refer to different and specific modes of dynamic embodiment.
>
> (Colebrook 2000, p. 87)

She cites Grosz's argument that the body is an 'open materiality, a set of (possibly infinite) tendencies and potentialities which may be developed, yet whose development will necessarily hinder or induce other developments and other trajectories' (Grosz 1994 cited in Colebrook 2000, p. 89).

Dynamic embodiment is a form of becoming that will differ according to the sexual attributes of each body and its interactions with mental or cultural representations of gender. In this respect, as Colebrook presciently notes, whereas Butler focuses primarily on Foucault's ideas about discourse, Grosz relies more on his conception of power in modes beyond the sites of knowledge and speech (Colebrook 2000, p. 84). The experiences of menstruation (Gatens 1996), or living 'breasted' (Young 1980), for example, are inflected both by patriarchal norms and judgments surrounding such physicality, as well as the actual lived experiences of such bodily realities. In this respect, although this approach insists upon sexual difference, this difference is not conceived essentially because we never know precisely what it is.

Gatens (1996) argues that we all inhabit socially and historically specific 'imaginary' bodies that will affect our lived experience in the world. It is in

The compensatory unconscious 57

this imaginary body that we evaluate relative perceptions of male or female bodies as informed by collective stereotypes or beliefs, or the value, stigma, or trauma of particular bodily experiences, such as menstruation, sex, or childbirth. This is why psychological issues such as hysteria or anorexia nervosa affect people in a collective, gender-specific way (p. 12). This conception of the imaginary body is similar to Jung's subtle body, but is much more specifically influenced by collective discourses of social and historical experience.

This is an important addition to Jung's ideas because it shows more specifically how desire becomes imagined when it works through the body. What happens in the subtle or imaginary body is both an effect of how desire filters through the flesh-and-blood body of hormones, organs, and neural pathways, and a reflection of how it plays out or becomes imagined in the realm of signification of discourses, institutions, and ideologies. The body and the realm of signification 'intra-act', affect each other, resulting in constantly changing manifestations of discourses, images, and ideologies and understandings of the body.

Although Gaten's account of the imaginary body is useful to the extent that it explains how bodily knowledge can be imagined on a collective level, however, it cannot really explain why the men described by Wollen and Reed in the previous chapter would be channelling feminine energy. Based as it is on the differing bodily experiences of men and women, Gaten's account can explain the specificity of a feminine and masculine imaginary, but not necessarily their contra-sexual attraction. This problem is less evident in Grosz's work, where she moves toward a more explicitly Deleuzean/Jungian understanding of sexual difference as forces that 'preexist the entities they produce' (Grosz 2005, p. 174).

In Grosz's concept of bodies as an open materiality, they are constantly changing in response to new understandings of male and female (and other) bodies and lived experience. As Colebrook argues, acknowledging the sexual difference of bodies in such a way goes beyond a strategic use of essentialism. In words identical to those used in Kerslake's discussion of the Jungian unconscious above, she describes sexual specificity as a *problem*, a way of 'dislodging thought from its Cartesian homeliness' (Colebrook 2000, p. 89).

Despite her critique of Deleuze and Guattari's becoming-woman, Grosz uses a similar approach in her attempt to develop an aesthetic conception of *a priori* forces of sexual difference, without labelling what these energies might look like. This is evident in her discussion of the relationship between sexual difference and aesthetics or art. Inspired by Deleuze and Darwin, Grosz argues that theories focusing on the politics of representation of art flatten and reduce the complexity of culture. Taking up the now familiar argument of both Deleuze and Jung with regard to the symbol, she argues that understanding art involves looking at forces *outside* the cultural, not inside it (Grosz 2005, p. 48). Rejecting the nature/culture division, she looks at the role of biological forces, among them Darwin's notion of sexual selection, and how they enable cultural production.

'The different arts are a consequence of the various experiments in intensification that have marked sexual life on earth' Grosz (2008, p. 9) argues. Biological difference opens us up to 'the indeterminancy of taste, pleasure, and sensation', evident in mating rituals in the natural world which produce artistic performances such as birdsong, erotic displays of dance and colour, or the emission of scents and perfumes. 'Sexuality', she argues, 'is not about the production of a norm but about the eruption of taste' (Grosz 2011, p. 130). Sexual activity is a manifestation of pleasure in itself, with reproduction merely a by-product of it.

These forces of sexual difference are pre-individual, *a priori*, ontological energies that become manifest in cultural production. Drawing on Deleuze, she argues that art in the form of music, dance, sculpture, painting, or architecture transmits resonant vibrations of a force that should be considered 'not as the product of mankind, an invention that distinguishes the human from the animal, but rather a nonhuman "unlivable Power"' (Grosz 2008, p. 19). Such pre-individual forces penetrate the permeable borders of the human and 'the personal gives way to the impersonal and the living connects with and is driven by events beyond it' (Grosz 2011, p. 38).

Grosz does not invoke gender in her definition of these forces of sexual difference, eschewing efforts such as Jung's to define aspects of the feminine, or Deleuze and Guattari's emphasis on the transformative impact of becoming woman. For her:

> Sexual difference implies that there are at least two ways of doing anything, from the most abstract forms of thought to the most concrete forms of production to the most intense practices of pleasure, without being able to specify in what ways they may develop or what form they may take. Which means that the production of concepts themselves must provide at least two paths of development, at least two (possibly incommensurable) modes of existence, not in competition with each other to find which is the best, nor in augmentation of each other to provide a more complete picture, but as two singularities that may either conflict with or complement each other, that may be altogether incomparable or simply different.
>
> (Grosz 2005, p. 176)

Darwin, she claims, was the first feminist of difference because of his argument that at least two irreducible morphologies of sexual difference were the engines for the variations that sustained life on earth (Grosz 2011, p. 142). To avoid attaching this to the presumption of heterosexuality, she separates Darwin's linked, but distinct, notions of sexual selection and natural selection. Natural selection is all about Darwin's famed aphorism of the 'survival of the fittest', and is therefore associated with reproductive mutations of genetic structure. Sexual selection is the non-functional, energic expression of life – the 'will to power' that Nietzsche argued emanated from every cell in the body, not just the sexual gametes (p. 119). Sexual selection is less about survival and more about excess, intensities, and choosing and attracting objects of desire, whether or not they are the fittest or most appealing (p. 125). Such expressions can take many forms, from heterosexuality to homosexuality, to a swan falling in love with a boat (p. 129).

There are several points where Grosz's approach and the Jungian perspective 'touch but do not touch'. For one, the Jungian understanding of the unconscious runs parallel to Grosz's conception of the relationship between sex and the Lacanian Real. For example, Colebrook claims that while Butler understands the Real as a logical effect of positing, Grosz sees the Real as a pre-semantic domain of sexual specificity. Like Jung's conception of the unconscious, for Grosz, the Real is *a priori* there to be symbolized; it is not an *ex post facto* effect of symbolization. It is known after, but exists prior to, symbolization (Colebrook 2000). Here Grosz does to Butler what, as in Zizek's quote above, Jung did to Freud, and Deleuze did to Lacan. In a comment that parallels Jung's critique of Freud's semantic approach to the symbol, Grosz notes:

> This image of the real enshrouded by the order of representations, an order which veils us from direct access to the real, is perhaps the most dominant residue of how 'postmodern feminists,' and especially those influenced by deconstruction, understand the real – as what can never be touched or known in itself, an ever-receding horizon. We need to reconceptualize the real as forces, energies, events, impacts that preexist and function both before and beyond, as well as within, representation.
>
> (Grosz 2011, p. 85)

Grosz's insistence that feminist theory needs to turn to the ontological, cosmological forces of the world is also compatible with the Jungian model of the feminine as a positive force of energy, as opposed to the Lacanian focus on lack. Grosz, however, specifically rejects the idea of defining what an ontological category known as the feminine might look like. Jung, as we know, defined both the masculine and the feminine in definite terms. Comparing these two approaches provides some insight into why an amended version of Jung's approach might prove superior.

Grosz's argument shows how and why the energies behind cultural production can be considered as libidinal and layered by sexual difference. Although her account clearly has political implications, however, she does not delineate in concrete terms what forms they might take. In fact, her ideas, although readily adaptable to political realities, are strangely apolitical, mostly because she ignores the collective dimensions of these libidinal energies – that they can affect many people similarly, at the same time, and take the same forms.

Partly because of this, and despite its biological grounding in Darwin, Grosz's Deleuzean-inspired analysis of sexual difference remains fairly molecular in form. While she makes an excellent case for the centrality of sexual difference in art and life, what is its relevance for the political situation of women or men? In her determination to avoid essentialism, she avoids defining or specifying what these two 'ways of doing anything' might be. One might justifiably ask, as she did of Deleuze, what is the relevance of these two 'ways of doing' for men or women? This has been a perennial problem for feminist analysis. As Chanter notes, on the one hand, there is a desire to resist any kind of reification, universalization, or generalization of the term woman. On the other hand, there is a need to recognize that being a woman informs one's experience, a practice that often leads to charges of essentialism (Chanter 1995, p. 28).

I respect Grosz's, and Deleuze and Guattari's, desire to avoid sending women back into the 'black hole' of a stratifying essentialism, but there are other ways to do this aside from denying that there is such a thing as essence at all. While their approach tends to avoid essentialism by refraining from saying what sexual difference looks like, there is the alternative, more Jungian approach of saying what it looks like, but bringing it into the *intermezzo* – that space between the body and the mind he called the subtle body. Here the energies of feminine *Eros* and masculine *Logos* can be re-imagined in forms apart from their purely biological and sexual associations. In the same way that Jung argued for understanding desire/libido/élan vital in a way that was not purely sexual, this involves understanding what is feminine or what is masculine in a way that is not strictly coterminous with, but still relevant to, the bodies of men and women.

In Jung's terms, I am calling for a *symbolic,* as opposed to a literal or *semiotic* interpretation of what the feminine is. A conscious appreciation of the symbolic energies of what Grosz calls the two 'ways of being' of sexual difference can be the basis for what Hardt and Negri (2009) would call biopolitics – a focus on the formation of alternative subjectivities. The kind of subjective exploration I am describing here corresponds to a sort of renegotiation of collective discourses of sexual and gender identity.

The compensatory unconscious 61

This approach relies on an *a priori* understanding of sexual difference while at the same time promoting the transferability of these energies. Rather than being essentialist, it allows for a fluid negotiation of these energies within both the individual and the collective psyches. As opposed to being limited to stratified identities, subjectivity can be viewed in a much more contingent, compensatory way that might change over time or in different circumstances. Such a configuration need not be strictly delineated in Jung's conception of the bisexual psyche – one can imagine a more liquid negotiation of these energies along a spectrum, where what is 'harmonious' to the self will depend on specific and contingent needs and compensations. This implies an understanding of identity, whether it is political, sexual, or gendered, in the same terms that Jung defined individuation: as an ongoing, negotiated process of transformation.

Negotiating identity

This process of negotiation involves a muddying of the strictly bisexual nature of the psyche proposed by Jung. In terms that parallel Foucault, Post-Jungians such as Samuels argue that sexual difference should be interpreted symbolically as something that is '*other,* strange, perhaps mysterious, but certainly full of possibilities and potentials' (Samuels 1985, p. 212). This *other* is contra-sexual because a woman or man will symbolize that which is *other* to them as an image of the opposite sex. 'Animus and anima', he notes, 'are ways of communicating otherness, difference, that which is momentarily unavailable because of unconsciousness. Animus and anima speak, then, of the unexpected, of that which is "out of order", which offends the prevailing order' (p. 214).

In this respect, one can view sexual difference as one of a series of complexes circulating around the ego. As Young-Eisendrath argues, animus and anima are attempts by individuals to explore the boundaries of their respective identities, the 'not-I' of the self. She argues that although a woman is limited in her subjectivity by culturally constructed notions of gender, she is also constrained by her form of embodiment. Parallel to the sexed embodiment approach outlined above, she argues that even if a woman tries to change her form of embodiment, it will always result in something other than a male body. How a woman imagines this limit of other, combined with her own interactions with actual male people, is central to the development of her selfhood (Young-Eisendrath 1992, p. 152).

Similarly, 'Anima is the expression of male people imagining what it means to be female, to give birth, to nurture, and to be embodied in a female form, as well as all else they experience as the female other' (p. 153). A man's anima is developed from his personal experience with women, but also his own embodiment and its meaning in the broader cultural situation of patriarchy. Anima is both idealized and feared and is projected onto real women, resulting in a consequent idealization or fear of actual biological women. She argues that it is important to recognize and withdraw this projection if men are to develop a healthy relationship with women in their daily lives.

Understanding a woman's animus or a man's anima from this perspective is a unique and personal process that involves examining patterns of unconscious symbols of the masculine and feminine in individuals and attempting to sort out what those symbols might mean in a contingent sense – the sense of both the collective they live in and their personal psyche. In this process, it is important for the individual to distinguish between their own projected 'not-I' and the actual *subjectivity* of members of other sex(es), races, or whatever other identity complexes they might be working through.

I would amend Young-Eisendrath's negotiation of the psyche to argue that anima is the expression of *all* people imagining what it means to be female, to give birth, to nurture, and to be embodied in a female form, as well as all else they experience as 'feminine'.

Although there is considerable potential in the contra-sexual exploration of the psyche Young-Eisendrath portrays, I think it is a mistake to make the distinct delineation of men possessing an anima and women an animus. Surely any person can use both aspects of sexual difference to guide them to a more complex development of identity. There is support for such an interpretation in Jung's work itself, when he acknowledges the broader role of the symbolic feminine, which has meaning for both women and men.

One can imagine here a creative exploration of various permutations of sexual difference within the individual psyche, where specific and contingent aspects of a person's life, including biological factors such as hormones, sexual organs, neurons, etc. will affect their imagined relationship to their body. Far from creating an assumption of heteronormativity, such an approach provides for a highly differentiated understanding of the formation of human sexual and gender identity. Further, it still provides for the overlapping and interactive impact with other complexes in the self that Young-Eisendrath underlines, involving issues such as race, class, or experiences of oppression or trauma.

In the exploration of the *other* within the psyche, sexual difference often overlaps with different complexes such as race or understandings of political hierarchies as they are played out in the realm of signification. This phenomenon is central to the arguments of Foucault (2001), Said (1979), and feminist authors such as Nochlin (2002) who have noted a frequent overlapping in the othering of women and non-Europeans that often takes the form of an opposition between reason and non-reason. Both women and those from outside the 'West', for example, are consistently associated with ornamental, 'unrestrained' aesthetics. This would account for the overlap between Orientalism and the feminine that is obvious in Wollen's sexually differentiated account of aesthetics outlined in Chapter 1.

In most social science accounts of the political role of difference, however, this process of *othering* is a negative phenomenon, generally used to exclude and demean those groups who are considered to be outside of socially constructed discourses of what is considered the norm. From a Jungian perspective, it becomes clear that this exploration of the *other* can be a positive thing – it involves an examination of compensatory forces far from consciousness that can open and transform the psyche. Jung himself had a profound respect for what he called 'Oriental wisdom', especially Buddhist and Taoist philosophical tracts that he argued most Westerners dismissed as religion. 'Texts of this kind do not consist of the sentimental, overwrought mystical intuitions of pathological cranks and recluses, but are based on the practical insights of highly evolved Chinese minds, which we have not the slightest justification for undervaluing' (Jung 1967, p. 7). In an interesting reversal of the typical European colonialist attitude outlined in Said's arguments regarding Orientalism, Jung argued that one explanation for the rigidly moral European interpretation of Christianity was that 'a highly developed Oriental religion' had been imposed on the minds of 'half-savages' (early Europeans) who were in no way spiritually developed enough to fully absorb its complexities (p. 47).

Such a model of an ego decentred in relation to other complexes provides for a more nuanced process of identity formation than that provided by the Freudian or Lacanian emphasis on penis envy or castration. Sexual difference as outlined here may not always be the most important complex an individual or collective is dealing with at all times, but it is certainly one of the most universal. It also provides a model for what I will describe in the following chapter as a biopolitics of the self. It is at the collective biopolitical level that defining the nature of these energies becomes important. If we assume, as I have argued following Deleuze and Jung, that collective aesthetic and political economic manifestations in the realm of representation *express* unconscious factors that are *compensatory*, how is it possible to interpret their relevance if there is not some 'essence' to their meaning? To be sure, this essence may become re-presented in some highly stereotypical ways, but the effect of assimilating such projected symbolic knowledge can be transformative. This, in turn, will feed back into the affordances of the unconscious, perhaps affecting how this knowledge will be projected in the future.

In my genealogy of the Rococo and *Art Nouveau* in Chapter 5, I argue that the conscious recognition of feminine energy characterized by the *Eros* of *moeurs douces* (gentle manners) and *volupté* (sensual pleasure) had concrete

64 Theory

political effects for women. Similarly, in Chapter 6 I argue that an appreciation of feminine energies was integral to the development of capitalist markets. Consciously acknowledging the impact of these feminine energies can have a) material consequences for those who identify as women and b) a broader ideological impact by influencing philosophical and political understandings of the impact of these energies. I am doubtful that denying any specific content to the energies of sexual difference would have the same effect.

Conclusion

I have made the case that a libidinal energy overlaid by at least two energies of sexual difference is integral to an understanding of not just the individual psyche, but to aesthetic and political change. I have defined these two energies in a basic way as *Eros/Luna* and *Logos/Sol*. In the chapters that follow, I will draw out these distinctions to show the many ways in which these energies manifest themselves in aesthetics, politics, and economics. My focus lies primarily on the energies of the feminine, however, which I will evoke in terms very similar to those used by Wollen in Chapter 1: as an energy that brings 'erotic' feelings of relatedness and sensual pleasure or *volupté*, and an aesthetic focus on the curve, on surface, and the anti-heroic everyday. The feminine can also be associated with ways of knowing that focus on the interval between the demarcated points of rationality, and a contingent, negotiated, often probabilistic, approach to politics and economy. In Chapter 4, I will develop Neumann's understanding of the elemental and transformative feminine to show how these are two indivisible aspects of feminine energies that are integral to understanding both the collective and individual psyche.

At this point, we have some notion of how sexual difference might enter the individual psyche and how it might interact with other aspects of identity such as race or class. But bringing politics into this perspective involves drawing some sort of collective relevance for these ideas, a task I will undertake in the following chapter.

Note

1 When I refer to the realm of representation, I am referencing approximately what Lacan called the Symbolic register. Lacan divided the process of acquiring subjectivity into three registers: the Real, the Imaginary, and the Symbolic. The latter two categories are the registers of conscious awareness. The Imaginary register is the realm of who one imagines oneself to be (as in the concept of ego) and how we relate to others, while the Symbolic register is the realm of language, laws, customs, mores, etc. His more elusive concept of the Real is roughly that which cannot be understood in the conscious apprehension characteristic of the Symbolic or the Imaginary. Zizek interprets the Real as something that precedes the

Symbolic order, but then is subsequently structured by it as it gets caught up in the network of signification inherent to the Symbolic register.

For Lacan, the unconscious communicates via the language of the Symbolic register. This linguistic reference indicates that Lacan's Symbolic is closer to Freud's semiotic interpretation of the word 'symbol' than to Jung's or Deleuze's conception of the symbol described here. To avoid confusion, therefore, I will refer to this register as the realm of representation or signification, to indicate its difference from the symbolic (in the Jungian sense) knowledge of the unconscious.

Bibliography

Barad, K. (2006) *Meeting the Universe Halfway: Quantum Physics and the Entanglement of Matter and Meaning*, Duke University Press, Durham, NC.

Bennett, J. (2010) *Vibrant Matter: A Political Ecology of Things*, Duke University Press, Durham, NC.

Berardi, F. "Bifo". (2009) *Precarious Rhapsody*, Minor Compositions, London, distributed by Autonomedia, New York.

Bergson, H. (2007) *Creative Evolution*, Palgrave Macmillan, New York.

Blackman, L. (2008) 'Affect, Relationality and the "Problem of Personality" ', *Theory, Culture and Society*, vol. 25, no. 1, pp. 23–47.

Braidotti, R. (1994) *Nomadic Subjects: Embodiment and Sexual Difference in Contemporary Feminist Theory*, Columbia University Press, New York.

Braidotti, R. (2003) 'Becoming Woman: Or Sexual Difference Revisited', *Theory Culture and Society*, vol. 20, no. 3, pp. 43–64.

Butler, J. (1999) *Gender Trouble: Feminism and the Subversion of Identity*, Routledge, London and New York.

Butler, J. (2000) 'Competing Universalities', in *Contingency, Hegemony, Universality*, eds. J. Butler, E. Laclau, and S. Zizek, Verso, London and New York, pp. 136–181.

Butler, J. (2011) *Bodies that Matter*, Routledge, London and New York.

Carey, Ford K. (2004) 'Portrait of Our Lady: Mary, Piero, and the Great Mother Archetype', *Journal of Religion and Health*, vol. 43, no. 2, pp. 93–113.

Chanter, T. (1995) *Ethics of Eros: Irigaray's Rewriting of the Philosophers*, Routledge, London and New York.

Colebrook, C. (2000) 'From Radical Representations to Corporeal Becomings: The Feminist Philosophy of Lloyd, Grosz, and Gatens', *Hypatia*, vol. 15, no. 2, pp. 76–93.

Deleuze, G. (1990) *The Logic of Sense*, trans. Mark Lester, Columbia University Press, New York.

Deleuze, G. (2000) *Proust and Signs*, University of Minnesota Press, Minneapolis.

Deleuze, G. (2004a) *Difference and Repetition*, trans. Paul Patton, Continuum, London and New York.

Deleuze, G. (2004b) 'From Sacher-Masoch to Masochism', trans. Christian Kerslake, *Angelaki*, vol. 9, no. 1, pp. 125–133.

Deleuze, G. and Guattari, F. (1983) *Anti-Oedipus: Capitalism and Schizophrenia*, University of Minnesota Press, Minneapolis.

66 Theory

Deleuze, G. and Guattari, F. (1987) *A Thousand Plateaus: Capitalism and Schizophrenia*, University of Minnesota Press, Minneapolis and London.

Deleuze, G. and Parnet, C. (2007) *Dialogues II*, revised ed. trans. Hugh Tomlinson and Barbara Habberjam, Columbia University Press, New York.

Despret, V. (2004) 'The Body We Care for: Figure of Anthropo-zoo-genesis', *Body and Society*, vol. 10, nos. 2–3, pp. 111–124.

Driscoll, C. (2000) 'The Woman in Process: Deleuze, Kristeva and Feminism', in *Deleuze and Feminist Theory*, eds. C. Colebrook and I. Buchanan, University of Edinburgh Press, Edinburgh, pp. 64–85.

Fabricius, J. (1976) *Alchemy: The Medieval Alchemists and their Royal Art*, Rosenkilde and Bagger, Copenhagen.

Faivre, A. and Needleman, J. (1992) *Modern Esoteric Spirituality*, Crossroad, New York.

Flieger, J. A. (2000) 'Becoming-Woman: Deleuze, Schreber and Molecular Identifications', in *Deleuze and Feminist Theory*, eds. C. Colebrook and I. Buchanan, University of Edinburgh Press, Edinburgh, pp. 38–63.

Foucault, M. (2001) *Madness and Civilization: A History of Insanity in the Age of Reason*, Routledge, London and New York.

Gatens, M. (1996) *Imaginary Bodies: Ethics, Power and Corporeality*, Routledge, London.

Grosz, E. (1994) *Volatile Bodies: Toward a Corporeal Feminism*, Indiana University Press, Bloomington and Indianapolis.

Grosz, E. (2005) *Time Travels: Feminism, Nature, Power*, Duke University Press, Durham, NC.

Grosz, E. (2008) *Chaos, Territory, Art*, Columbia University Press, New York.

Grosz, E. (2011) *Becoming Undone: Darwinian Reflections on Life, Politics, and Art*, Duke University Press, Durham, NC.

Haraway, D. (2008) *When Species Meet*, University of Minnesota Press, Minneapolis and London.

Hardt, M. and Negri, A. (2009) *Commonwealth*, The Belknap Press of Harvard University Press, Cambridge, MA.

Harris, J. (2001) *Jung and Yoga: The Psyche-Body Connection*, Inner City Books, Toronto.

Hauke, C. (2000) *Jung and the Postmodern: The Interpretation of Realities*, Routledge, London and Philadelphia.

Hillman, J. (1985) *Anima*, Spring Publications, Dallas, TX.

Jardine, A. (1985) *Gynesis: Configuration of Woman and Modernity*, Cornell University Press, Ithaca.

Jung, C. G. (1954) *Collected Works*, vol. 16, trans. R. F. C. Hull, Bollingen Series, Princeton University Press, Princeton, NJ.

Jung, C. G. (1958) *Collected Works*, vol. 11, trans. R. F. C. Hull, Bollingen Series, Princeto University Press, Princeton, NJ.

Jung, C. G. (1959) *Collected Works*, vol. 9, pt. 2, trans. R. F. C. Hull, Bollingen Series, Princeton University Press, Princeton, NJ.

Jung, C. G. (1960) *Collected Works*, vol. 8, trans. R. F. C. Hull, Bollingen Series, Princeton University Press, Princeton, NJ.

Jung, C. G. (1964) *Collected Works*, vol. 10, trans. R. F. C. Hull, Bollingen Series, Princeton University Press, Princeton, NJ.

Jung, C. G. (1967) *Collected Works*, vol. 13, trans. R. F. C. Hull, Bollingen Series, Princeton University Press, Princeton, NJ.

Jung, C. G. (1973) *Memories, Dreams, Reflections*, Pantheon Books, New York.

Jung, C. G. (1977) *Collected Works*, vol. 14, trans. R. F. C. Hull, Bollingen Series, Princeton University Press, Princeton, NJ.

Jung, C. G. (1980) *Collected Works*, vol. 9, pt. 1, Bollingen Series, Princeton University Press, Princeton, NJ.

Jung, C. G. (1981) *Collected Works*, vol. 17, trans. R. F. C. Hull, Bollingen Series, Princeton University Press, Princeton, NJ.

Jung, C. G. (2009) *The Red Book: Liber Novus*, ed. Sonu Shamdasani, W.W. Norton & Company, New York.

Kerslake, C. (2007) *Deleuze and the Unconscious*, Continuum, London and New York.

Kerslake, C. (2008) 'The Somnambulist and the Hermaphrodite: Deleuze and Johann de Montereggio and Occultism', *Culturemachine*, n.p., www.culturemachine.net.

Knox, J. (2003) *Archetype, Attachment, Analysis: Jungian Psychology and the Emergent Mind*, Brunner-Routledge, Hove and New York.

Kristeva, J. (2002) 'The Powers of Horror', in *The Portable Kristeva*, updated edition, ed. Kelly Oliver, Columbia University Press, New York, pp. 229–263.

Latour, B. (2004) 'How to Talk About the Body? The Normative Dimension of Science Studies', *Body and Society*, vol. 10, nos. 2–3, pp. 205–229.

McKenzie, S. (2006) 'Queering Gender: Anima/Animus and the Paradigm of Emergence', *Journal of Analytical Psychology*, vol. 41, pp. 401–421.

Neumann, E. (1974) *The Great Mother: An Analysis of the Archetype*, trans. Ralph Manheim, Bollingen Series, Princeton University Press, Princeton, NJ.

Nochlin, L. (2002) 'The Imaginary Orient', in *Race-ing Art History*, ed. Kymberly Pinder, Routledge, London and New York, pp. 69–85.

Pint, K. (2011) 'Doubling Back: Psychoanalytical Literary Theory and the Perverse Return to Jungian Space', *S: Journal of the Jan van Eyck Circle for Lancanian Ideology Critique*, vol. 4, pp. 47–55.

Plato. (2001) *Symposium*, trans. S. Benardete, University of Chicago Press, Chicago.

Protevi, J. (2010) 'Adding Deleuze to the Mix', *Phenomenology and the Cognitive Sciences*, vol. 9, pp. 417–436.

Ramey, J. (2012) *The Hermetic Deleuze: Philosophy and the Spiritual Ordeal*, Duke University Press, Durham, NC.

Rowland, S. (2002) *Jung: A Feminist Revision*, Polity, Cambridge, UK.

Said, E. (1979) *Orientalism*, Vintage Books, New York.

Samuels, A. (1985) *Jung and the Post-Jungians*, Routledge & Kegan Paul, London.

Schwartz-Salant, N. (1995) *Jung on Alchemy*, Princeton University Press, Princeton, NJ.

Shamdasani, S. (2003) *Jung and the Making of Modern Psychology: The Dreams of a Science*, Cambridge University Press, Cambridge, UK.

Stein, M. (2005) 'Individuation: Inner Work', *Journal of Jungian Theory and Practice*, vol. 7, no. 2, pp. 1–14.

Taylor, C. (2007) *A Secular Age*, The Belknap Press of the Harvard University Press, Cambridge, MA and London.

von Franz, M. L. (1964) 'The Process of Individuation', in *Man and His Symbols,* ed. C. G. Jung, Dell Publishing, New York, pp. 157–254.

von Franz, M. L. (1980) *Alchemy: An Introduction to the Symbolism and the Psychology,* Inner City Books, Toronto.

Woodman, M. (1982) *Addiction to Perfection: The Still Unravished Bride,* Inner City Books, Toronto.

Young, I. M. (1980) 'Throwing Like a Girl: A Phenomenology of Feminine Body Comportment Motility and Spatiality', *Human Studies,* vol. 3, no. 2, pp. 137–156.

Young-Eisendrath, P. (1992) 'Gender, Animus and Related Topics', in *Gender and Soul in Psychotherapy,* eds. N. Schwartz-Salant and M. Stein, Chiron, Wilmette, IL, pp. 151–177.

Zizek, S. (1989) *The Sublime Object of Ideology,* Verso, London and New York.

Zizek, S. (2004) 'Notes on a Debate "From Within the People"', *Criticism,* vol. 26, no. 4, pp. 661–666.

Chapter 3

Venus ♀

Toward a biopolitics of the unconscious

Understanding the collective aspects of the archetypal energies of sexual difference involves an explanation of the connection between aesthetics, the unconscious, and their material relationship to political economy in the realm of representation. In this chapter I will build on my description of the porous boundaries inherent to Jung's and Deleuze's understandings of the relationship between psyche, cosmos, body, and the realm of representation. Examining this complex relationship also offers insights into the collective political and economic effects of the unconscious, and the symbolic feminine. I argue that aesthetics, politics, and economics 'intra-act' in a space that Kant called the *sensus communis* – a psychic space where the affective aspects of art and political economy are felt. Kant talked of this space in terms of how it affected our judgments of taste, but as the work of Jung, Zizek, and Polanyi shows, it can also be a very political, at times dangerous space. Drawing on the work of Rancière, I demonstrate that this can also be a space of positive politics, but add a layer of sexual difference that both challenges and enhances his concept of the aesthetic regime. I then draw on the work of Hardt and Negri to argue that acknowledging the politics of this space is the first step toward a biopolitics where the forces of sexual difference can be assimilated in a more productive way.

Venus ♀

On March 10, 1914, Mary 'Slasher' Richardson smuggled a meat cleaver into the National Gallery in London and attacked a Velázquez painting known as the Rokeby Venus (Figure 3.1), hacking it several times before a museum guard could stop her. A Canadian suffragist, she was disgusted by the contrast between the voluptuous idleness of the Venus portrayed in the painting and the situation of Emmeline Pankhurst, then on hunger strike in jail.

Figure 3.1 Diego Velázquez, *The Toilet of Venus* ('The Rokeby Venus'), 1647–51, National Gallery, London

Photo Credit: National Gallery, London/Art Resource NY

Richardson's justification for her action was printed the following day in *The Times*:

> I have tried to destroy the picture of the most beautiful woman in mythological history as a protest against the Government for destroying Mrs Pankhurst, who is the most beautiful character in modern history . . . If there is an outcry against my deed, let every one remember that such an outcry is an hypocrisy so long as they allow the destruction of Mrs Pankhurst and other beautiful living women, and that until the public cease to countenance human destruction the stones cast against me for the destruction of this picture are each an evidence against them of artistic as well as moral and political humbug and hypocrisy.
> ('Miss Richardson's Statement', 1914)

Whether one considers Richardson's slashing a feat of courage or a raging act of censorship (note that she later became a member of the British Union of Fascists), it raises some interesting questions regarding the relationship between ostensibly aesthetic matters and political expression. Richardson's act was both political and aesthetic in content as well as form. It was Venus's *image* that Richardson contrasted with the image of Pankhurst on hunger strike and enduring force feedings in prison. The act of slashing the painting was itself aestheticized, intended to have a symbolic, emotional impact. Her act was meant to show how images of women were controlled by the projections of men, and how debilitating this was for women trying to assert themselves as political subjects.

In Rancière's (2004) terms, Richardson was trying to challenge the 'distribution of the sensible', or decisions about what is considered inside or outside of art and politics, including how these things should be portrayed, and what can be said about them. Her act was symbolic of the broader mission of the suffragist movement at that time: to force men to consider women as equal political subjects and include them in the universal conception of those who bear political rights. As Pankhurst noted, 'a thought came to me in my prison cell . . . that to men, women are not human beings like themselves' (quoted in Plonowska-Ziarek 2012, p. 27).

Richardson's act makes clear both the political nature of aesthetics and the aesthetic nature of politics. As Alliez and Osborne note, the assertion of a connection between aesthetics and politics dates back to the Enlightenment (Alliez and Osborne 2013, p. 7). From a political economy perspective, however, this focus became particularly intense from the 1930s on, primarily in neo-Marxist or post-structuralist perspectives. One of the earliest accounts came from Frankfurt School theorists such as Adorno and Horkheimer (2002) who examined the transformations of cultural production associated with the expansion of mass production, arguing that the development of a culture industry had usurped artistic expression and turned it into an ideological, commodified tool of corporate capitalism. Engaging with his Frankfurt School colleagues, Benjamin (2007) countered that there could be revolutionary potential in the technical innovations associated with mass production. At the same time, he noted a dark side to the relationship between aesthetics and politics, arguing that a dangerous 'aestheticization of politics' seemed to be occurring in fascist Germany. Politics, including war, appeared increasingly as aesthetic concepts – what Rancière describes in a critique of Benjamin as 'a perverse commandeering of politics by a will to art' (Rancière 2004, p. 13).

Subsequent neo-Marxist accounts such as Harvey (1990) and Jameson (1995) focused on the aesthetic transformations occurring in the transition from Modern to Postmodern aesthetics and their relationship to the development of late, or post-Fordist, capitalism. Post-structuralist accounts, such as Baudrillard's (2004), also addressed the post-Fordist period, invoking semiotics to show how late capitalism was implicated in a political economy of the sign, arguing that the image as simulacrum had come to form a new reality. In Postmodern economics, he argued, signifiers become detached from their 'signifieds' and become free-floating images used to construct alternative hyper-realities. Lash and Urry (1993) later developed Baudrillard's ideas into a comprehensive analysis of the growing influence of aesthetic concepts such as images, symbols, or brands on capitalist production. From this more consumption-oriented perspective Bourdieu (1984) also showed how aesthetic choices, or the distinctions involved in 'taste', corresponded to a form of cultural capital implicated in both social and economic hierarchies.

With the exception of Benjamin, who evokes a sort of Nietzschean 'will to art' behind politics, all of the above analyses remain in the realm of representation or signification. By this I mean that they focus on the semiotic manipulation of images or signifiers (or in Baudrillard's case their detachment from the signified) and their relationship to underlying changes in the means and relations of production. These approaches provide important insights into the relationship between aesthetics and economy; however, they might be described as necessary, but not sufficient explanations for this association. For one, although some of them (especially Benjamin, Jameson, and Harvey) can conceive of the possibility that unconscious factors could be at play here, these unconscious factors are considered to be reflections or manifestations of economic factors. Second, there is little or no attention to sexual difference in these accounts.

Richardson's act clearly points to the importance of incorporating sexual difference into aesthetics, an approach already taken by feminist art historians. In fact, her statement neatly summarizes many of the criticisms feminist art historians have levelled against male representations of women in art. Velázquez's projection of his ideal woman onto the canvas might be a sublime vision of Venus, but he also portrays her as languorous and vain – looking at herself in a mirror, her nude body sexualized, signifying her as an object designed for the pleasure of the implicit male viewer, including the artist himself. According to this critique, the painting is not a veneration of woman, but an attempt to control her, limit her status to that of sexual object, and dominate her. Rather than celebrating the sublime power of the feminine, it is yet another tool in the vast panoply of representative techniques that oppress women. From this perspective, Velázquez's lush brush strokes are not sincere adulation, but to use Richardson's words, moral and political humbug and hypocrisy.

These arguments highlight the social and cultural construction of sexual and gender identities. In Butler's terms (1999 & 2011), such images can be viewed as men's culturally inflected positing of the ontological nature of women, and Richardson's objections to Velázquez's projection of Venus provides a material rejection of the phenomenon Butler describes. What Richardson was trying to say with her violent action was that this projection of Venus had nothing to do with her lived experience as a woman, nor Emmeline Pankhurst's. Her action disrupted Velázquez's projection of what the feminine meant to him.

This process of deconstruction is a necessary but not sufficient step in analyzing Richardson's act, however. Although she provides a rationalization for what she did, on a symbolic level Richardson's act seems bewilderingly self-destructive – the symbol of Venus (♀) is, after all, the symbol for woman. The opening line of her statement says it all: she is killing one beautiful woman in the name of another. Even metaphorically, slaying a woman is certainly a curious action for someone claiming to fight for women's rights. In a way, her action symbolically captures a central dilemma for feminism: breaking free of the male-dominated definition of women's subjectivity involves a figurative deconstructive 'slashing' of such images. But categorically rejecting the possibility of a symbolic Venus associated with feminine power metaphorically destroys a 'beautiful' woman. Once the image has been deconstructed, why not re-imagine it? Why is it necessary to reject it?

Surely we can work through the sexist projections of the symbolic feminine in the realm of representation to reclaim its meaning and power for both men and women, and do so in a way that does not involve such a categorical rejection and censorship of men's projections, nor some panglossian form of goddess worship. Men, of course, have every right to aesthetically express their projections of the feminine. What is objectionable is that typically, these are the only projections that have been considered art, and they have been allowed to define feminine subjectivity. The consequence, as Plonowska-Ziarek (2012, p. 2) notes, is a situation where women's aesthetic subjectivity is often rendered as dumb muteness or dying tongues. My suggestion is to find a way into a process that allows the symbolic feminine to speak for herself; this, in turn, might allow us to consider how the aesthetic interpretation of such energic flows might be re-negotiated to provide alternative subjectivities necessary for political change. Such an 'aesthetic' or symbolic understanding of *a priori* forces could have transformational results, in effect changing both individual and collective perspectives on their involvement in the realm of representation surrounding them.

Applying this approach to the forces of sexual difference means working in both the realms of representation and the *a priori* world of Kant's *sensus communis*, playing with the representation of energies in a way that transforms our understanding of them. It is short-sighted to reject the potential of symbolic forces simply because of the politicized nature of their meaning in the realm of signification. Perhaps we cannot 'know' the actual meaning of the ontological, but we can dream, fantasize, imagine.

In this respect, constructionist approaches tend to make an artificial distinction between the ontological and the representational realms. To return to Velázquez's Venus, the deconstruction enacted by Richardson and later expanded upon in feminist art history is a necessary but not sufficient way of analyzing such images and their political importance. Applying deconstructive tools is a necessary first step, which points out that what Velázquez painted was informed by patriarchal norms. But should we dismiss the value of his projection entirely? What was he trying to express, as distorted as this message may have been by cultural and ideological artefacts? What 'problem' was he compensating for? His portrayal of Venus does portray a very limited and stereotypical view of the feminine, but if one considers this painting to be a projection of the feminine aspects integral to his own psyche, a different interpretation might ensue. A critical response to men's projections of the feminine does not simply deny them, but reads through them to find the affective, symbolic meanings they are trying to express. In many cases this message is a negative one, but its very presence indicates that something is *there* that is attempting to be *presented*. This is the analysis I attempt to undertake in the genealogies that comprise Part II of this book.

In Chapter 2, I discussed the entanglement of body and psyche inherent to Jung's notion of the subtle body. Here, I want to extend this practice of entanglement to the intra-action between the symbolic and representative realms. I borrow these concepts of intra-action and entanglement from the work of Barad (2006). Speaking in the molecular language used by both Jung and Deleuze, Barad recognizes that physical and physiological systems do not possess clear boundaries or follow consistent linear patterns or rules; their internal systems (e.g. atoms) are dynamic, not static. This means that systems can 'intra-act' – creating phenomena not through causal means but through chaotic entanglements of forces. Her idea of intra-action draws on Niels Bohr's insight that the physical and theoretical apparatus used to measure quantum phenomena essentially determines what is observed or measured. If the apparatus 'determines' the object being measured, how can the object and apparatus be ontologically separate? The meaning of each 'object' depends on mutually constitutive, what she calls intra-active practices, in contrast to interaction, which relies on a 'metaphysics of individualism' that assumes prior existence of separately determinate entities (p. 128). This introduces, she notes, a fundamental inseparability between what Kant distinguished as *noumena* (things that cannot be known through the senses) and *phenomena* (things that can be physically sensed). '[T]here are no determinately bounded or propertied entities existing "behind" or as the causes of phenomena.' (p. 128)

Intra-action suggests that meaning is not a property of individual bodies or technologies, but is a process or 'an ongoing performance of the world in its differential dance' in which 'part of the world becomes determinately bounded and propertied in its emergent intelligibility to another part of the world' (p. 149). Physical and immaterial influences intra-inform to establish phenomena, including understandings of subjectivity, perception, and cognition. I argued in Chapter 2 that Butler's separation between the body and its representation effectively mimics the same sort of metaphysics of separability that Barad rejects, but Butler's emphasis on the phenomenology of performance is highly pertinent here, as is the phenomenology of both Jung and Deleuze.

I want to use Barad's terminology to clarify the relationship between this symbolic concept and the actual bodies of women, as well as relations between the unconscious and the realm of representation. Jung believed that the body and psyche performed a differential dance similar to Barad's concept of intra-action in the space of the subtle body, where psyche and soma 'touch but do not touch'. In the space of the subtle body, body and mind become entangled in a mutually constitutive way. A similar phenomenon occurs in the manifestation of symbolic knowledge in the realm of representation. There is not a circular, but rather a mutually constitutive relationship here. Both Jung and Deleuze viewed symbolic knowledge as unrepresentable, as knowable only in its projected form. These projections, in turn, were to be interpreted contingently in terms of what they meant for a particular person or collectivity at a particular point in time. They were not identical to the symbolic knowledge they were projections or manifestations of, but metaphorically related to it.

Jung, to reiterate, argued that the symbolic feminine was manifested as *Eros* and the symbolic masculine as *Logos*. I will take Jung at his word that these linguistic projections of the energies of sexual difference are not the *same* as symbolic knowledge, but only metaphorically express them. They are related to, but not the same as, the actual bodies of women and men. If this is the case, where is the perceived meaning of these energies being made? Is it made in the unconscious, or is it made in the projection of this un-representable knowledge into images and words in the realm of representation where it becomes known? A noumenous feeling or unconscious image is sent to us that will be projected in terms we understand from the highly political and socially constructed forms of communication we 'know' in the realm of representation. This means that as the politics and social constructions of the realm of representation change, symbolic knowledge might be manifested in different ways, at different times, even for different individuals. The meaning, in Butler's terms, is 'posited', not absolute. Recall that for Jung the interpretation of symbolic knowledge is always contingent, depending on the particular circumstances in which it is projected.

But does this mean that that political realities or changes in the realm of representation then determine the meaning of symbolic knowledge? If we accept Jung's and Deleuze's understanding of the unconscious as ontological and compensatory, this is not clear. The unconscious sends a message by communicating it as best it can, using the images and words of the realm of representation, but always with a particular, unknowable message in mind.

Rather than trying to resolve this 'chicken and egg' dilemma, can we not acknowledge the mutual intermingling of these two realms? In Barad's terms, this meaning making is entangled, produced in the intra-action of these realms. In the genealogies that comprise the second half of this book, I will show many examples where unconscious energies are conceived aesthetically and metaphorically expressed as feminine. This unconscious message, projected in the socially influenced images of a particular time and space, in turn changes the political meaning of this image, and those materially associated with it in the realm of representation, with real, material implications for both women and men. In other words, the politics, sexual relations, language, and knowledge inherent to the realm of representation intra-act with unconscious symbolic knowledge to produce new phenomena. Such is the nature of the Jungian/Deleuzean phenomenology of the assimilation of symbolic knowledge, and Deleuze's belief in the ability of the symbol to change reality in conformity with itself. It also makes clearer my claim that even though the symbolic feminine is not the same as woman, the assimilation of this knowledge can have political effects for those metaphorically associated with it.

But as I showed in my analysis of the phenomenology of Deleuze's ontology of difference in Chapter 2, these manifestations in the realm of representation, or what he called the Actual, have a feedback loop that in turn affects the affordances of Ideas. It is entirely possible that actions in the realm of representation intra-act with the unconscious to change the nature of archetypal knowledge itself. Barad's attention to the simultaneous, mutually constitutive nature of molecular relations has clear relevance for both Jung's and Deleuze's thinking here.

This means that aesthetics, and their political and economic dimensions, can never be fully understood through analysis purely based in the realm of representation, nor with a singular focus on the unconscious. Instead, a consideration of the unconscious aspects of aesthetics, politics, and economics, as well as the feedback mechanism between the materialization of these factors and the unconscious, is necessary. Rancière's work on the political relevance of aesthetics is a first step in this direction, despite the fact that I will argue he needs to more specifically account for the impact of unconscious forces such as the energies of sexual difference on the politics of aesthetics.

Rancière argues that art, and aesthetics more generally, often involve highly political acts that urge a reconsideration of what is considered politically or aesthetically visible or 'sensible'. For example, the painting of everyday scenes and working class people that came to be commonplace in Modern art, or what he claims might more appropriately be called the 'aesthetic regime', was inconceivable in the classical 'representative regime' of art that preceded it. That artists dared to portray such things in art, whether in painting or in literature, was both a reflection of, and a contribution to, changing political configurations of power. This change began in literature, he claims, where writers wrote about ordinary people (Balzac), or the 'civilization of the sewers' (Hugo) (Rancière 2004, p. 33). These artistic acts rendered 'invisible' people who previously were not even considered to be political actors 'visible', a practice that added legitimacy to their material battles for political rights.

Rancière considers artistic practices that challenge political delineations of what can be seen or said to be 'primary aesthetics'. It is at this level of 'sensible delimitation', he argued, that aesthetics and politics are related. Artistic practices are 'ways of doing and making' that intervene in more general practices of doing and making, affecting relationships both to 'modes of being and forms of visibility' (p. 13). His understanding of aesthetics is inherently Kantian in that he views it as 'the system of a priori forms determining what presents itself to sense experience. It is a delimitation of spaces and times, of the visible and the invisible' (p. 13). As Tanke describes it, it involves a sort of 'making sense of sense' (Tanke 2011, p. 1).

Rancière's Kantian definition of aesthetics as a priori has parallels with the ideas of both Jung and Deleuze, despite his singular focus on the realm of representation. Kant's idea of the *sensus communis* as a psychic 'space' where aesthetics are felt involves a sort of pre-understanding of understanding – a presumption that an object or experience is capable of capturing our imaginations and evoking feelings in those who are exposed to it. It assumes the universal human ability to be *affected* by something. It does not involve specific judgments concerning any objective criteria about the actual positive or negative merits of something, but rather is the assumption that there is a realm of communication based on affect or feeling that everyone is capable of possessing. The fact that humans are able to communicate their ideas indicates that 'the way our cognitive powers are attuned for cognition generally' must be universal, a 'subjective condition of the act of knowing', a 'necessary condition of the universal communicability of our knowledge' (Kant 2007, p. 69).

Thus, the *sensus communis* is not agreement on whether or not something is beautiful, but a common element of humanity that makes us capable of sharing in the emotions evoked by a certain representation. It is not in the realm of empirical assessment, but another faculty of cognition above the level of the senses, a feeling that is communicable, like Jung's and Deleuze's symbol, 'without the mediation of a concept' (pp. 123–5). Jung's and Deleuze's idea that an unconscious symbol is capable of evoking *feelings* that can be transformative in a material sense bears much in common with Kant's *sensus communis*, and in this respect can be considered an *aesthetic* experience. It is here that we can begin to analyze the links between aesthetics and politics in a manner that will be relevant to the genealogies in the second part of this book, where we will repeatedly see individual men and women, and collectivities of people, channelling the vibrations of an apparently 'feminine' aesthetic force.

But material or sensible phenomena in the realm of representation are not the only source of political influence here. Unconscious energies also come into play that intra-act with these material factors, which in turn affect phenomenal outcomes. It is possible to view Kant's *sensus communis* as a 'space' analogous to Jung's conception of the subtle body – a place where the realm of representation and the unconscious intra-act in an entangled manner. In this space, actions in the realm of representation affect the affordances of Ideas or archetypal energies such as sexual difference in Deleuze's Virtual or Jung's collective unconscious, but they in turn are prompted and influenced by these energies from the unconscious.

As useful as I find Rancière's understanding of the *a priori* nature of aesthetics, injecting the energies of sexual difference into his analysis challenges not only his conception of the sources of political change, but also his periodization. As noted above, he argues that a major aesthetic 'regime' change occurred at the end of the 18th and beginning of the 19th century. Prior to this period, art obeyed the rules of what he calls the representative regime, which loosely corresponds to what is known in art history as classicism. In this classical representative regime, the *beaux arts* and *belles lettres* were heavily regimented in terms of what subjects or people could be represented, and how they were to be represented. At the end of the 18th century, artists began to challenge these regulatory assumptions in movements such as Realism and Romanticism that rejected the preordained rules of what it was appropriate to paint or write about (Tanke 2011, p. 3). Painting or writing about working-class people, prostitutes, or dancers and portraying them in an abstract, fragmented way were all characteristic of this new approach. This new regime of 'aesthetic art' is the real point of change to look at for fundamental transformation, in Rancière's view, not the transition between the Modern and Postmodern, which are merely variations on the same theme.

Toward a biopolitics of the unconscious   79

In Chapter 5, I will take issue with this periodization, showing that from the perspective of sexual difference, an even more transformational 'regime' (I will not use this term outside of my discussion of Rancière because it suggests a far more structured and delimited conception than what I am talking about) began in the 17th century Baroque period and culminated in the 18th century Rococo. I will further argue, in contrast to Rancière, that the post-revolutionary period he regards as transformational was initially regressive in terms of sexual politics, simply reinstating the masculine energies that predominated prior to the Baroque period. Adding sexual difference to his analysis also provides an idea of what might be *provoking* the kinds of changes he discusses, something that remains rather vague in his argument.

Without rejecting Rancière's ideas about the transformative political aspects of primary aesthetics, I think it is necessary to emphasize that the highly political nature of aesthetics is in part due to their relation to the unconscious. To summarize my argument in advance, for Jung and Deleuze unconscious symbols are communicated in an affective manner, similar to the way Kant described aesthetic judgements as being 'felt' in his concept of the *sensus communis*. Politics and economics, insofar as they are affected by the unconscious, are 'felt' in the same way as art. To be sure, politics are played out in the realm of representation and must be understood as responses to concrete material issues such as repression, inequality, or violence. Investigating the discourses and social constructions inherent to the realm of signification provides a necessary, but not sufficient, explanation of the mass basis of politics, however. As I will show, Jung, Zizek, and Polanyi argue that such discourses often coalesce in the form of unconscious complexes that are symptoms of something that is missing or unknown. Often, they are a reflection of unconscious factors that are felt and manifested aesthetically.

This, in part, explains Benjamin's concern with the phenomenon he described as 'the aestheticization of politics' (Benjamin 2007, pp. 241–2), which he held responsible for the spread of fascism in Germany. Writing in 1936 in the context of the carefully choreographed Nazi rallies designed by Albert Speers and the dynamic film images of Leni Riefenstahl, it is not surprising that Benjamin sensed an ominous connection between art and politics. Rancière claims that his own conception of

> an aesthetics at the core of politics has nothing to do with Benjamin's discussion of the 'aestheticization of politics' . . . as a perverse commandeering of politics by a will to art, by a consideration of the people qua work of art.
>
> (2004, p. 13)

He further criticizes Benjamin's emphasis on the ritual nature of art, inter-preting his concept of the sacred 'aura' of art in a fairly narrow fashion (p. 103).

In contrast, I will argue that although aesthetics can be used in the transformational manner that Rancière suggests, Benjamin's warnings about the symbolic connections between aesthetics and what appears to be an unconscious 'will to power' should be taken very seriously. Such an approach invites a consideration of the role of the unconscious in the collective activity of political economy. It also opens the door for an understanding of politics and aesthetics that incorporates sexual difference.

Richardson's act, for example, is very concerning in light of Benjamin's arguments. That years after this incident Richardson joined the British Union of Fascists is also very troubling in this respect. It highlights the attention that must be paid to the role of unconscious forces in what Kant referred to as the *sensus communis* of aesthetics.

Politics, the unconscious, and the collective

Jung and Zizek (from a psychoanalytical perspective) and Polanyi (from a political economy perspective) have all provided analyses of collective political responses, primarily revolving around what Jung described as the collective complex. Both Jung and Freud shared a profound distrust of such collective reactions, believing that they generally dragged people to their lowest common denominator. Both the Jungian and Freudian approaches to psychoanalysis are based on the idea that individuals strug-gle with various complexes: unconscious 'patterns of interlocking asso-ciations' that express themselves through repetitive behaviours or moods (Kimbles 2000, p. 159). These complexes, shaped by various life experi-ences, operate unconsciously and become split off from conscious behav-iours, often expressing themselves in an emotional reaction. Unless they are made conscious, they take the form of an automatic reaction where the individual will act compulsively on the basis of unconscious projec-tions (Gellert (1998, pp. 76–77). Although a person's psyche is shaped by complexes unique to the individual, it is also structured by beliefs and experiences that operate at a group level. Sometimes these collective com-plexes take innocuous forms; at other times, they express deeply rooted fears or archetypal associations that emerge in spontaneous, and often violent, reactions.

Both Jung and Zizek have argued that such unconscious forces can cause serious and violent political phenomena. From his Lacanian perspective, Zizek's (1989, pp. 57–92) argument begins with the understanding that subjectivity emerges partly on the basis of foreclosures. This hinges on the idea that there is always something unknown, always a void or lack that the signifiers of the Lacanian Symbolic or realm of signification are organized around. When such unknown meanings become foreclosed from signification, they return in the Lacanian Real as a symptom. The symptom is like a coded message, a kind of 'communication by other means'. In the context of psychoanalysis, the symptom is always addressed to the analyst as an appeal by the analysand to find its hidden meaning. This hidden meaning always reveals some sort of 'kernel of enjoyment' that the subject has a perverse interest in maintaining, even though the symptom that reveals it may bring discomfort or shame. The meaning of the symptom is thus retroactively inferred by the analyst.

Once discovered, Lacan insisted that this kernel of enjoyment should only be identified by the analysand; it should never be broken apart or disposed of. In certain cases, which Lacan referred to as 'sinthomes' rather than symptoms, it could be the only positive support of the analysand's being, and destroying it would effectively obliterate a central source of the patient's subjectivity, resulting in a sort of 'psychic autism'. The key then is for the subject to recognize the symptom as a pathological 'inert stain' resisting communication and integration into the social bond network, but at the same time forming a positive condition of it.

Zizek (1989) pushes the political implications of this psychic phenomenon in his use of Lacan's concept of the '*point de capiton*'. The *point de capiton* is what Zizek refers to as a rigid signifier – a signifier that holds a place or an identity in the signifying chain, while the meanings or 'signified' associated with it may change over time. This means, paradoxically, that it designates and constitutes identity at the same time. His example is the signifier 'democracy'. Democracy can have numerous meanings, for example, there can be socialist democracy or liberal democracy, both of which are very different. It is impossible to exhaustively delineate all the possible permutations of democracy, some of which are completely opposing. The *point de capiton* is the place where this 'metonymic sliding' of the signified stops, the point at which the subject becomes 'sewn' to this rigid signifier (p. 112). This does not mean that the actual meaning of the signifier is discovered, but rather that it holds a structural position that enunciates its own meaning by attaching itself to a signified.

Ideology is where this 'empty' signifier suddenly becomes saturated with meaning; it becomes a sort of Master signifier that then gives meaning to other points, which then become totalized into an ideological system (p. 110). For Zizek, there may be 'a series of floating signifiers like freedom, state, justice, peace and then their chain is supplemented with a master-signifier like Communism that retroactively determines their meaning'

82 Theory

(p. 113). The key to analyzing an ideology, therefore, is to find the lack or void this ideology is a symptom of. Says Zizek,

> If we look at the element which holds together the ideological edifice, at this 'phallic', erected Guarantee of Meaning, . . . we are able to recognize in it the embodiment of a lack, of a chasm of non-sense gaping in the midst of ideological meaning.
>
> (p. 110)

Merging this concept with Lacan's notion of the void/lack as some sort of pre-ideological kernel of enjoyment, Zizek argues that ideology must be analyzed on two levels: 1. a symptomal reading that deconstructs how floating signifiers become totalized at various nodal points or *point de capiton*; and 2. extracting the kernel of enjoyment, 'the way in which – beyond the field of meaning but at the same time internal to it – an ideology implies, manipulates, produces a pre-ideological enjoyment structured in fantasy' (p. 140). He uses the example of anti-Semitism, arguing that the Jew becomes the fetishistic embodiment of a certain blockage/void that holds society together (p. 143). Something that has been foreclosed or excluded from the Symbolic returns in the Real as the figure of the Jew. The Jew becomes a symptom that reveals the true functioning of the system, the same way Freud viewed dreams and slips as symptoms that reveal underlying psychological issues (p. 144). All of this gives the illusion that the master-signifier has an immanent essence or meaning that unfolds, when in fact its meaning was *retroactively* fixed by the master-signifier itself. So, instead of a 'linear, immanent, necessary progression according to which meaning unfolds itself from some initial kernel, we have a radically contingent process of retroactive production of meaning' (p. 114).

In line with the Lacanian notion of foreclosure, Jung likely would have agreed that becoming 'conscious' inevitably involves putting up walls or letting most elements of the unconscious remain unconscious. Like Bergson, Jung (1958, p. 551) had an understanding of the unconscious as the potential totality of all psychic factors, from which consciousness singles out small pieces or fragments from time to time. Jung's unconscious obviously is not the same as the Lacanian concept of the Real, but for both Jung and Lacan, these concepts were defined as total, or complete.[1] Since it is impossible to fully convey the meaning of the Real in symbolic terms, there is always something left over – 'the scraps'. This sense of something being left out propels us to know more, but despite this sense of 'lack', Zizek notes, the Real itself contains 'the fullness of inert presence; it is only the signifier that opens the hole, the gap. The symbolic order organizes itself around this gap (Zizek 1989, p. 191).

Zizek's idea that the meaning does not 'unfold' but is produced retroactively may appear to be a major contrast with Jung's concept of the symbol and the *a priori* basis of archetypal meaning. In practice, however, Jung's insistence on the contingent interpretation of archetypal symbols makes his ideas closer to Zizek's concept of the *point de capiton* than one might think. Recall Jung's emphasis, outlined in Chapter 2, on the necessity of interpreting symbolic knowledge contingently in the context of individual and collective experience. Unlike Lacan, however, Jung believed that when the unconscious source of a neurosis or psychosis was discovered, it was possible and essential to acknowledge it and assimilate it, even if it was something undesirable or dark, so that its power could be defused. As Zizek (2004) notes, this is precisely what Lacan warned *not* to do.

In contrast, Jung believed that the tendency to foreclose or deny unconscious energies was a negative phenomenon that had become even more attenuated on a collective level in modern European cultures because of the predominance of scientific rationality, and a highly rigid and moral form of Christianity that was unable to countenance the unconscious. Indeed, for him this denial was central to understanding the collective complex, and overcoming it was key to the resolution of complexes.

Jung believed that the stronger and more fierce the 'cult of consciousness' focusing on rationality and morality becomes, the more unconscious elements are thrust to the background, creating a dangerous situation. The problem, in his view, was not with rationality or *logos* in itself, which is obviously a necessary aspect of being, but that it had become 'uncontained', so to speak, having 'set itself free and proclaimed itself the ruler' (Jung 1967, p. 244). In words that will become clearer in the next chapter, he speaks of the lack of a *temenos*, a sort of sacred boundary that used to be provided by otherworldly, eschatological images that reason always remained embedded in. In such uncontained circumstances, the unconscious elements become split off from consciousness and gain an autonomy of their own. Says Jung:

> If we deny these autonomous systems, imagining that we have got rid of them by a mere critique of the name, then the effect which they still continue to exert can no longer be understood, nor can they be assimilated to consciousness. They become an inexplicable source of disturbance which we finally assume must exist somewhere outside ourselves. The resultant projection creates a dangerous situation in that the disturbing effects are now attributed to a wicked will outside ourselves, which is naturally not to be found anywhere but with our neighbor *de l'autre côté de la rivière*. This leads to collective delusions, 'incidents' revolutions, war – in a word to destructive mass psychoses.
>
> (Jung 1967, p. 36)

84 Theory

At this point, the ego relinquishes its importance and the individual becomes 'mass man, the ever-ready victim of some wretched "ism"'(Jung 1960, p. 219). His most famous example of this is his essay 'Wotan', which describes the rise of National Socialism in Germany. He writes that the Germans were in *Ergriffenheit* – a state of seizure by their ancient god of war, wandering, and poetry (among other things) – a sort of Dionysian character known as Wotan whose followers were known as berserkers. In line with Benjamin's concerns regarding the aestheticization of politics, he argued that aesthetic portrayals of 'Jesus as a blond and blue-eyed hero, the Greek mother of St. Paul, the devil as an international Alberich in Jewish or Masonic guise' were all symptoms of a 'mighty rushing wind' that had taken hold of Germany. Writing in 1936, the same year Benjamin wrote his critique of the aestheticization of politics, Jung lamented that 'A hurricane has broken loose in Germany while we still believe it is fine weather' (Jung 1964, p. 186.)

The fact that such unconscious factors were denied by the conscious attitude of rationality prevalent in Europe made the situation all the more powerful. The more dominant the ideas of the collective conscious become, he argued, the more the contents of the collective unconscious become repressed. The energy of the repressed factor moves to the repressing factor, whose effect becomes even more fanatical, until eventually it causes an *enantiodromia* – a psychic conversion to its opposite (Jung 1960, pp. 218–19). The unconscious breaks free of its bonds and takes over in the realm of signification like a marauding berserker.

Generally speaking, an *enantiodromia* is a phenomenon whereby any force that becomes too strong or dominant turns on itself, creating the seeds of its opposite and swinging back in that direction. In the context of Jung's usage of the term, it involves the reversal of a psychic situation. His understanding of this concept was clearly influenced by Taoism. In his introduction to Wilhelm's translation of the Taoist alchemical text *The Secret of the Golden Flower,* Jung describes the *enantiodromia* in the context of the dynamic between *yin* and *yang* energies:

> The wise Chinese would say in the words of the *I Ching:* When *yang* has reached its greatest strength, the dark power of *yin* is born within its depths, for night begins at midday when *yang* breaks up and begins to change into *yin*.
>
> (Jung 1967, pp. 12–13)

The momentum of the *enantiodromia* is compensatory – it means that at some unconscious, cosmic level, an attempt to balance will occur (p. 245). As one side of the pendulum becomes predominant, it attracts its opposite and will swing back in the opposite direction. Whenever the unconscious takes over in the form of fanaticism, it is likely to be opposed in an equally fanatical way, often resulting in catastrophic violence.

Von Franz provides a fascinating example of how the energies of sexual difference may have enacted a cosmic religious *enantiodromia* in her description of a change in the collective psyche from the masculine to the feminine at the end of the ancient Egyptian patriarchal order in 3000–2800 BCE. Religiously, this was a time period where the worship of the masculine sun god *Ra* was at its peak. Then, she notes, 'because these things come to an end, to an *enantiodromia*, the masculine mode of consciousness tires' (von Franz 1980, pp. 61–62). The myth of the goddess Isis then became dominant in a mythical story where an angel hands over knowledge to Isis and she, in exchange for having sexual relations with him, learns the alchemical secrets. Note that these swings clearly are not changes between matriarchy and patriarchy, but a change in the collective psychic dynamic of sexual difference. She saw another swing toward the feminine during the development of dialectical materialism, with its focus on the feminine *mater* (mother/matter) of production and everyday life in the early 20th century.

Jung's use of the *enantiodromia* may seem like some sort of mystical *deus ex machina*, but it actually bears many similarities to Karl Polanyi's (1944) political economy approach contrasting the double movement of laissez-faire capitalism and protectionist social responses. Polanyi argued that the harsh, instrumental rationality of laissez-faire capitalism elicited automatic, socio-cultural responses to protect society against the market's potentially annihilating forces. On one side was the relentlessly expanding, self-regulating market, based on the principles of economic liberalism. On the other side, and moving in tandem with the expansion of the self-regulating markets, was the principle of social protection, designed to cushion society from the ravages of unimpeded capitalist competition. Despite their vastly different motives, Polanyi argued that these two movements were Janus-faced, comprising two sides of the same coin. They moved together organically; society attempted to 'embed' markets in social values even as the universal spread of the market sought to escape or 'disembed' itself from social strictures. To this point, Polanyi presents an account with parallels to Jung's argument that rationality had become disembedded from the *temenos* of a broader cosmology. The difference, of course, is that in Polanyi's ideas the *Logos* of the market has become disembedded from society, not from the cosmos.

In Polanyi's view, much of the harshness of capitalism, and political reactions to it, could be explained by the fact that in contrast to previous forms of trading, capitalist markets had become completely disembedded from society. Unimpeded by the norms and protections of society, the implacable logic of the market would have destroyed land, labour, and the financial realm had not spontaneous, political reactions occurred to protect and preserve them. Polanyi's sense of disembedded markets parallels Jung's sense of a disembedded unconscious above – and interestingly they wrote these comments at almost exactly the same time (Jung in 1943 [see Jung 1967] and Polanyi in 1944). In contrast to Jung's interpretation, however, Polanyi argued that fascism could be explained as a protectionist reaction to the harsh austerity Germany experienced under the free trading Gold Standard policies of the late 19th and early 20th century.

Jung's idea of the *enantiodromia* also appears relevant to Wollen's story of the rise, then swift repression, of the feminine *Art Nouveau* by an aesthetic 'masculine renunciation' outlined in Chapter 1 (followed, incidentally, by World War I). It also seems relevant to the rise and repression of the Rococo I will describe in Chapter 5 (followed by the French Revolution), and the repression of the feminine aspects of Modern art inherent to the Bloomsbury movement of the first half of the 20th century (followed by World War II). I do not want to make any simplistic parallels between these aesthetic events and the apocalyptic violence that followed them, but these 'coincidences' are rather unnerving. This notion of a pendulum-like swinging back and forth suggests a regularly occurring, potentially violent collision between the energies of sexual difference.

It also makes one slightly despairing for any sense of either individual or collective political agency. Polanyi's theory can be criticized for its apparent denial of human political agency, which appears to be subsumed by an apparently unavoidable, organic dynamic between society and the market. He at least identifies, however, a way to mitigate this phenomenon: enact policies that contain or embed people in something larger than the *Logos* of the market. Deny this basic human need, and you can expect the kinds of 'identitarian' politics (such as racism or nationalism) that Hardt and Negri (2009, pp. 182–197) claim happen when love goes 'bad'.

Jung's ideas, however, seem to indicate cosmic forces manipulating humans in a manner that they are not able to resist. His solution was to acknowledge the paradoxes and polarities of life contained in these oppositions and 'hold' them in their very contradictions, but this took years of special preparation and training, either through psychoanalysis in a Western context or through practices such as yoga, Zen Buddhism, or Taoism outside the West. Even in these cases, not everyone is capable of developing the kind of psychological distance that enables one to hold the opposites and resist an identification with the collective consciousness that controlling the *enantiodromia* would involve (Jung 1960, pp. 219–222). Consequently, he did not hold out much hope for building the bridge between the conscious and unconscious necessary to avoid such fanatical reactions on a collective level.

Despite this pessimism, I believe there is potential for the integration of Jung's ideas into a more concrete approach to political change. To compare the psychoanalytical approaches of Jung and Zizek, for Zizek understanding ideology involves finding the signifier that constitutes the stitching point or *point de capiton*, then finding the pre-ideological 'kernel of enjoyment' it addresses. This kernel of enjoyment is evidence of some lack or void that the subject has foreclosed from consciousness. For Jung, a search for the repressed unconscious symbolic knowledge associated with the collective complex is necessary, accompanied by a becoming conscious of the affects caused by these symbols. In both cases, the lack of control such unconscious forces elicit are 'felt' in Rancière's *sensus communis* and expressed both in aesthetics and politics in the realm of representation, making it clear why Benjamin regarded the 'aestheticization of politics' with such fear.

But Zizek's Lacanian approach rotates around a concept of lack or void that in turn ultimately relates to the Phallus and castration, and thus can never be fully known or resolved. For Jung, this lack is related to the absence of an unconscious, identifiable force that is being repressed or denied and keeps seeping back into our consciousness. This difference leads to widely differing potential for political action. From Zizek's perspective, for example, we might describe the persistent popularity of the 'feminine' styles of art, architecture, and fashion described by Wollen in Chapter 1 as the appearance of 'woman as symptom'. This in turn points to a replaying of the original traumatic castration, an attempt to fill the lack left by the impossibility of being the mother's object of desire. It is an incestuous return to the womb, which will likely be followed by an equally fanatical revulsion and repression of that desire. This could explain why a collective fascination with the aesthetic feminine often precedes extremely violent events like the French revolution or World War I. It is a fantastical playing out of the desire to fill the unknowable void, to be the original love object for some cosmic mother figure, which in turn is harshly interrupted by the Law of the Father in the form of a violent political crushing of such hopes.

As interesting as this explanation might be, even if it provides a possible analysis of a situation, what political program would it recommend? If the original castration complex and the perpetual sense of void or lack that surrounds it are foundational, how can a Lacanian perspective ever be translated into a political agenda for change? And if this symptom is not to be 'messed' with, so to speak, how will it ever be fully resolved? Zizek's Lacanian approach provides an understanding of sexual difference and its association to a lack of subjectivity for women, but what is the way out of this situation, given the foundational status of the original trauma in Lacanian theory? What is to be done about it?

From a Jungian perspective, a collective taste for feminine aesthetics might be considered compensatory – an attempt to make up for the lack of the symbolic feminine in contemporary life through use of imagery. This focus on compensation could explain why the curvaceous eroticism of aesthetics such as the Baroque, Rococo, or *Art Nouveau* coincided with the focus on scientific rationality that emerged in the Renaissance and became integral to the politics of the Enlightenment period. The aspects of knowing and being that Jung described as feminine – *Eros* and *Luna* – are precisely those aspects of knowing and being that were being decried as nonsense and superstition at the time. As I will argue further in Chapter 6, in the late 16th century the anti-heroic sensibility of these feminine *moeurs douces* (gentle manners) were consciously considered necessary to compensate for the 'heroic' dedication of the aristocracy to violence and warfare. Jung's concept of the *enantiodromia* also helps us understand why the fascination with the feminine is often followed by a focus on a more masculine aesthetic and vice versa, given the inherent tendency to a compensatory reversal of psychic energies. Further, his discussion of the one-sidedness of the masculine focus on rationality and consciousness in the contemporary *zeitgeist* provides an understanding of why such feminine aesthetics become denigrated as inferior and kitsch.

It is here that the superiority of the Jungian approach in terms of its ability to countenance the power disparity between the aesthetic conception of the masculine and feminine becomes apparent. In this context, one could acknowledge from a Jungian perspective that woman is 'lack' because her repression leaves a void – not the lack that represents an unfulfillable desire, but the repression of a feminine energy that people are compensating for in searching for her symbols. The answer to this problem is clear: consciously acknowledge this lack, then hold it in opposition with the masculine aspects of the collective unconscious in order to avoid the *enantiodromia*. Such an interpretation reveals that the lack of political agency that appears to be inherent to the *enantiodromia* is not as inevitable as it seems.

All the same, I do not like the automaticity of Jung's *enantiodromia*. If this is a natural, cosmic phenomenon, is it possible to control it? This is a fairly simplistic understanding of power that appears to be in contradiction to the more immanent, purposive sense of power Jung develops in his conception of individuation. A greater appreciation for such immanent conceptions of power, still embedded in the concept of a collective unconscious, would be more useful. In this respect, the work of Hardt and Negri, which in turn is influenced by both Deleuze and Foucault, offers an approach that differs from, but is compatible with, the immanent, embodied views of desire offered by both Deleuze and Jung. My contribution will be to overlay their views with the energies of sexual difference.

From a theoretical perspective, Hardt and Negri's trilogy *Empire* (2000), *Multitude* (2005), and *Commonwealth* (2009) was greatly influenced by Deleuze and Guattari's adoption of the Jungian concept of the rhizome. As a political program, it is closely aligned with the Italian stream of political economy known in English as autonomism, and in Italian as *autonomia operaia* or *operaismo* (literally translated as 'workerism'). Together, these works comprise an alternative imagining of subjectivity, politics, and resistance.

Hardt and Negri reconfigure Jung's rhizome as the dispersed, networked world of multinational capital – a space they refer to as Empire. In their view, the rhizomic flows of capital, materials, and people around the world are rendering the 'constituted' or heteronomous power inherent to institutions like sovereign states, political parties, and trade unions obsolete. This is not necessarily a negative thing for Hardt and Negri, who reject the delegation of individual power required by such organizations in favour of an immanent, autonomous, 'constituent' concept of power. To borrow Purcell's distinction of these concepts of power, it is useful to think of the Latin basis of these terms: if *auto* = self, *hetero* = other, and *nomos* = law, we have a contrast here between an understanding of an immanent, *autonomous*, constituent law of the self that contrasts with the *heteronomous*, constituted power of organizations such as the state and unions, which ultimately only exist because individuals have handed their own autonomous power over to them (Purcell 2013, p. 13, fn).

Autonomists thus reject the liberal political economy tradition originating in Hobbes and Locke, where humans' inherent tendency to violence (for the former), or the need to protect private property (for the latter), renders the handing over of their constituent power to a sovereign, via a social contract, necessary for the good of society. Instead, it looks for power in 'the multitude' – the ability of 'singularities', in relation to multiple other singularities, to creatively interact and produce collectively, instead of delegating their power to the constituted organizations listed above. The social then becomes, in Negri's words 'a constellation of singularities' which, in following their own telos, come into contact with others to spontaneously create, and re-create, the Common.

Not surprisingly, one of the questions posed by this alternative vision of democracy is how a multitude unburdened by governing institutions can possibly co-exist in a peaceful and productive manner. Negri has responded to this concern in the language of *Eros*. Life in the rhizome must be ruled by love. Love is the 'law' of the multitude – without it there is chaos. Negri's Spinozist understanding of the phenomenology of love bears significant parallels to both Jung's and Deleuze's ideas of how symbolic knowledge moves through the body to become actual or material, and to an alchemical understanding of the mind/body connection.

For Spinoza, immanent power or *potentia* unfolds through a series of transitions that begin with *conatus* – the striving of and for life (Hardt and Negri 2009, p. 192). *Conatus* is the rough equivalent of Nietzsche's will to power; it traverses the body through desire (*cupiditas*) where it takes the form of 'all man's endeavours, impulses, appetites and volitions' (Spinoza quoted in Negri 2013, p. 88) and ultimately ends in the intellectual idea of *amor*. As *conatus* becomes corporal and moves in conjunction with the embodied desires of the individual, it produces imagination, where the potential institutions of social experience become expressed (p. 8). But for Spinoza, love (he calls it love of God) is the most basic of human emotions. As Negri shows, in Spinoza's view there are no emotions that can be directly opposed to this love and it cannot be destroyed without destroying the body as well. This, in turn, indicates that love is the most constant of all emotions (p. 90).

Negri's description of the transitions and transformations of *cupiditas* evokes a sense of the repeated process of the alchemical *coniunctio*:

> ... this cupidity immediately undergoes a process of transition, of movement toward greater or lesser perfection, in a process of singular imagination of the future that displaces *cupiditas* from a given level of composition to another, which is superior to it. And thus, from threshold to threshold – dispersing any interrelational physics of the social through the immanent constitutive character of the development of *cupiditas*.
>
> (p. 89)

How do politics and economy emerge from this? In terms of Hardt and Negri's Spinozan concept of the multitude, the striving of singularities 'of and for life' constantly moves in a nomadic fashion both *within* and *against* Empire. As in Deleuze and Guattari's Jungian-inspired understanding of the nomadic nature of desire in the rhizome, monadic singularities become nomads constantly manifesting the energies of desire. They are both constrained by the networks and ideologies of Empire, and resist these same forms of power:

> New figures of struggle and new subjectivities are produced in the conjuncture of events, in the universal nomadism, in the general mixture and miscegenation of individuals and populations, and in the technological metamorphoses of the imperial biopolitical machine. These new

Toward a biopolitics of the unconscious 91

figures and subjectivities . . . are not posed *merely against* the imperial system – they are not simply negative forces. The also express, nourish, and develop positively their own constituent projects; they work toward the liberation of living labour, creating constellations of powerful singularities. This constituent aspect of the movement of the multitude, in its myriad faces, is really the positive terrain of the historical construction of Empire.

(Hardt and Negri 2000, p. 61)

As Negri notes, one of the central questions posed by this understanding of the global political economy is how to guarantee that the production of new subjectivities by the multitude is a positive, as opposed to negative experience. 'What proof is there that the multitude, instead of being productive of democracy, isn't just a mob, a pure upsurge of plebeian disorder?' (Negri 2013, p. 29). In response to critics who charge that he has simply created a utopian political theology that magically 'believes' in the ability of the multitude to create love and freedom, Negri counters that Hobbes' emphasis on the necessity of controlling the multitude through sovereign power is closer to theology than Spinoza's model. In the context of Jung's emphasis on the destructive implications of the dominance of the rational *logos* implicit to a concept such as the social contract, Negri's claim gains further credence. The rational social contract guaranteeing the heteronomous power of the state is itself a historically contingent social, and as Jung points out, psychic phenomenon. As such, what makes it more innately just or viable than alternative forms of power?

Foucault called the discursive forms of power over life created by heteronomous forms of power *biopower*, which is close to the form of power Spinoza called *potesta*. Opposing this is what Hardt and Negri call *biopolitics* – a focus on the formation of alternative subjectivities, or what Spinoza would call *potentia*. Using Foucault's understanding of power as something that does not so much repress, but rather *produces* subjectivities, Hardt and Negri (2009) define biopolitics as 'the power of life to resist and determine an alternative production of subjectivity' (p. 57). For Foucault, 'Power is not something that is acquired, seized, or shared, something that one holds on to or allows to slip away; power is exercised from innumerable points, in the interplay of nonegalitarian and mobile relations' (Foucault 1980, p. 94). Configured this way, power is not just decentralized, but immanent to various relations of power/domination in society (such as sexual relations, economic relations, family relations, and various institutional relations such as schools and hospitals). He considered biopower to be the forms of power that evolved to restrict and mould the immanent power emerging from bodies. Such forms of power work in part through a variety

92 Theory

of discursively created 'disciplines' that are absorbed and accepted by individuals, who to a large extent self-regulate in accordance with such discourses. In Foucault's words 'Power is everywhere; not because it embraces everything, but because it comes from everywhere' (p. 93).

Foucault's biopower is far more pervasive and invasive than the forms of sovereign power conceived by Hobbes or Locke, where a government effectively gains 'power over' large collectivities of people. To borrow another of Foucault's terms, such techniques of power can be seen as forms of 'governmentality' that can be used, both by the state directly or via other institutions, to make order in society. Power, in this view, is not necessarily ideological – it constrains, represses, and conforms individuals in accordance with multiple logics of control.

Negri maintains that it is actually such attempts to repress and control the immanent power of individuals that create uncontrollable political reactions. He argues that while Spinoza feared the potential 'barbarities' of the multitude, he also believed that attempts to address such fears by repressing immanent power in fact *create* barbarities. In an argument similar to Polanyi's, he claims that it is actually political moves to oppress and repress the immanent, biopolitical movement to form alternative subjectivities against heteronomous power that creates mob behaviour, not movements that encourage the elaboration of singular desires (Negri 2013, pp. 30–32). As Lazzarato (2002) points out, although Foucault's decentralized of webs of biopower appear to trap individuals with inescapable limits to their freedom, in his later work Foucault emphasized that such forms of biopower are *responses* to the expression of power emanating from free subjects. In other words, the attempts to discipline and control inherent to biopower *presuppose* the immanent, biopolitical power of acting subjects. Singularities are constantly pushing forward to express themselves, but are then faced with attempts to contain their power. They can go along or resist, but there is always the possibility of change.

Lazzarato's work emphasizes the creative aspects of such resistance. Power becomes condensed into a dynamic of 'strategic relations' where attempts to contract or control the spaces of freedom are met with constant resistance. Life and living become a process of working through this dynamic, 'that simultaneously resists power and creates new forms of life' (Lazzarato 2002, p. 109). In Foucault's words 'To create and recreate, to transform the situation, to participate actively in the process, that is to resist' (quoted in Lazzarato 2002, p. 109).

My analysis of the insights of Jung, Zizek, and Polanyi into the causes of mob behaviour, or what Jung called collective complexes, offers a complementary perspective on this question of mob verses multitude. Negri and Polanyi both view 'mob' behaviour as reactions to the imposition of power – for Negri this imposition comes from the discourses and institutions of biopower, for Polanyi it derives from the instrumental logic of the market. For Jung and Zizek, on the other hand, collective complexes emanate from unconscious causes, and the refusal to acknowledge this only exacerbates the problem.

I want to draw on all of these approaches in a way that integrates sexual difference into this problem. To draw out Polanyi's argument further, what he is effectively arguing is that the inherent relationship of caring necessary to the social bonds of life – *Eros* – turns negative when an excessive form of *Logos* is imposed on it. Just as he argues that conscious attempts to re-embed the *Logos* of the market in society can keep this impulsion toward social protection from turning negative, I believe that an approach involving a conscious cultivation of both energies of sexual difference can result in a sort of 'plateauing' phenomenon that avoids unconscious phenomenon such as the *enantiodromia*. I use the word plateauing in Bateson's use of the word (later adopted by Deleuze and Guattari) – a sort of levelling of energies in a relationship that is not allowed to come to a climax. In Deleuze and Guattari's (1987, p. 21) terms, it is always 'in the middle, not at the beginning or end'.

Polanyi's concept of collective, spontaneous, protectionist reactions that have the potential to take negative forms such as fascism parallels Jung's understanding of the collective complex, or Hardt and Negri's concept of 'identitarian' love, such as race love, or nation love, populisms or fascisms, and religious fundamentalism. Such dark forms of love, in Hardt and Negri's (2009, pp. 182–3) words, urge us to love those most like us more and those who are not like us less, in contrast to what Nietzsche claimed was the highest form of love: love of the 'farthest' or the stranger. Hence, although it is clear why Negri (2013, p. 98) claims that 'Democracy is an act of love', it also obvious that this love or *Eros* has negative, devouring aspects. Such negative forms of love clearly need to be tempered by not just tolerance, but by consciousness. This means rationally acknowledging the inherent desire for *Eros*, our need to be embedded or contained in relatedness, but also accepting that there might be standards applied to it, such as the principal of inclusivity.

I am arguing here for a conscious recognition of the immanent manifestations of desire that both inhabit and connect us, layered by sexual difference. In this, I acknowledge the unconscious pressures that are created when the two archetypal energies that Jung identified as *Eros* and *Logos* are not equally assimilated. In Negri's terms, think of *conatus* as layered by these energies of sexual difference as it works through *cupiditas* to become the intellectual concept of *amor*. Defining this concept of *amor*, Negri develops a manifestation of love that sounds very much like a conscious assimilation of *Eros* and *Logos*; of a rational, erotic collective action based on singularities:

> How difficult it is to wrench love away from the psychological vanity of romanticism, or the ferocious utopia of mysticism . . . For me, on the contrary, love as defined by Spinoza introduces us to the rational and constructive rapport between constituent ontological potency and the collective action of the singularities. In this sense, a possible Spinozan sociology would constitute a sort of laboratory working against and beyond the modern, against and beyond possessive individualism. I would embrace *amor* as a subversive force, showing society as the constitution of the common, *as the intersecting of the rationality and desire of singularities*, as the trajectory of common liberty.
>
> (Negri 2013, p. 97, my emphasis)

One might call Negri's conception of *amor* a rational *Eros*. As I will argue in Chapter 6, Marcuse referred to this as 'sensuous rationality' or the development of a '*rationality of gratification* in which reason and happiness converge. It creates its own division of labor, its own priorities, its own hierarchy' (Marcuse 1966, p. 224, his emphasis). Negri's Spinozan-based phenomenology of *conatus/cupiditas/amor* – so similar to the phenomenologies of Jung and Deleuze described in the previous chapter – differs from classical liberal theory in that it assumes *amor/Eros* is a significant aspect of the integrity and liberty of the human psyche that must be protected and ensured. This complicates the classical liberal understanding of human interaction, where *Eros* (relatedness or love in a non-reproductive sense) is either considered an inessential human need (as in Rousseau), or where it is a presumed natural morality (as in Locke) that does not need to be protected by law, unlike private property or individual liberty. Another complication is that such energy cannot be directly contractually created – it is a feeling that must arise immanently and should be tempered by rationality but not repressed.

In contrast, our current biopolitical situation is characterized by a pervasive contractualization of human relations that stretches from the economy into the home (Mitropoulos 2012). While I do not completely discount the importance of the contract, its influence in the contemporary political economy has become pervasive. A parallel constitutional commitment to the development of *Eros* would undoubtedly change the tenor of contemporary politics and economics, yet a full commitment to what effectively involves a continual process of negotiation between the forces of sexual difference is not something that can be easily accommodated in contemporary political theory or institutions. Part of this is a lack of political development of such concepts. Between the extensive development of the social contract in classical liberal political theory, and the prominence of the contract in legal theory, everyone has an idea of what contractualism is. But can the same be said of *Eros*? Jung described the *Eros* of the symbolic feminine as relatedness and pleasure, but what does this mean in practical, experiential terms? This will be the central question of the following chapter.

Note

1 Zizek interprets the Real as something that precedes the Lacanian register of the Symbolic Order or (realm of signification), but then is subsequently structured by it as it gets caught up in the network of signification inherent to the Symbolic register.

Bibliography

Adorno, T. and Horkheimer, M. (2002) *Dialectic of Enlightenment*, Stanford University Press, Stanford, CA.

Alliez, E. and Osborne, P. (2013) *Spheres of Action: Art and Politics*, MIT Press, Cambridge, MA.

Barad, K. (2006) *Meeting the Universe Halfway: Quantum Physics and the Entanglement of Matter and Meaning*, Duke University Press, Durham, NC.

Baudrillard, J. (2004) *Simulacra and Simulation*, trans. Sheila Faria Glaser, The University of Michigan Press, Ann Arbor.

Benjamin, W. (2007) 'The Work of Art in the Age of Mechanical Reproduction', in *Illuminations*, ed. Hannah Arendt, trans. Harry Zohn, Schocken Books, New York, pp. 217–251.

Bourdieu, P. (1984) *Distinction: A Social Critique of the Judgment of Taste*, Harvard University Press, Cambridge, MA.

Butler, J. (1999) *Gender Trouble: Feminism and the Subversion of Identity*, Routledge, London and New York.

Butler, J. (2011) *Bodies that Matter*, Routledge, London and New York.

Deleuze, G. and Guattari, F. (1987) *A Thousand Plateaus: Capitalism and Schizophrenia*, University of Minnesota Press, Minneapolis and London.

Foucault, M. (1980) *The History of Sexuality*, vol. 1, Vintage Books, New York.

Gellert, M. (1998) 'The Eruption of the Shadow in Nazi Germany', *Psychological Perspectives*, vol. 37, no. 1, pp. 72–89.

Hardt, M. and Negri, A. (2000) *Empire*, Harvard University Press, Cambridge, MA.

Hardt, M. and Negri, A. (2005) *Multitude: War and Democracy in the Age of Empire*, Penguin Books, New York.

Hardt, M. and Negri, A. (2009) *Commonwealth*, The Belknap Press of Harvard University Press, Cambridge, MA.

Harvey, D. (1990) *The Condition of Postmodernity*, Blackwell, Cambridge, MA and Oxford.

Jameson, F. (1995) *Postmodernism: Or, the Cultural Logic of Late Capitalism,* Duke University Press, Durham, NC.

Jung, C. G. (1958) *Collected Works,* vol. 11, trans. R. F. C. Hull, Bollingen Series, Princeton University Press, Princeton, NJ.

Jung, C. G. (1960) *Collected Works,* vol. 8, trans. R. F. C. Hull, Bollingen Series, Princeton University Press, Princeton, NJ.

Jung, C. G. (1964) *Collected Works,* vol. 10, trans. R. F. C. Hull, Bollingen Series, Princeton University Press, Princeton, NJ.

Jung, C. G. (1967) *Collected Works,* vol. 13, trans. R. F. C. Hull, Bollingen Series, Princeton University Press, Princeton, NJ.

Kant, I. (2007) *Critique of Judgement,* revised, trans. James Creed Meredith, ed. Nicholas Walker. Oxford University Press, Oxford and New York.

Kimbles, S. (2000) 'The Cultural Complex and the Myth of Invisibility', in *The Vision Thing,* ed. Thomas Singer, Routledge, London and New York, pp. 157–169.

Lash, S. and Urry, J. (1993) *Economies of Signs and Space,* Sage Publications, London.

Lazzarato, M. (2002) 'From Biopower to Biopolitics', *Pli,* vol. 13, no. 2002, pp. 99–113.

Marcuse, H. (1966) *Eros and Civilization: A Philosophical Inquiry into Freud,* Beacon Press, Boston.

'Miss Richardson's Statement', *The Times,* March 11, 1914.

Mitropoulos, A. (2012) *Contract and Contagion: From Biopolitics to Oikonomia,* Minor Compositions, Wivenhoe, New York and Port Watson.

Negri, A. (2013) *Spinoza for our Time: Politics and Postmodernity,* Columbia University Press, New York.

Plonowska-Ziarek, E. (2012) *Feminist Aesthetics and the Politics of Modernism,* Columbia University Press, New York.

Polanyi, K. (1944) *The Great Transformation,* Beacon Press, Boston.

Purcell, M. (2013) *The Down-Deep Delight of Democracy,* Wiley-Blackwell, Malden, MA and West Sussex, UK.

Rancière, J. (2004) *The Politics of Aesthetics: The Distribution of the Sensible,* trans. Gabriel Rockhill, Continuum, London and New York.

Tanke, J. (2011) 'What is the Aesthetic Regime?' *Parrhesia,* no. 12, pp. 71–81.

von Franz, M. L. (1980) *Alchemy: An Introduction to the Symbolism and the Psychology,* Inner City Books, Toronto.

Zizek, S. (1989) *The Sublime Object of Ideology,* Verso, London and New York.

Zizek, S. (2004) 'Notes on a Debate "From Within the People"', *Criticism,* vol. 26, no. 4, pp. 661–666.

Chapter 4

Containment/transformation

Eros as interval

The mother/child relationship is the Rosetta Stone of psychoanalytic theory. It is the incestuous love for the mother and the necessary separation from the mother that determine the central complexes (for Freud) or the constitutional sense of lack (for Lacan) that are foundational to psychological development. This understanding of the central, yet elided role of the feminine also permeates philosophy. As Derrida writes:

> The displacing of the relationship with the mother, with nature, with being as the fundamental signified, such indeed is the origin of society and languages. But can one speak of origins after that? Is the concept of origin, or of the fundamental signified, anything but a function, indispensable but situated, inscribed, within the system of signification inaugurated by the interdict [of incest]? Within the play of supplementarity, one will always be able to related the substitutes to their signified, this last will be yet another signifier. The fundamental signified, the meaning of the being represented, even less the thing itself, will never be given us in person, outside the sign or outside play.
>
> (Derrida 1976, p. 266)

In other words, 'mother' *is* origin, but the limitations of language mean we will never be able to understand her; the nature of her power can only be described by a series of endlessly deferred signifiers.

Derrida's comment insinuates that meaning can only be known, or forces such as 'mother' can only be expressed, through language. This, as we know from Jung's and Deleuze's emphases on affect, is not the case. Mother, as any infant (obviously incapable of linguistic skills) would 'know', is a *feeling*. It is an energy, possibly a bodily energy hardwired into the brain. This possibility is reinforced by decades of neurological research into the nature of the mother/child interaction.

In what follows, I will review Jungian approaches that show how this embodied, relational energy might be related to the concept of the archetypal feminine. I will take this argument further, however, to show the broader political and economic implications of the simultaneously containing and transformational energy Jung and Deleuze have characterized as feminine. This exercise is important not only in terms of redressing the predominant conception of the feminine in psychoanalysis as 'lack', but also to a reconsideration of the supposedly passive energy of woman as container inherent to classical philosophy. I will show the necessary connection of containing energies to psychic development and transformation, not only for individuals, but in a collective sense as well.

My characterization of archetypal feminine energy as containment/transformation references the very different work of two Jungian analysts: the more classical Jungian ideas of Erich Neumann (1974), and the post-Jungian approach of Jean Knox (2003 & 2011). I will begin with an exploration of the post-Jungian work of Knox and her emphasis on the importance of neuroscience to understanding the Jungian concept of the archetype.

Containment

Jungians such as Connolly (2013), Knox (2003 & 2011), and Wilkinson (2006) draw on insights from interpersonal neuroscience and development studies to argue that the development of the self is a relational process. As such, they incorporate an important aspect of Jung's understanding of *Eros* to their approach. As I argued in Chapter 2, for Jung *Eros* was not purely sexual as it was for Freud, but also involves a more Platonic understanding of relatedness and connection.

The central premise of the relational neuroscience Knox draws on is that the self and a sense of self-agency are developed interpersonally by relating to others, both physically and psychically. Drawing on approaches such as attachment theory, she argues that the development of the self is in effect a negotiated process that occurs in the context of our interactions with other people and the social environment. Generally, relational approaches tend to focus on the early mother–infant interaction, although in Knox's interpretation there is attention to both parents' interactions with a child, in addition to environmental influences such as trauma.

Both Knox and Wilkinson use the work of neuroscientists such as Damasio (1999), Johnson (1987), Meltzoff (2005), Schore (2003), and Sinigaglia (2008) to emphasize the importance of physical mirroring in the development of self. Knox argues that we have a basic sense of body, referred to as a body schema, that precedes a sense of self-agency. This genetically inherited body schema provides us with the potential for action, although it does not explain the content of self-agency and action itself. Here Knox is borrowing Johnson's notion of the image schema formed from early bodily experience of the physical world.

According to Meltzoff, a sense of agency and action develops through personal interactions with early caregivers. Through this physical interaction with adults, the child develops an 'extended body scheme consisting of body movements, postures, and acts' that provide the basis for human interaction *as well as* a notion of the self (quoted in Connolly 2013, p. 643). For Meltzoff's collaborator Gallagher (2005), these embodied practices become our primary access to understanding others, even after mind abilities are considerably more developed (Connolly 2013, p. 644). Hence, corporeal awareness is fundamental to the development of the self and to self-agency.

According to Sinigaglia, this process is facilitated by mirror neurons – neurons that fire simultaneously in different people's brains when someone is carrying out an action *or* observing another person performing an action. As Knox explains, 'When mirror neurons fire, we know what we ourselves would intend if we performed the action and therefore attribute the same intention to the person we observe'. This process, which occurs unconsciously and automatically, does not attribute mental states, desires, or beliefs, but is a means for action understanding that 'provides a direct matching of the others' observed behavior to our own motor repertoire' (Knox 2011, p. 62).

On the basis of these interactions the child has early on in life, various 'internal working models' are developed and held in neuronal networks in the brain. They then implicitly guide individual action and reaction in the world. From early infancy we develop such internal working models – schematic patterns stored in implicit memory and therefore not consciously available. In Schore's more technical language, 'neurodevelopmental processes of dendritic proliferation and synaptogenesis which are responsible for postnatal brain growth are critically influenced by events at interpersonal and intrapersonal levels' (quoted in Knox 2003, p. 95).

Knox argues that body schemas are comparable to what Jung referred to as the archetypes, while the internal working models are similar to the Jungian notion of the complex. Like the archetypes, body schemas do not have any content in themselves (i.e. the symbolic content of the image is not passed on genetically) but provide a kind of 'scaffolding' on which future meaning is organized and constructed. These body schemas involve some degree of learning, but because the pattern of early learning is nearly identical for all children regardless of culture (i.e. sucking on a breast) they are universal inclinations. In this context, Knox proposes that the archetypes be considered as 'reliably repeated early developmental achievements' (p. 60).

100   Theory

Symbolic meaning is subsequently attached to these biological, archetypal schemas through a process of metaphor that Lackoff and Johnson referred to as polysemy – the 'extension of a central sense of a word to other senses by devices of the human imagination, such a metaphor and metonymy' (Johnson quoted in Knox, p. 60). To use an example from Knox that is central to my argument,

> 'Mother' is a concept, but the body schema of 'containment', the bodily experience of being held and accompanying physiological sensations of warmth, comfort and security, are not initially symbolic although they become so with the metaphorical elaboration of the image schema.
>
> (p. 62)

The parallels between Jung's and Deleuze's phenomenological understandings of the bodily assimilation of symbolic knowledge outlined in Chapter 2 mean that Knox's insights are as relevant to Deleuze's work as they are to Jung's. Protevi (2010) makes this link explicit in his discussion of Deleuze's relation between the Virtual/Intensive/Actual, and what he calls the 4EA (embodied-embedded-extended-enactive-affective) approach to cognitive science, arguing that Deleuze's work can provide an ontology for it. The 4EA approach, which draws on many of the theories discussed by Knox, conceives of the nervous system as a massive internal feedback loop where the brain develops coherent wave patterns out of a chaotic background of nervous system activity. In this respect, a person is continually 'leaning' or reaching out to things or experiences in the environment and organizing these stimuli in the context of the internal working models and body schema Knox refers to.

This bodily sensibility or openness to the environment merges with internal system messages based on existing subliminal patterns or neural pathways that 'compete' with one another for dominance (Protevi, p. 425). The system that emerges 'victorious' from this chaotic competition then becomes a determinate pattern of brain activity that can then be used as a 'basin of attraction' for further behaviour. The sensory input from an ever-changing environment either reinforces existing patterns, or in some cases shocks the brain into the creation of new patterns of behaviour. Hence, the system is not linear but rather a chaotic feedback loop that is in constant mutation. Linking this to Deleuze's ontology of *virtual* Ideas, *intensive* embodied experiences, and *actual* experience, Protevi argues that the neuro-somatic-environmental interaction corresponds to Deleuze's concept of the Idea or pre-individual virtual field, and the dynamics of the nervous system as it works through this sensory input in the body is comparable to his conception of 'intensive' processes or impersonal individuations (p. 426).

Knox takes this argument further, however, to argue that the nature of a child's early containment experience can affect her/his process of individuation. When parent/child interaction is 'good enough', to borrow Winnicott's term, this process is the basis for a negotiated process that leads to the development of the self, as well as a coherent sense of self-agency. 'Secure' parents make the child feel safe, contained, and enabled. A sense of self-agency develops when the infant tries to express something or make something happen and the parent responds appropriately, making the child feel that they have had an impact through their actions.

When parents are non-responsive (due to neglect or depression, for example), or tend to impose on their infant instead of responding to her/his communications, an image schema of 'force' or 'splitting' is activated, as opposed to that of containment (p. 66). As Knox notes, such an absence of parental attunement can be devastating, 'leading to lifelong states of mind in which people feel that they do not really exist, that they have a kind of psychic black hole at their very core' (Knox 2011, p. 11). Because such misattunement often results in the parent reacting to a child's emotional distress or vital bodily movements by withdrawing, it constitutes a 'profound assault on the infant's experience of agency in the relationship' (p. 49). Consequently, inadequate practices of containment have also been associated with psychological issues such as eating disorders, self-harm, addictions, and sexual perversions (Connolly 2013, p. 643). Connolly, for example, describes an analysand with containment issues who developed a sense of 'inner deadness', with frequent dreams involving coldness, snow, and ice, as well as masochistic fantasies where he is immobilized and enslaved by women.

The relevance of Knox's research for my purposes is that the nurturing, containing energy that has been associated with the feminine for millennia is actually central to the process of individuation – in other words, individual transformation. In extreme cases, the absence of an adequate sense of containment results in cases where there is a fundamental sense of non-being (Connolly 2013). In cases where containment incorporates violence, it results in a tendency to legitimate this sort of behaviour later in life. In other words, containment and transformation are two sides of the same coin; they form a sort of double movement where the individual draws on the embodied sense of containment throughout their life to encourage a further sense of change and transformation.

Importantly, when Knox discusses this primary relationship of caring and *Eros*, she consistently uses the word 'parent', as opposed to 'mother'. Not just the mother, but anyone regularly interacting with an infant is responsible for developing her/his sense of contained transformation. This indicates that all humans, regardless of gender identification, are capable of performing this embodied, yet psychic, action of containment. If we want to rely on a more Darwinian interpretation of this capability, it is entirely possible that women, as the bearers of children, might possess more of the hard wiring that inclines them to undertake this role. This tendency would be enhanced by the broader social assumption that this caring role should primarily undertaken by women. This, effectively, is the argument of feminists in the 'ethic of care' tradition who maintain that women have superior *Eros* or relational skills due to their experiences caring for children and other family members (Chodorow 1978; Gilligan 1982; Held 1993; Ruddick 1980). It is also possible that Jung's association of pleasure with this archetypal energy derives from this mother/child relationship, given the primal bliss a newborn infant must feel when experiencing the protection and tactile sensuality of this containing experience.

My conception of the feminine energy of *Eros* differs from the ethic of care approach, however, in that I consider it analogous to, but not coterminous with, this sort of mothering relationship. Although *Eros* as relatedness may be metaphorically associated with the kinds of caring relationships primarily undertaken by women, it can be more accurately described as what Grosz calls 'another way of being' that applies to all humans, whether they undertake caring relationships or not. This, in turn, is related to its status as a fundamental aspect of the human relational experience. In other words, it is metaphorically associated with, and sometimes feels like, the affective labour such as childcare primarily performed by women, but it is not limited to this. As will become clearer below, I also maintain that *Eros* alone cannot ensure an appropriate containment experience; instead a negotiation with the energies of *Logos* to create a 'plateau' or interval is necessary. Particularly as we move beyond Knox's focus on the individual containment experience to look at collective ones, the transformative role of containing energies and their necessary relation to *Logos* will become more apparent.

Relational psychology identifies the centrality of the process of containment for healthy individual psychic development, but it has little to say on the transpersonal aspect of the embodied, psychic act of containment. The individual focus of this literature does not mean that there is no macrocosmic aspect to this phenomenon, however. The widespread nature of relational disorders such as anorexia or self-harm indicates that although they may have roots in individual experience and may be best treated on an individual level, there is a transpersonal aspect to them.

Given the murkiness of the inside/outside boundary in Jung's ideas, the possibility of a transpersonal dimension to the phenomenon of containment is clear. As noted above, the necessity for containment is pervasive in a person's life. It has a longitudinal dimension in that it is necessary to invoke this feeling of containment throughout one's life, but it is also latitudinal in that it applies to a variety of different circumstances other than the mother/child interaction. It is entirely possible that circumstances that affect individuals in a collective way, such as the form of their economic interactions or the nature of their political or work environment, could affect their sense of containment. In such circumstances, it would not be surprising to see collective behaviour related to this physiological/psychological phenomenon.

In fact, a collective manifestation of the need for containment and human interconnection is implicit in Polanyi's (1944) emphasis on the need for the *logos* of capitalism to remain embedded in society, or in Negri's (2013) Spinozan interpretation of the natural movement of power in the form of *conatus/cupiditas/amor* in the previous chapter. It is possible to see how a collective of individuals could feel a sense of alienation (a 'black hole' as Knox puts it) due to the preponderance of the instrumental rationality inherent to many contemporary political and economic relationships and metaphorically regress to the mother to address it. They might look for alternative sources of containment that can have a broad range of manifestations – from starting a yoga collective on one end of the spectrum, to joining the Nazi party on the other. It stands to reason, therefore, that understanding the compelling nature of this affective force and dealing with it appropriately can have significant political implications.

Venus in furs

Deleuze provides a compelling example of the collective aspects of inadequate containment in his exegesis of Sacher-Masoch's novel, *Venus in Furs*. Before I relate this story, I want to underline the parallels between the fantasies of Sacher-Masoch's hero Severin and the masochistic fantasies of Conolly's analysand mentioned above. In both case, there are feelings of anomie, fantasies of being enslaved and immobilized by women, and constant references to cold, ice, and freezing. Sacher-Masoch's novel, I believe, can be taken as a kind of metaphorical parable describing the effects of what happens when containment must be created contractually, as opposed to being allowed to evolve naturally. Although I will ultimately criticize his conclusions, Deleuze's analysis of this novel reinforces Kerslake's argument regarding the Jungian influence on his ideas, and also shows the entangled relationship between aesthetics (this time in the form of writing), bodies, and sexual difference.

Although I agree with Deleuze's analysis tying the desire of the story's hero, Severin, to the archetypal feminine, I argue that ultimately Severin's role-playing of the revival of feminine power fails because of its overly contractual recreation of the feminine energy Jung defined as *Eros*. Yet this failure in itself still gives us some clues as to what a collective biopolitics that genuinely seeks to incorporate *Eros* might look like, insofar as it highlights the contrast between the erotic experience of containment, and the *Logos* of the contract.

Sacher-Masoch's semi-autobiographical story of a man whose sexual experiences were heightened when he was brutally mistreated by a woman begins with a dream in which the story's narrator converses with a 'sublime', marble skinned Venus wrapped in furs. When he awakens from the dream, the narrator visits an acquaintance named Severin von Kusiemski, who tells him that he has actually lived this dream with a real woman, showing him a painting modelled after Titian's *Venus with the Mirror* (a painting strikingly similar to Velázquez's Venus, Figure 3.1). Severin proceeds to tell his story. Although his real-life Venus (named Wanda) was hesitant at first, he convinced her to treat him as her slave by whipping and humiliating him. To ensure that he abided by this agreement, Wanda made Severin sign a contract stating that he would be her slave. Wanda's only commitment was that she must wear fur.

Deleuze provides an archetypal reading of this story that owes much to the ideas of Jung and Bachofen, setting his reading apart from most interpretations of Sacher-Masoch's work, which turn to Freud or Lacan (for example, Jacob 2007; Sigler 2011; Silverman 1988. See Kazarian 2010; Kerslake 2007; Zizek 2004 for analyses that include Jung). Deleuze saw the novel as a regressive fantasy based on the return of a primitive feminine communism presided over by Venus-Aphrodite. Sacher-Masoch, Deleuze claims, was obviously influenced by Bachofen, who viewed gynocracy as a state of humanity that had been overwhelmed and destroyed by patriarchy in three stages. The first stage that Deleuze outlines is the primitive hetaeric or Aphroditic era when women were dominant, their relations with men highly promiscuous, and pleasure was the only law. But the chaotic sensuality of this era embedded in nature was transformed by a 'glacial epoch', when sensuality was repressed and a strict severity emerged. This ushered in the Demetrian era, the time of the Amazons, another matriarchal epoch characterized by a strict agricultural order in which men had some status, but still were dominated by women. The third era was the Apollonian – the era of rational patriarchy in which we now live, in which matriarchy is severely repressed and survives only in degenerate forms (Deleuze 1991, pp. 52–53).

In this transformation from hetaeric matriarchy to patriarchy, men gradually succumbed to a hyper-rationality and became 'children of reflection', losing their nature or soul. Even before that, however, the feminine principle had started to become cold, transformed into a despotic and devouring Mother. In Sacher-Masoch's novel, Deleuze points out, Venus is constantly shivering and sneezing, wrapped in furs to protect her from the cold of 'our abstract northern climate, in the icy realm of Christianity' (Sacher-Masoch quoted in Deleuze 2004, p. 127).

Sacher-Masoch's masochism, Deleuze argues, should be seen as a regression to this cold mother, and Wanda, Severin's whip-bearing mistress, is a devouring mother figure. The symbols of the bear and fur throughout the novel are further evidence of this chthonic, devouring mother. From this perspective, Deleuze claims, Severin's journey is one of transformation and rebirth, a regression to the mother in order to escape the cold contradictions of Judeo-Christian patriarchy. This is a dangerous journey: 'He who unearths the Anima enters on this regression: all the more terrible for being repressed, the Anima will know how to turn patriarchal structures to its own advantage and rediscover the power of the devouring Mother' (Deleuze 2004, p. 127).

According to Deleuze, a key aspect of Sacher-Masoch's masochism is his use of the contract to restore the repressed Anima. Using a fairly essentialist argument, Deleuze maintains that the contract is fundamentally bound up with patriarchal society as a non-material, spiritual guarantee of relations of authority between men. In contrast, women are more united by the material and chthonic bonds exemplified by the union between a mother and child, which 'by its nature seems to rebel against contractual expression' (p. 126). Deleuze claims that Sacher-Masoch used the patriarchal contract against itself to restore the power of the feminine; Wanda (Venus) uses a contract to ensure that Severin remains enslaved to her. 'Masochism cannot be separated from the contract, but at the same time as it draws up the contract for the dominant woman, it pushes it to the extreme by dismantling its machinery and exposing it to mockery.' (p. 127)

Deleuze turns to Jung to critique the Freudian interpretation of masochism as fundamentally lying in the realm of the Father. In the Freudian view, Deleuze argues, Wanda's whips and ferocious power are an exteriorization of the Father; he quotes the Freudian theorist Reik as arguing that in every case of masochism 'we found the father or his representative hidden behind the figure of the beating woman' (p. 132). One has to perform some extraordinary gymnastics, Deleuze argues, to see Wanda as a masculine figure. But this interpretation is typical of the Freudian approach, he claims, which inflates the masculine and remains in the realm of the individualized unconscious. By ignoring the pre-individual, collective, maternal unconscious, Deleuze argues, Freud remained stuck in the superficial hysterical

106 Theory

unconscious caught up in the Oedipal struggle, ignoring the deeper realms of the unconscious where the symbol of the Mother reigns in its own terms (p. 128).

Instead, the unconscious symbol of the Mother inherent to masochism is emblematic of the relations of 'opposition, compensation and reorganization' inherent to the unconscious regressions of Jungian psychology (p. 128).

> It is the image of the Mother, it is the regression to this image, which is constitutive of masochism and forms its unity. On condition that one interprets this original image after the manner of Jung, as an archetype from the deep strata of the unconscious.
>
> (p. 130)

Symbols cannot be reduced or made composite as Freud did, Deleuze argues, referring them back to desires or instincts. Sexuality and death are symbolic in themselves. Hence the threat of death looming throughout Sacher-Masoch's story is not real death, but a symbolic death and rebirth via regression to the mother.

Here Deleuze is referring to Jung's understanding of images of incest with the mother as a symbolic rebirth, in contrast to Freud's more literal view of incest derived from the Oedipal story. In disputing Freud's tendency to explain psychological development causally instead of symbolically, Jung used the process of regression to the mother as an example. For Freud, such a regression might be caused by a mother fixation. From this angle, Jung (1960, p. 23) notes, 'the whole edifice of civilization becomes a mere substitute for the possibility of incest'. From a symbolic perspective, however, the libido regresses to an *imago* of the mother that evokes memory associations that allow further psychological development to take place, 'for instance from a sexual system into an intellectual or spiritual system' (p. 23). Hence, for Jung the image of incest in a dream or myth usually refers to a process of re-birth, as opposed to a repressed desire for a sexual relationship with one's mother. 'Mother' in this instance is not fact, but symbol. 'Everything that is real and essential to |the Freudian causal perspective| is unreal and inessential to the |symbolic perspective|,' Jung maintained (p. 24). In other words, the regression to the mother may be a form of incest, but it is a symbolic incest and should not be taken literally. It is necessary for an often painful process of re-birth, which makes further progression possible. Severin's performance of masochism, as Deleuze pointed out, is an attempt to symbolically address the repression of the divine feminine under patriarchy; it is not a coincidence that Wanda becomes the goddess Venus.

Sacher-Masoch's novel, combined with his sexual practices, can be viewed as a fantasy narrative in which the author tries to re-create a more erotic (in the Jungian sense) environment of containment or *temenos* for himself. He does this by seeing his own story reflected symbolically in a broader sexo-cosmic narrative. He creates an entire alternative cosmology based on Bachofen's interpretation of matriarchal history that provides the background for his personal role-playing narrative with Wanda. But instead of re-enacting it with genuine *Eros* or relatedness, he seals it all with a contract, a legal document binding him to others as opposed to an emotional bond. The contract and Wanda's whip are his only connections to interpersonal relatedness.

Deleuze makes much of the importance of the contract in *Venus*, contrasting it with the mother/child bond, which is the opposite of the legal document that lies within the realm of the Father. He views it as a mocking attempt to use paternal law to support the power of the Mother: 'the contract here expresses the material predominance of the woman and the superiority of the maternal principle' (Deleuze 2004, p. 126). Zizek criticizes Deleuze for not realizing that although the masochist may be acting out a desire to give power to a Woman, this Woman remains ensconced in the paternal contract, as one of the 'Names-of-the Father'. I think Zizek's critique has merit. The bond between Severin and Wanda is not authentic *Eros*, but contractual. She is effectively a puppet in a game where the rules are made by the slave, even if she turns the tables on him by enforcing her dominance with a contract (Zizek 2004, pp. 663–664).

This also reveals why Severin's containment strategy – being bound and whipped – is not appropriate to the task. The sort of *Eros* he needs cannot be instilled by whip nor contract. Rather than flaunting the symbolic Law of the Father, Sacher-Masoch attempts to use the contract to cement a process that in its primal form is the *antithesis* of a contract. His contractual notion of the symbolic feminine is a pale comparison to the more organic process of embodied *Eros*. In the end, the feminine is repressed and the whole scenario remains firmly within the realm of the paternal. The 'supersensualist' Severin, over whom 'reason has little power' (Sacher-Masoch 1991, p. 172), ends up getting Apollonian reason whipped into him by a male character that Sacher-Masoch literally calls Apollo. Severin's quest for the archetypally feminine process of erotic containment is abandoned; he ends up taking Apollo's whip and turning it on his 'peasant girls' (p. 271).

Deleuze's interpretation, although over-optimistic in its claim that the archetypal feminine overthrows patriarchy by using the masculine Logos of the contract, succeeds in highlighting one of the central loci for biopolitical change: the distinction between creating *Eros* or relatedness by embedding or containing it in a genuine *temenos*, versus the artificial containment of *Eros* in *Logos* via the implementation of rule-based contractualism.

Cultivating an *appropriate*, affective sense of containment is central to the re-negotiation of identity inherent to what Hardt and Negri (2000 & 2009) call biopolitics: the creation of alternative subjectivities necessary for political transformation. By containment I mean a sense of relatedness to others that is encouraged by concrete actions of caring and interaction. There is nothing new or revolutionary to this statement. Humans have been unconsciously trying to replicate this feeling on a collective level for millennia, sometimes with so much success that it obliterates all conscious feelings of rationality. Clearly, the potential to resort to fascist, sexist, nationalist, or fundamentalist forms of containment is a danger here. Hence the second aspect of this relation is that it should be tempered by reason. It does not prohibit rational or contractual limits or provisos, but delimits them in the sense that they should be embedded in human interaction, not the other way around. The conceptions of 'rational *Eros*' or sensuous rationality as evoked by Negri and Marcuse respectively in the previous chapter is central to what I am describing here as an appropriate containing experience.

A return to becoming-woman

Deleuze's analysis of *anima* in this early work seems a giant step away from his later concept of becoming-woman/girl developed with Guattari (1987). Yet in this fairly essentialist analysis he alludes to something missing in his later work: the coldness involved in being uncontained and deprived of *Eros*. Recall from my discussion in Chapter 2 that Deleuze and Guattari's (1987, p. 277) becoming-woman makes explicit links between transformation and the transpersonal political aspects of the feminine: 'All becomings begin with and pass through becoming-woman'. But I have argued that their molecular focus makes it difficult to see the possible relation of becoming-woman to the actual bodies of women. Here I will extend this critique to note that their version of *anima* is also 'uncontained'. Deleuze's later fascination with the world of universal, molecular images that transcend every experience is reflected in a one-sided immersion in a sublime world to the neglect of the embodied experiential. Deleuze brilliantly analyzes the universal symbolic inherent to feminine energies. In contrast to Jung, he is less interested in their embodied, molar aspects. This is emblematic of an inclination toward the sublime in all of Deleuze's work with Guattari that contributes to the sense of 'horror of the ordinariness of flesh' that Haraway (2008, p. 3) complains of.

Deleuze and Guattari's becoming-woman avoids the charges of essentialism evident in his early work that also have been levelled at Jung, but she is uncontained, molecular, unmoored from any grounding that might impact her transformational status of becoming. Given that the sublime is typically considered to be a masculine force, while the feminine is generally associated with the much more passive 'beautiful' (Heymans 2011, pp. 14–15), Deleuze and Guattari's inclusion of 'becoming-woman' into their sublime approach does move away from Burke's and Kant's understanding of the aesthetic feminine as passive. Yet becoming-woman's ungroundedness means that the girl is also set adrift, sacrificed in the name of her status as sublime.

Deleuze and Guattari's (1987, p. 291) reliance on the transformative impact of becoming-woman is related to woman's minoritarian status as 'other' relative to the majoritarian subjectivity of men. But it is also because the idea of imposing a dominant history begins with the 'stealing' of the body of the girl. It is the girl who is first disciplined into behaving according to the discourses of history, or to use their example, is told 'you're not a little girl anymore, stop behaving like . . .' (p. 276). The boy is subsequently disciplined by reference to the girl as the object of desire, through which a dominant history becomes imposed on him too. The molecular girl doesn't belong to an age or sex or any other kind of order, but rather the in-between. She lives in the *intermezzo* – she is the 'block of becoming that remains contemporaneous to each opposable term, man, woman, child' (p. 277).

There is no question that part of the excitement of Deleuze and Guattari's approach derives from its association with the sublime. As Heymans notes, Deleuze and Guattari's ideas are by turns exhilarating and terrifying, precisely how Burke and Kant described the effects of the sublime. But their molecular notion involves a disembodiment that romanticizes the realities of the material girl/woman. In the double-sided sublime, the exhilaration of the molecular girl can rapidly flip to terror. Given the importance of the process of containment outlined above, what child, even a molecular one, would willingly live in such an uncontained, sublime world? The girl's sublime nature is denied any grounding by her location in the *intermezzo* – she is in constant movement, never standing still. The girl becomes sacrificed to Deleuze and Guattari's unwavering, heroic commitment to transformation.

Finding a balance between Deleuze and Guattari's sublime molecular approach and Jung's more molar one is key to developing a dynamic notion of the symbolic, transformative feminine that has meaning and transformative power for both men and women. Understanding how and why the girl might be revolutionary involves more than just seeing her as an anonymous 'girl', for she is key not just to the process of transformation, but to a negotiated peace of the symbolic forces of sexual difference. Illustrating this involves compromising her molecular nature to stratify her, at least partially, by giving her a name. Because she does have a name: Kore.

Demeter/Kore/Persephone: *Eros* as interval

The Demeter/Kore/Persephone myth goes a long way to explaining the attractiveness of the girl in the imaginations of men such as Deleuze and Guattari (or, in Heyman's example, the poet Robert Blake). It is the story of two sublime women: Demeter and Persephone – both goddesses and both evidence of the relationship between the feminine and containment/transformation. When deconstructed from a Jungian perspective, one finds in their story not just a tale of feminine transformation, but an even more compelling description of the 'original trauma' of separating from the mother so foundational to Freudian and Lacanian analysis.

The Oedipal story is not the only myth that describes the traumatic separation of mother and child. The Demeter/Kore/Persephone myth provides an alternative version of the original trauma that highlights the potential for transformation based on sexual difference. Unlike the Oedipal myth, it portrays desire not as lack or void, but as a positive force that must be negotiated relative to others, providing insights not just into the mother/child relationship, but also: 1. relationships between men and women as differing collective political entities; 2. relationships between partners (regardless of sexual or gender identity); 3. the negotiation of difference within the individual psyche; and most importantly for my purposes, 4. the collective negotiation of the energies of sexual difference. In fact, its approach to the trauma of separating from mother/origin is so vastly more comprehensive and complex than the Oedipal myth, it makes one question how the latter gained such foundational status in psychoanalysis. Understanding the importance of the Demeter/Kore/Persephone myth involves a look at how sexual difference is explained in psychoanalytic models based on the Oedipal theme of castration, such as Lacan's.

For Lacan, sexual difference revolves around identification with the signifier of the Phallus. Lacan argued that the Phallus is a symbol of the mother's desire that comes to represent a 'rupture' between the mother and child once the child realizes that her/his incestuous desire for the mother cannot be satisfied. The child's wish to be the object of the mother's desire is prohibited by the mother's desire for the father, or what Lacan called the Name or Law of the Father, a conceptual entity that the actual father effectively stands in for. Unable to represent this prohibited desire, the child only understands it as a primordial void. This rejection of the child's incestuous desire is what Lacan refers to as 'castration', and is experienced by both male and female children. Castration effectively involves cutting off the child's *jouissance* (an element of the Real that roughly translates as an almost unbearable pleasure), leaving a void or 'lack' symbolized by the Phallus.

Sexual difference then becomes defined through the relationship of males and females to the Phallus. The child attempts to signify this lack in a way that involves sexual differentiation: boys 'have' the Phallus and girls masquerade as 'being' the Phallus. In the process of signification set off by the child's rupture from the mother, the boy assumes the mother's desire for the father means that the father has the Phallus. The boy then associates with the father, pretending to have the object of desire himself. Girls, on the other hand, cannot make this association of 'having' the Phallus and begin to identify with the mother as the object of the father's desire, in effect pretending they are the unknowable desire symbolized by the Phallus. But the Phallus is only void; it is a negative object that does not exist. For this reason, Lacan famously declared that given her masquerade as the Phallus, woman does not exist.

Butler criticizes this account for the foundational, 'quasi-transcendental' status it gives to the primordial trauma of castration. She questions how this primordial trauma can be separated from the terms of sociality in which it is framed: an idealized kinship that presumes the heterosexual family. For Butler (2000, p. 147), the primordial myth is clearly discursively constructed, yet for Lacanians such as Zizek it is 'radically uncontestable', 'immune from critical examination, yet necessary and essential: a truly felicitous instrument of power', despite that fact that the historical incidence of such a nuclear family is a relatively recent phenomenon. Thus, she claims, 'This most unverifiable of concepts' (p. 145) acquires a sort of theological status that effectively proscribes anything outside of the heterosexual family such as 'intersexuality, transsexuality, lesbian and gay partnership' (p. 148). She goes on to use this argument as the basis for her categorical rejection of the notion of sexual difference.

Jungians similarly reject the primacy of the Phallic signifier. In a critique of Freud with many parallels to Butler's assessment of Lacan, Neumann argues that the reduction of the castration threat to anything that bears parallels to the 'patriarchal bourgeois family of the nineteenth century, is scientifically impossible' (Neumann 1969, p. xxii). Young-Eisendrath further argues that this description of sexual difference, like the Freudian notion of penis envy, is a distortion of women's psyche into a narrow, bio-political envy of masculine power and desire. As a developmental psychologist, she argues that a young girl at the age of four or five does not yet understand the exclusivity of gender, hence her questions regarding why she does not have a penis do not represent a sense of lack, but a positive sense of desire to discover her masculine other and an incomprehension that she has already been assigned a 'gender club' (Young-Eisendrath 1992, p. 170). It is also at this age, Young-Eisendrath points out, that children are initiated not just into gender groups, but the three great classes of being: persons, animals, and inanimate objects (p. 171). These divisions characterize a process of othering that individuals must negotiate for the rest of their lives.

There is a central irony involved in the use of the Oedipal story as a foundational myth for psychoanalysis. The entire story revolves around the trauma of separating from the mother, yet an understanding of 'mother' is basically irrelevant to any subsequent theorization. Somehow, the importance of the symbolic feminine morphs into the centrality of the undefinable Phallus. This sleight of hand, in turn, results in the denial and mystification of the integral role of psychological forces associated with the mother, such as containment and its relationship to becoming or the process of individuation. I want to focus on reinforcing the importance of the relationship between the energies of becoming and containing as illustrated in the myth of Demeter/Kore/Persephone.

The Demeter/Kore/Persephone myth is a story of the separation from mother that actually provides a conception of the power of at least two forces of sexual difference. It also describes the process of negotiation involved in the development of self in a far more complex way than the Oedipal castration story. Jung believed this myth had such importance for women that it applied to them exclusively. It is easy to see why he would argue this – the *Homeric Hymn to Demeter* is one of the few myths that places female experience and power at the centre of the narrative. I believe, however, that it is a myth that applies universally, regardless of gender identification, because it effectively describes the process of containment, individuation/transformation, and identity formation itself, as well as the negotiation of relationships between individuals and collectivities of people.

This said, the myth also explores the trauma of separating from the mother and negotiating an individual identity in a way that highlights the difficulty of this process for women in the context of patriarchy. The male figures in the myth use their power in an arbitrary way that is analogous to Lacan's Law of the Father. In the end, however, there is compromise: a negotiated settlement that has important repercussions for any individual, regardless of gender or sexual identity. Demeter and Persephone resist and transform patriarchal power in a way that leaves what might be regarded as a 'void' from a Lacanian perspective, but which I will refer to more positively as an interval. This interval is not an empty space or lack, but the positive space of love or *Eros*. Explaining this involves examining the myth in greater detail.

To briefly summarize,[1] Zeus decides without consulting Demeter, goddess of grain, to give their daughter Kore (which means 'girl-child') in marriage to the god of the underworld, Hades. One day Kore is in a field with other girls (including Elektra and Artemis), engaging in the blissful, untroubled pleasure of childhood play. She finds a particularly large and beautiful narcissus (a phallic symbol) and picks it, which causes Hades to spring up from the earth in a chariot and carry her back with him to the underworld, where she is raped and becomes his wife. Unaware of how her daughter has disappeared, Demeter frantically looks for her until Helios the sun god tells her what has happened. Helios tells Demeter that this is an appropriate marriage for Kore and she must accept it.

Devastated with grief, Demeter disguises herself as a human and wanders the countryside. Hekate, who heard Kore's cries but does not know who took her, tries unsuccessfully to comfort Demeter. While wandering, Demeter meets three mortal daughters who treat her kindly and convince their mother (Metaneira) to take her in as a nursemaid. Eventually, Demeter reveals her true identity to Metaneira and orders the mortals to build her a temple at Eleusis, where she goes into a deep mourning that leaves the earth without grain and in stark famine. Alarmed, Zeus realizes that unless he compromises, all mortals will perish, and he tells Hades he must return Kore to her mother. Before Kore leaves the underworld, however, Hades tricks her into eating a pomegranate seed (another phallic symbol), which means she must return to the underworld for one third of each year. Mother and daughter are blissfully reunited and the crops once again begin to grow, but Kore, now known as Persephone, must return each winter to play her role as Queen of the underworld.

It is easy to see why Jung identified this as an important myth for women, focusing as it does on the mother/daughter relationship, the ordeals faced by women under patriarchy, and ultimately the depth of women's power and patriarchal jealousy and fear of it. It also highlights the transformative role of the feminine. On the one hand, as Irigaray (1994, p. 110) notes, the myth illustrates how patriarchy is founded upon the theft and violation of the girl's virginity and the use of her virginity as commerce among men. Little girls, Irigaray remarks, are often 'caught up in the dealings, contractual or otherwise, between men, between men and male gods' and it is important that they are kept away from such dealings until their virginity can be assured (quoted in Gray 2008, p. 126). On the other hand, it also underlines Demeter's power. By going on strike and demanding that Zeus return her kidnapped daughter from Hades, Demeter effectively 'stops the traffic in women' among the gods. In addition, during her time of mourning she forms a unique alliance between a female god and mortal women (Foley 1994, p. 112). She also brazenly defies Zeus, coming very close to total victory in thwarting his patriarchal authority.

Persephone, initially a victim of rape and an unwilling bride, ultimately is transformed into the Queen of the underworld (p. 126). In Kerényi's (1970, p. 172) view, she comes to symbolize the 'eternally unique', or the *uniqueness* of the individual and its *enthrallment to not-being* (his emphasis). Persephone's not-being is connected to her relation to the underworld – paralleling

Deleuze and Guattari's emphasis on the molecular nature of the girl and her importance to becoming. Her power, not-being, and eternal uniqueness also make her sublime. As Kerenyi points out, whenever Persephone is mentioned in the Iliad she is referred to as 'awful', which implies both praise and fear in equal measure (p. 173). In this respect, Kore/Persephone is the mythological equivalent of Deleuze and Guattari's girl/becoming-woman – two sides of the same coin of transformative becoming.

This transformation is also evident in the symbol of the pomegranate seed from Hades, consumed underground and watered by her mother's tears. Persephone protests that she was forced or tricked into eating the seed, but whether the seed is perceived literally as the masculine seed or more broadly as sexuality (Neumann 1974, p. 308) there is the sense that she may be hiding her willingness to eat the pomegranate seed in order to save her mother's feelings (Foley 1994). Her eating of the pomegranate seed can be interpreted as 1. entering the sexual world; 2. entering the Law of the Father inherent to the Symbolic realm of representation as understood in Lacan's or Kristeva's terms; or 3. in Jungian terms, the development of her own masculine aspects within her psyche. The masculine seed gives her power and Persephone bursts forth from the underworld transformed into a powerful goddess. Every year she goes back to the underground world of the masculine Hades, away from her mother, to begin the transformation anew.

Her new status leaves her with a position both in the non-being of the Underworld and the grounded being of the earth. Persephone must leave her mother to be in the masculine/sexual realm of signification, but she does not reside there always. In contrast to the Oedipal triangle, we have a symbolic image of a cosmos that is stratified (earth/underworld) but fluid. Underworld and earth are separate, but merged through Persephone. Hades is kind to Persephone when she leaves, offering her inducements to return. Masculine and feminine are differentiated, but coexist in a peace negotiated by Zeus and Demeter.

Effectively, aided by her mother's actions, Persephone has regained her 'virginity'. As Warner points out, in pre-Christian mythology the concept of a virgin rarely had anything to do with the ascetic abstention from sex portrayed in Christianity. Venus, Ishtar, Astarte, and Anat were all considered virgins despite the fact that they had numerous lovers. Instead, Warner argues, the term usually referred to a person who was 'autonomous', who had the freedom to reject lovers or accept them (Warner 1976, pp. 47–48). As Harding puts it, a goddess who is virgin 'is essentially one-in-herself. She is not merely the counterpart of a male god with similar characteristics and functions, modified to suit her female form. On the contrary, she has a role to play that is her own' (Harding 1975, p. 125). For Woodman, the transformative virgin archetype is 'that aspect of the feminine, in man or in woman, that has the courage to Be and the flexibility to be always Becoming' (Woodman 1985, p. 78). Irigaray (2004, p. 152) also notes that the concepts of Virgin and mother could correspond to a female becoming, if understood in a spiritual as opposed to a literal sense. Note that for both Warner and Woodman, the term virgin is also relevant for men.

Persephone regains her virginity in three ways: the negotiation of an interval between herself and her mother, herself and her husband, and herself and her father. This ties her to Hades and the underworld, but only for a third of the year. For the rest of the time, she is free to do as she pleases in Demeter's realm of the feminine. Yet as goddess of the underworld, she is no longer under the control of her mother. There are other intervals negotiated in this story as well. Demeter, allied with Hekate (and in some versions Baubo), as well as the mortal women Metaneira and her daughters, creates a space of power between the women in the story and the male gods (Zeus, Helios, and Hades), symbolized by her success in making Zeus change his mind.

In sum, in spite of the traumatic sacrificial kidnapping of the Kore into the masculine realm of Hades, a negotiated peace emerges that can be described as a 'plateauing' in Bateson's (1972, p. 113) use of the word (later adopted by Deleuze and Guattari) – a sort of levelling of energies in a relationship that is not allowed to come to a climax. In Deleuze and Guattari's (1987, p. 21) terms, a plateau is always 'in the middle, not at the beginning or end'. In Bateson's original application of the plateau in the context of Balinese culture, one gets a sense of tantra-like, pre-orgasmic harmony, a capturing of energies that prevents a climactic event. At this point, there is an eddying of energies and forces, a gentle whirlpool that combines them in a circle, in contrast to Jung's notion of the violent swinging back and forth of the *enantiodromia* described in Chapter 3. This plateauing might also be applied to what Jung calls 'assimilation', or a mutual penetration of the conscious and unconscious.

This plateauing or assimilation does not involve a one-sided evaluation of the unconscious by the conscious mind (Jung 1954, p. 152) but is more a negotiation or coming to terms with the unconscious in which its fragmented aspects (the gods) begin to 'forfeit their autonomy' (Jung 1967, p. 35). The analysand views them in a more detached way, rather than being immersed in them in the form of a *participation mystique*. Adopting this term from Lévy-Bruhl, Jung defined it as a non-differentiation between subject and object, where the unconscious is projected onto a particular object (it could be another person) and the object then becomes part of the subject's psychology. If the unconscious can be assimilated in the sense of the plateau described above, the centre of gravity of the personality shifts from the ego, which becomes decentred to a new point between the unconscious and conscious that, according to Jung 'might be described as the self' (p. 45). The delineation between subject and object reappears – as if an interval is created between them.

Thinking of the self being developed in this way, one might characterize the whirling space in the middle of this plateau as an interval. This interval can be seen as integral to psychic development in various ways: it can be viewed as the space that must be maintained between the conscious and unconscious aspects of the psyche, or it can be understood as the differentiated space between subject and object necessary to avoid *participation mystique*. It can also be seen as the exploration between self and other within the psyche. And, as mentioned above, it also constitutes the negotiated peace between mother/child, partners in a relationship, or men and women as collectivities.

More fundamentally, however, it can be considered as the space of love or *Eros* – the interval necessary to both join and separate self and other, whether it be mother and child, or between adult lovers, or even within aspects of the individual psyche. Even more relevant for my purposes, it also has a collective aspect – creating an interval of love between the archetypal energies of the masculine and feminine that can be conceived as a metaphor for the *amor* that Hardt and Negri (2009) argue is integral to the negotiation of the Common – an *amor* that Negri (2013) describes as the intersection of the rationalities and desires of singularities. Offering a conception of love based on Levinas and Derrida, Caputo describes love not as possession, but affirmation, 'letting the other be precisely in his or her alterity, tout autre', coming toward the other without 'crossing the threshold' (Caputo 2004, p. 41).

The image here is of a space or interval, a 'third thing' as Schwartz-Salant calls it, noting that in alchemy the creation of such a space is referred to as 'slaying the dragon' (Schwartz-Salant 1995, p. 31). In the alchemical *coniunctio*, the destruction of this space is a constant danger known as 'negative fusion'. The hermaphrodite represents a *coniunctio* where negative fusion has been overcome, and the male and female polarities have been preserved (p. 33). It may also be considered the space or interval of desire. As Woodman notes, the trick in understanding the hermaphrodite is not to neuter it. 'The true androgyne embodies the conscious union of the differentiated masculine and the differentiated feminine, something quite different from the neutered hermaphrodite, in which the opposites are symbiotically joined.' (Woodman 1982, p. 122)

For Irigaray, the negotiation of relationships to others (mothers, husbands, children) is one of the central questions of a woman's life. In mythical terms, she must learn how to retain her 'virginity'. In her words:

> The problem for feminine subjectivity is how to escape from what is only a natural state, at the level of birth but also at the level of relations

with the other(s) – be they the mother, the lover, or the child, for example. What a woman has to do is to maintain an irreducible difference between the other and herself, while preserving her natural origins or roots. This can happen by arranging and keeping a transcendental dimension between the other and herself, particularly the other who belongs to a different origin – the masculine other. The matter, for a woman, is one of interposing between the other and herself a negative that cannot be overcome.

(Irigaray 2008, p. 228)

The challenge here is to retain the symbolic feminine as a marker of irreducible difference that affects women, while at the same time acknowledging its importance for those who are not women. The Demeter/Kore/Persephone myth reveals the great travail necessary to find this interval, symbolized on many levels as between mother and daughter/child, earth (life/being) and underworld (death/not-being), partners in a relationship, between masculine and feminine, or between individuals and collectivities in a political commons. These relationships, some of which are not dyads but multiples, must further find intervals as multiples relative to each other, a practice that finds meaning not only in relation to these particular dyads, but other considerations such as race, class, ethnicity, or sexuality.

Butler has criticized Irigaray for her emphasis on relations between men and women, considering this an overt heterosexualism that is 'all about mom and motherhood and not at all about post-family arrangements or alternative family arrangements' (Cheah et al 1998, p. 28). The Demeter and Persephone myth, with its metaphorical reliance on heterosexual relationships, might also be interpreted in this way. This would be a very narrow reading of this story, however. To begin, Zeus, Demeter, and Persephone can hardly be considered a traditional nuclear family, nor can Persephone's subsequent coupling with Hades be described this way. Demeter is not Zeus's wife (they are siblings and apparently mated in the form of intertwining serpents) – she is the mother of his child. It is not really a story about sexuality, but rather focuses on the negotiation of both desire and power. Second, whether or not one accepts the Jungian understanding of the sexually differentiated psyche, there is no question that everyone, regardless of sexual identification, has to negotiate the challenges of separating from the mother, entering the sexual realm, separating themselves from partners and children, as well as the political divide in the realm of signification between women and men.

Both Demeter's and Persephone's power and perseverance reveal the autonomous influence of feminine energies. Consider Neumann's description of 'mom' as the transformative feminine. Persephone's transformation is symbolic of the feminine as an active, creative force. Neumann poetically describes this sublime world of the transformative feminine, describing it as growth.

> In perpetual transformation, the humble 'rotting' seed lengthens into stalk and sprouting leaves, long stem grows into dense bud, whence the blossom burst forth in all its diversity and colour . . . Everywhere [this vegetation] grows: roots and tubers under the earth, a sea of fruit on trees attainable and unattainable.
>
> (Neumann 1974, p. 51)

In an apt reference to Demeter, he describes the Great Mother as 'the protectress, the good mother, who feeds man with fruits and tubers and grains, but also poisons him and lets him hunger and thirst in times of drought, when she withdraws from living things' (p. 52).

Animals live in and are dependent on this feminine world of vegetation,

> bringing danger and salvation; under the ground the snakes and worms, uncanny and dangerous; in the water fishes, reptiles, and aquatic monsters; birds flying through the air and beasts scurrying over the earth. Roaring and hissing, milk-giving and voracious, the animals fill the vegetative world, nestling in it like birds in a tree.
>
> (p. 52)

This animal world is also in perpetual transformation,

> bursting eggs and crawling young, corpses decomposing into earth, and life arising from swamp and muck. Everywhere mothers and suckling cubs, being born, growing, changing, devouring and devoured, killing and dying' all overshadowed by the Great Mother as World Tree 'which shelters, protects, nourishes this animal world to which man [sic] feels he belong(s). Mysterious in its truthfulness, the myth makes the vegetative world engender the animal world and also the world of men,' decentering humans and portraying them as mere leaves on the tree.
>
> (p. 52)

Neumann further points out that this process of feminine transformation pertains not just to the natural, but to cultural development as well. The transformative life principal is 'creative nature and a culture-creating principal in one' (p. 305). In contrast to the typical nature/culture divide, he argues that many forms of cultural transformation that are considered 'technical' processes are actually aspects of the transformative feminine (pp. 59–60).

In Neumann's poetic description of the transformative nature of feminine energy, we see not only the decentring of the human in the *anima mundi*, but a reversal, with reference to Bachofen, of the Judeo/Christian/Islamic tradition. Man as spirit does not come first, but last. In the rites of the Eleusinian Mysteries, a divine son is born of Demeter/Persephone – either Dionysus or Iacchus. 'In other words', he claims, 'masculine *spirit* is born of the feminine and would not exist without it' (pp. 305–311). In contrast, Neumann notes, 'patriarchal consciousness starts from the standpoint that the eternal spirit is *a priori*; that the spirit was in the beginning', and what was mythically the final stage, somehow becomes the first one. 'This modern consciousness', he maintains, 'is threatening the existence of Western mankind, for the one-sidedness of masculine development has led to a hypertrophy of consciousness at the expense of the whole man' (p. 57).

Whether the feminine comes first or last is not particularly relevant to my argument, but Neumann's insistence on the relevance of this myth to those who do not identify as women is. Jung argued that 'Demeter-Kore exists on the plane of mother – daughter experience, which is alien to man and shuts him out' (Jung cited in Gray 2008, p. 122). Although the cult of the Eleusinian Mysteries based on the Demeter/Persephone ordeal was important to some rituals that were exclusive to women, however, it attracted initiates of both sexes from around the ancient world. Jung's friend and collaborator Karl Kerényi disagreed that this myth only held importance for women. For Kerényi (1967, p. 12) the Eleusinian rituals were fundamental to Greek society as a whole and were considered so important that they were thought 'to hold the entire human race together'. Although he acknowledged their importance for women, he argued that associating them solely with women's 'self-understanding' was too narrow. Instead, the Mysteries should be envisaged as the '*feminine source of life*, but not in an intellectual way' (p. xxviii). Similarly, Neumann argued that the attraction of this female-centred myth for male initiates was the possibility for them to relate to their pre-patriarchal and feminine sides (Foley 1994, p. 121).

Comparing Deleuze and Guattari's description of the girl as transformative feminine to the Demeter/Kore/Persephone myth reveals the depth and political relevance their 'fragment of a tale' loses by insisting on her anonymous, molecular status. Given their antipathy to the stratifying power of myth, Deleuze and Guattari explode Demeter and Kore into a molecular flow. The results may be fascinatingly destratifying, but in doing so they disregard the important symbolic importance of this story for both men and women. As Irigaray notes, obscuring the stories of the divine feminine effectively erases traditions of feminine spirituality (Irigaray 1994).

More importantly, however, Deleuze and Guattari's molecular becoming-woman fixates on the transformative aspects of the feminine without

120 Theory

recognizing its elemental or containing roots. Neumann divides the symbols of the Great Mother broadly between those that are elemental or 'containing', and those that are transformative. These, in turn, are divided into positive and negative manifestations and arranged into a set of concentric circles that reveal a vast differentiation in the understanding of the feminine (Neumann 1974, p. 82a). Neumann argues that transformative and elemental/containing energies cannot be understood in isolation from one another, 'the symbols of the transformative character almost always retain a connection with the elementary character of the Feminine' (p. 47). Transformation begins in the 'lower' level of the containing elemental and encompasses it. 'In the matriarchal world, it is never a free-floating, rootless, "upper" process, as the abstract male intellect typically imagines.' (p. 47) Deleuze and Guattari's girl/becoming-woman resides solely in this 'upper' register.

Demeter's power brings symbolic meaning to the process of containment in Sacher-Masoch's *Venus in Furs*, showing why Severin's contractual relationship with Wanda pales as a containing experience. Demeter's containing energy and power is the source of Kore's transformation into the 'awful' Persephone. Her 'passive' resistance as she sat contained in her temple at Eleusis was effectively the bargaining chip that turned the tides of Kore's sacrifice. As Kerényi notes, Demeter's containment and Persephone's transformation are two sides of the same coin. Yet Deleuze and Guattari's molecular focus on the transformative properties of the Kore/girl set her adrift from this containing rootedness. The importance of elemental, containing energies in the development of the individual and collective psyche will be apparent throughout this book. As I will show, the importance of containment is also relevant to an understanding of the relationship between the individual and capitalist markets, a point that will be further developed in Chapter 6.

When I speak of containing energies, I will use them in a much more abstract sense than the parenting relationship. Containment can be described more generally by what Jung called a *temenos*. On the verge of his own breakdown after his break with Freud and on the eve of World War I, he realized the 'talking cure' would not be sufficient to draw himself out of his looming potential psychosis. Instead, he tried to ground himself spatially, collecting stones and building a miniature village with them. This space became what he called his '*temenos*' a 'demarcated, sacred place where the powerful forces of the unconscious could be experienced' (Pint 2011, p. 51). This *temenos* was both creative and protective – it allowed images to appear that would not have emerged outside of this sacred place, but it also gave him, in Deleuze and Guattari's (1987, p. 161) words, 'a small plot of new land' at all times to avoid the dangers of explosive destratification. In Jung's words, it draws a boundary in order to prevent 'an "outflowing" or to guard by apotropaic means against distracting influences from outside' (Jung 1967, p. 24). Throughout his life, Jung was gravely aware of this issue, taking great care to ground himself in his profession and family in order to avoid the psychological fate he believed had befallen Nietzsche. In this respect, containing energies should be seen as integral to the stability of the lines of flight necessary for transformation.

The notion of the *temenos* is replicated in Deleuze and Guattari's (1987, p. 311) notion of 'the refrain' – the organization of a limited space where the forces of chaos can be kept out as much as possible. Indeed, the uncontained, molecular status of their girl is at odds with their insistence that transformation should be undertaken only in the context of a delicate balance with the forces of stratification. Instead, they suggest a delicate experimentation with forces of stratification and the molecular forces of transformation that bears many similarities to Knox's ideas concerning containment and Jung's concept of the *enantiodromia*:

> The BwO is always swinging between the surfaces that stratify it and the plane that sets it free. If you free it with too violent an action, if you blow apart the strata without taking precautions, then instead of drawing the plane you will be killed, plunged into a black hole, or even dragged toward catastrophe. Staying stratified – organized, signified, subjected – is not the worst that can happen; the worst that can happen is if you throw the strata into demented or suicidal collapse . . .
>
> (p. 161)

Rather than exploding the strata, they give the following instructions:

> This is how it should be done: Lodge yourself on a stratum, experiment with the opportunities it offers, find an advantageous place on it, find potential movements of deterritorialization, possible lines of flight, experience them . . . have a small plot of new land at all times. It is through a meticulous relation with the strata that one succeeds in freeing the lines of flight.
>
> (p. 161)

This relationship between the feminine as gently containing and the feminine as transformative is implicit in Leonardo's painting *St. Anne and the Virgin* (Figure 4.1), a work that was also the subject of Freud's famous 'vulture' reading of Leonardo's psyche. In this painting, which in many respects can be viewed as the Christian version of the Demeter/Persephone relation, St Anne is the elemental, containing feminine. Her daughter, Mary, who sits gently contained on her lap, is the transformative virginal *anima*

122 Theory

Figure 4.1 Leonardo da Vinci, *St. Anne, the Virgin Mary, and the Christ Child*, 1452–1519, Musée de Louvre, Paris

Photo Credit: Alfredo Dagli Orti/The Art Archive at Art Resource, NY

of becoming who gives birth to Jesus, the word, *Logos*, here portrayed as a child.

Expanding upon this understanding of the 'feminine' energies of containment and transformation, we can reframe Jung's understanding of the feminine as *Eros*. The energies of containment and transformation, configured as feminine in the representative realm of myth or art, are integral to the *creation* of *Eros*; they are not co-terminous with it. This distinction may seem purely semantic, but it is not. It means that *a priori* energies, connected to women in the realm of representation primarily because they are enacted in the mother/child relationship, are integral to the plateauing of energies I have characterized here as the interval of love. 'Woman' is not *Eros*, the energies involved in the negotiation of this relationship are. Additionally, the women do not create this interval themselves, but set off a process of negotiation with the masculine figures in the myth, indicating that the archetypal masculine is also integral to the creation of the interval. Finally, although the original erotic relationship was configured as that between mother and child, Kore/Persephone's transformation becomes much more than this. Politically, it enacts the interval or space of love necessary for peaceful cohabitation, illustrating Negri's (2013) claim that 'democracy is an act of love'. As a form of agonizing and contingent negotiation, it also sets an alternative model of the social contract.

This conception of the feminine as an energy also throws light on Hillman's (1985) emphasis on Jung's conception of *anima* as butterfly that will become important to my analysis of the Rococo and Postmodern aesthetics. This reference resonates with Deleuze's emphasis on the simultaneity of becoming, and the paradoxes inherent to staying on the surface and rejecting false depth, a point that will be explored in greater detail in Chapter 7. Imagine the interval created in the negotiation of sexual difference enacted by Demeter/Persephone as a sort of circular, concave cloth that is held loosely at the edges by the characters in the myth, dropping to a curve in the centre. This circular cloth is pulled taut and flat by the plateauing of energies, so that what was previously held in the depth of that concave curve is still there, but spread out. As Deleuze (1990) argues, these contents do not disappear but rise to the surface. What was previously a 'false depth' brings meaning to the surface. The same sense of a meaningful surface is implicit in the Hillman/Jung understanding of *anima* as butterfly, although here it is not clear whether it is *anima* alone that creates this phenomenon, or if it is an effect of the plateauing of the energies of sexual difference that follows from a conscious acceptance and recognition of *anima*.

These *a priori* feminine forces or energies can flow across any body. Anyone can 'channel' them, so to speak. They may have special meaning for those who identify as women, however, because they are metaphorically associated with the containing, transformative energy that is felt in the mother/child relationship. A valuation of these energies, I believe, will also result in a re-valuation of this affective labour. And as this affective energy is increasingly valued and social relationships between mothers, fathers, and children continue to evolve, the imagery related to this symbolic energy may

124 Theory

change. It is entirely possible that as men become more involved in this primal relationship, the imagery through which this symbolic knowledge is projected might evolve as well. Such is the nature of the intra-active concept Jung and Deleuze called the symbol.

When one considers the implications of the Demeter/Kore/Persephone myth for all people, it seems incomprehensible (at least, outside of the male-biased projections of psychoanalysis) that it has not played a more fundamental role in an understanding of the human psyche. From a broader political/philosophical perspective, however, it can be regarded not as a story that was once told, but a story that is still in the telling. If Lacan's castration complex figures the status quo – women as void, or 'not One', in Irigaray's terms – Demeter/Kore/Persephone heralds a future where the forces of sexual difference achieve a plateau or interval co-terminous with love or *Eros*. This interval has little to do with contracts – social or otherwise. This negotiation of power between the symbolic energies of the masculine and feminine, and the formation of an interval that both separates and joins, is nothing less than the story of a new political economy, a new philosophy, in Olkowski's (2010, p. 46) words, based on a respect for the energies of sexual difference.

A conscious appreciation of the symbolic energies of the these two 'ways of being' that Jung designated the archetypal feminine and masculine, *Eros* and *Logos,* or *Luna* and *Sol,* can be the basis for what Hardt and Negri (2009) would call biopolitics – the development of alternative subjectivities necessary to engage in new kinds of social experience. The kind of subjective exploration I am describing here corresponds to a renegotiation of collective discourses of sexual and gender identity with highly political effects. In the chapters that follow, I will explore situations that confirm my argument that such intra-actions actually occur. The material manifestations of these intra-actions can only be played out in the actual entangled practices of biopolitics working themselves out in the cosmos as we speak.

Note

1 My account is based on the translation of Foley (1994).

Bibliography

Bateson, G. (1972) *Steps to an Ecology of Mind,* Chandler Publishing Co., San Francisco, Scranton, London and Toronto.

Butler, J. (2000) 'Competing Universalities', in *Contingency, Hegemony, Universality,* eds. J. Butler, E. Laclau, and S. Zizek, Verso, London and New York, pp. 136–181.

Caputo, J. (2004) 'Love among the Deconstructibles: A Response to Gregg Lambert', *Journal for Cultural and Religious Theory,* vol. 5, no. 2, pp. 37–57.

Cheah, P., Grosz, E., Butler, J. and Cornell, D. (1998) 'The Future of Sexual Difference: An Interview with Judith Butler and Drucilla Cornell', *Diacritics,* vol. 28, no. 1, pp. 19–42.

Chodorow, N. (1978) *The Reproduction of Mothering,* University of California Press, Berkeley.

Connolly, A. (2013) 'Out of the Body: Embodiment and Its Vicissitudes', *The Journal of Analytical Psychology,* vol. 58, pp. 636–656.

Damasio, A. (1999) *The Feeling of What Happens: Body, Emotion and the Making of Consciousness,* Heinemann, London.

Deleuze, G. (1990) *The Logic of Sense,* trans. Mark Lester, Columbia University Press, New York.

Deleuze, G. (1991) 'Coldness and Cruelty', in *Masochism,* ed. Gilles Deleuze, Zone Books, New York, pp. 9–142.

Deleuze, G. (2004) 'From Sacher-Masoch to Masochism', trans. Christian Kerslake, *Angelaki,* vol. 9, no. 1, pp. 125–133.

Deleuze, G. and Guattari, F. (1987) *A Thousand Plateaus: Capitalism and Schizophrenia,* University of Minnesota Press, Minneapolis and London.

Derrida, J. (1976) *Of Grammatology,* trans. Gayatri Chakravorty Spivak, Johns Hopkins Press, Baltimore and London.

Foley, H. (1994) *The Homeric Hymn to Demeter,* Princeton University Press, Princeton, NJ.

Gallagher, S. (2005) *How the Mind Shapes the Body,* Oxford University Press, Oxford and New York.

Gilligan, C. (1982) *In a Different Voice,* Harvard University Press, Cambridge, MA.

Gray, F. (2008) *Jung, Irigaray, Individuation: Philosophy, Analytical Psychology, and the Question of the Feminine,* Routledge, London and New York.

Haraway, D. (2008) *When Species Meet,* University of Minnesota Press, Minneapolis and London.

Harding, E. (1975) *Women's Mysteries: Ancient and Modern,* Harper Colophon Books, New York, Hagerstown, San Francisco and London.

Hardt, M. and Negri, A. (2000) *Empire,* Harvard University Press, Cambridge, MA.

Hardt, M. and Negri, A. (2009) *Commonwealth,* The Belknap Press of Harvard University Press, Cambridge, MA.

Held, V. (1993) *Feminist Morality: Transforming Culture, Society and Politics,* University of Chicago Press, Chicago.

Heymans, P. (2011) 'Eating Girls: Deleuze and Guattari's Becoming-Animal and the Romantic Sublime in William Blake's Lyca Poems', *Humanimalia,* vol. 3, no. 1, pp. 1–30.

Hillman, J. (1985) *Anima,* Spring Publications, Dallas, TX.

Irigaray, L. (1994) *Thinking the Difference: For a Peaceful Revolution,* trans. Karen Montin, Routledge, New York.

Irigaray, L. (2004) 'The Redemption of Women', in *Key Writings,* ed. L. Irigaray, Continuum, London and New York, pp. 150–164.

Irigaray, L. (2008) 'The Return (May 2005)', in *Luce Irigaray: Teaching*, eds. Luce Irigaray with Mary Green, Continuum, London and New York, pp. 219–220.

Jacob, B. (2007) 'The "Uncanny Aura" of *Venus im Pelz*: Masochism and Freud's Uncanny', *The Germanic Review*, vol. 82, no. 3, pp. 269–285.

Johnson, M. (1987) *The Body in the Mind: The Bodily Basis of Meaning, Imagination and Reason*, University of Chicago Press, Chicago.

Jung, C. G. (1954) *Collected Works*, vol. 16, trans. R. F. C. Hull, Bollingen Series, Princeton University Press, Princeton, NJ.

Jung, C.G. (1960) *Collected Works*, vol. 8, trans. R. F. C. Hull, Bollingen Series, Princeton University Press, Princeton, NJ.

Jung, C. G. (1967) *Collected Works*, vol. 13, trans. R. F. C. Hull, Bollingen Series, Princeton University Press, Princeton, NJ.

Kazarian, E. (2010) 'The Revolutionary Unconscious: Deleuze and Masoch', *SubStance*, vol. 39, no. 2, pp. 91–106.

Kerényi, C. (1967) *Eleusis: Archetypal Image of Mother and Daughter*, Bollingen Series, Pantheon Books, New York.

Kerényi, C. (1970) 'Kore', in *Introduction to a Science of Mythology: The Myth of the Divine Child and the Mysteries of Eleusis*, eds. C. G. Jung and C. Kerényi, Routledge and Kegan Paul, London, pp. 119–183.

Kerslake, C. (2007) *Deleuze and the Unconscious*, Continuum, London and New York.

Knox, J. (2003) *Archetype, Attachment, Analysis: Jungian Psychology and the Emergent Mind*, Brunner-Routledge, Hove and New York.

Knox, J. (2011) *Self-Agency in Psychotherapy: Attachment, Autonomy, and Intimacy*, W.W. Norton and Company, New York and London.

Meltzoff, A. (2005) 'Imitation and Other Minds: The "Like Me" Hypothesis', in *Perspectives on Imitation: From Neuroscience to Social Science*, eds. S. Hurley and N. Chater, vol. 2, MIT Press, Cambridge, MA, pp. 55–77.

Negri, A. (2013) *Spinoza for Our Time: Politics and Postmodernity*, Columbia University Press, New York.

Neumann, E. (1969) *The Origins and History of Consciousness*, trans. R. F. C. Hull, Bollingen Series, Princeton University Press, Princeton, NJ.

Neumann, E. (1974) *The Great Mother: An Analysis of the Archetype*, trans. Ralph Manheim, Bollingen Series, Princeton University Press, Princeton, NJ.

Olkowski, D. (2010) 'Kore, Philosophy, Sensibility, and the Difference of Light', in *Rewriting Difference: Luce Irigaray and 'the Greeks'*, eds. Elena Tzelepis and Athena Athanasiou, SUNY Press, Albany, NY, pp. 33–50.

Pint, K. (2011) 'Doubling Back: Psychoanalytical Literary Theory and the Perverse Return to Jungian Space', *S: Journal of the Jan van Eyck Circle for Lancanian Ideology Critique*, vol. 4, pp. 47–55.

Polanyi, K. (1944) *The Great Transformation*, Beacon Press, Boston.

Protevi, J. (2010) 'Adding Deleuze to the Mix', *Phenomenology and the Cognitive Sciences*, vol. 9, pp. 417–436.

Ruddick, S. (1980) *Maternal Thinking: Toward a Politics of Peace*, Beacon Press, Boston.

Sacher-Masoch, L. (1991) 'Venus in Furs', in *Masochism*, ed. Gilles Deleuze, Zone Books, New York, pp. 9–142.

Schore, A. (2003) *Affect Regulation and Disorders of the Self*, W.W. Norton and Company, New York.

Schwartz-Salant, N. (1995) *Jung on Alchemy*, Princeton University Press, Princeton, NJ.

Sigler, D. (2011) ' "Read Mr. Sacher-Masoch": The Literariness of Masochism in the Philosophy of Jacques Lacan and Gilles Deleuze', *Criticism*, vol. 53, no. 2, pp. 189–212.

Silverman, K. (1988) 'Masochism and Male Subjectivity', *Camera Obscura*, vol. 6.2, no. 17, pp. 30–67.

Sinigaglia, C. (2008) 'Mirror Neurons: This Is the Question', *Journal of Consciousness Studies*, vol. 15, nos. 10–11, pp. 70–92.

Warner, M. (1976) *Alone of All Her Sex: The Myth and the Cult of the Virgin Mary*, Alfred A. Knopf, New York.

Wilkinson, M. (2006) *Coming into Mind: The Mind-Brain Relationship: A Jungian Clinical Perspective*, Routledge, London and New York.

Woodman, M. (1982) *Addiction to Perfection: The Still Unravished Bride*, Inner City Books, Toronto.

Woodman, M. (1985) *The Pregnant Virgin*, Inner City Books, Toronto.

Young-Eisendrath, P. (1992) 'Gender, Animus and Related Topics', in *Gender and Soul in Psychotherapy*, eds. N. Schwartz-Salant and M. Stein, Chiron, Wilmette, IL, pp. 151–177.

Zizek, S. (2004) 'Notes on a Debate "From Within the People" ', *Criticism*, vol. 26, no. 4, pp. 661–666.

Part II

Genealogies

Chapter 5

Channelling the feminine
Rococo

Edmond de Goncourt and his brother Jules believed in the compensatory healing properties of visual experience. Astute 19th century commentators and art collectors, the *frères* de Goncourt filled their mansion in the Parisian suburb of Auteuil with a collection of furniture and artefacts explicitly designed to elicit stimulating psychological 'vibrations'. According to Silverman (1992), they would stand in their *salon* and revel in the currents of vibrating energy coursing just beneath the surface of their skin. The wall colours and the carefully positioned objects within the room were assembled into a unity of 'artistic harmony' which sent their inhabitants into what Edmond described as a 'feverish' and heightened state that was a precondition for his writing. It is as if each brother was merely a medium, channelling the vibrations emitted from their preferred Rococo aesthetic onto the page.

The collection that emanated this healing energy consisted primarily of the sensuous, feminine curves of 18th century Rococo, a time period when 'women reigned', according to the Goncourts. These Rococo objects were complemented by a broad collection of Japanese and contemporary *Art Nouveau* objects with a similar sinewy aesthetic. The brothers saw the soft curves inherent to these objects as an antidote to the cold brutality of modern life. Edmond wrote, 'My Paris, the Paris where I grew up is disappearing . . . I am a stranger to what is coming, to what is there, like these new boulevards, lacking in all curves, implacable axes of the straight line. It makes me think of some American Babylon of the future' (quoted in Silverman, p. 20).

Precisely what was it that the *frères de Goncourt* were channelling? An energy force, a feeling, or as they might have called it at the time, a 'sensibility'? Mary Wollstonecraft defined the concept of sensibility in a manner that aligns both with Edmond's description of his experience and Jung's and Deleuze's understandings of the nature of art: 'I should say that it is the result of acute senses, finely fashioned nerves, which vibrate at the slightest touch, and convey such clear intelligence to the brain, that it does not require to be arranged by judgment' (Wollstonecraft 1972, p. 135). In what follows, I make a case for considering the feminine energy the Goncourts were channelling as a force that it is different from, but related to, the actual bodies of women. In brief, my argument is that libidinal forces of desire overlaid by sexual difference, and often expressed in aesthetic terms such as the Rococo, operate unconsciously to animate events in the material world. The energies of sexual difference, including those considered 'feminine', are affective forces that flow through all bodies, influencing not just aesthetic, but political sensibilities. Viewed in this manner, it becomes clear that such forces of sexual difference have an influence beyond considerations of gender identity and sexual preference. They can be considered aspects of what Hardt and Negri (2009) call biopolitics – the exploration of alternative subjectivities necessary for material, political change.

The negotiation of complexes revolving around sexual difference and class that will become apparent in this genealogy also reveal the highly political nature of discourses that appear to solely address aesthetics. The overlap of the feminine with the aristocracy as a class, and the substitution of the feminine (in the form of Pompadour) for the King, is evidence of the highly political nature of the projection of feminine energies. Further, the history of Rococo's extensive and gradual rise, followed by a dramatic and violent fall, then a flip-flopping between the forces of sexual difference during the Terror, appears to be a clear example of a collective complex and the horrific consequences of the pendulum swing Jung defined as an *enantiodromia*.

For all of these reasons, examining the Rococo, its so-called 'defeat' by neo-classicism, and its reprise in the Goncourt's era in the form of *Art Nouveau*, is instrumental to understanding both the relation of sexual difference to politics, and the perils of remaining unconscious of these forces. Parenthetically, although my argument will confirm Rancière's (2004) claims regarding the political nature of primary aesthetics, it will also challenge his emphasis on the progressive nature of the Aesthetic regime he saw percolating in the late 18th century. From the perspective of sexual difference, the start of Rancière's Aesthetic regime also corresponded with a harsh repression not just of feminine aesthetics, but also women's political rights.

The feminine as a compensatory aesthetic force

The apparently hypnotic absorption of the *frères* de Goncourts' Rococo vibrations lends credence to Silverman's argument that they were opening themselves up to the workings of their unconscious. In this, they were influenced by the first incursions into the world of psychoanalysis and hypnosis by their friend Dr Jean-Martin Charcot, one of the original mentors of

Sigmund Freud. Edmond and Jules were not the only men of their time influenced by these vibrations. The glass artist Emile Gallé and sculptor Auguste Rodin both saw their work as the direct expression of vibrations that came directly out of their unconscious into their art. Gallé described his works as 'vibrating presences' that he hoped would stimulate similar vibrations in the spirits of those who saw them, produced by the release of unconscious forces and the rejection of reason. Rodin sought to bring the dynamic, erotic force of nature into his works, emphasizing the neurotic tension between reason and dreams in his sculptures (Silverman 1992, pp. 235–245).

All four men were immersed in, and consciously influenced by, the psychological theories of the unconscious developed by Charcot at the L'hôpital Salpêtrière outside of Paris, and Dr Hippolyte Bernheim in the French city of Nancy. Charcot was especially known for his studies of hysteria, which appeared to disproportionately affect women from rural areas. He developed the technique of hypnosis in an attempt to heal the various hysterics, both male and female, being treated at the Salpêtrière. The basic assumption of this treatment, developed further by Breuer and Freud (who spent time working with Charcot), was that some incident or memory related to the symptoms was being repressed. If it could be identified in a state of unconsciousness, the symptoms of hysteria would dissipate. Although neither the Goncourts, nor Rodin or Gallé, were ostensibly hysterics, all four men were influenced by the ideas of the healing nature of the unconscious Charcot and Bernheim had uncovered.

The Goncourts explicitly viewed their curvaceous objects as an antidote to the aesthetic horrors of modern capitalist society. It was a 'feverish, tormented' time, Edmond wrote, and the people of France suffered a transpersonal nervous tension because of it. It was widely perceived that the cause of this nervous tension was industrialization and the constant stimulation and rapid pace of urban life. Psychologists referred to this nervous condition as neurasthenia: a state of nervous exhaustion that culminated in irritability and physical lassitude, often diagnosed today as chronic fatigue syndrome. The American physician George Miller Beard first diagnosed neurasthenia, linking it to an excessive American zeal for the Protestant work ethic (interestingly, Max Weber suffered from it). Charcot considered this nervous disorder to be a transpersonal phenomenon, suggesting that it might be an incurable condition of modernity that resulted in widespread degeneration. The German physician Max Nordau, who studied under Charcot, argued it was a sort of collective pathology caused by war, and the speed and sensory overload of the city (pp. 80–81).

Although there was probably some truth to this diagnosis, none of it explains why the antidote these men craved was avowedly 'feminine'. If the purpose of Charcot's hypnotic trances was to release repressed thoughts or memories, why were they releasing a Rococo memory described as feminine? Freud, no doubt, would have diagnosed it as a sexual symptom. While this is entirely possible in their individual cases, it doesn't explain why *all* of these men were channelling it, nor why the aesthetic they appreciated continued to grow as a collective aesthetic preference for decades to come.

If we accept Nordau's diagnosis of a collective pathological response to a country in the throes of an industrial revolution, the Goncourts' channelling of the feminine can be viewed as a sort of 'hysterical symptom' similar to Marx's concept of commodity fetishism (Zizek 1989, p. 22). If, as Marx (1949, p. 43) argued, commodity fetishism involves repressing the truth of class inequalities inherent to the products of labour, thereby creating a 'the fantastic form of a relation between things', what the Goncourts, Rodin, and Gallé were doing was projecting the repressed feminine aspects of sexual difference onto their Rococo and *Art Nouveau* objects. In Jung's terms, we could view it as *compensatory*. In response to the alienating destratification of social forces ushered in by the rapid expansion of capitalism and the urbanization that accompanied it, they longed for the containing, erotic, sensual pleasures of their idealized version of the Rococo.

In line with Wollen's argument in Chapter 1, the Goncourts portrayed this Rococo energy as contrasting with what their protégé Paul Mantz called the 'cult of the straight line' (Silverman 1992, p. 125). The feminine warmth and eroticism of the serpentine and curvaceous Rococo symbolized not just a better time, when things were slower and more soothing to the nerves, but also the epitome of French craft and interior design skill. As Silverman notes, it was as if reviving the Rococo, represented in contemporary design by *Art Nouveau*, would usher in a renewal of French culture and the reunion of craft and art that was destroyed with the elimination of the pre-capitalist guilds.

These considerations prompt a number of questions. What precisely was this Rococo energy, and why did it lose its influence in post-revolutionary France, only to re-emerge a century later in the Goncourts' time? More importantly for my purposes, exactly what about it is 'feminine'? This association is so frequently repeated as to make it appear automatic and obvious, but what *precisely* is the basis for this metaphoric association? Understanding this connection involves a broader understanding of the 'genus' of which Rococo can be considered to be a 'species': the Baroque. In particular, I will focus on an understanding of the Baroque as a transpersonal force that appears to be associated not just with the time period designated in art history texts (the 17th and 18th centuries) but reappears across time and spaces. My approach to this will be to pull the energies of sexual difference away from bodies into the space of Jung's subtle body or Deleuze's *intermezzo*, to portray them as interpersonal energies.

Baroque and Rococo

As Conley notes, Deleuze believed that the characteristics of the Baroque should not be restricted to 17th and 18th century European art, but recognized as a more generalized cultural trope characterized by 'proliferation of mystical experience, the birth of the novel, intense taste for life that grows and pullulates, and a fragility of infinitely varied patterns of movement' (Conley 1993, p. x). While Deleuze's description does not explicitly evoke the feminine, many other analyses of the Baroque as a transpersonal force make this connection clear. Lambert develops Deleuze's argument to show that many others have regarded the Baroque as some sort of transhistorical force. In a 1935 essay, for example, d'Ors described the Baroque as an 'eon', a metaphysical category that has a history, but not in the art history sense of a periodization of styles. Instead, it is 'a category of spirit that has been ripped from any historical narrative and is made to stand on its own' (Lambert 2004, p. 41). Rather than being a moment in the stages of art history, 'the Baroque is a living and archetypal category inserted into the fabric of History' (p. 41). As such, it is not limited to any single time period, but can reappear. Of particular interest for my purposes is his argument that the Baroque 'eon' that culminated in the Rococo is compared to the 'Ewig-weibliche' or the eternal feminine (p. 48).

Interestingly, Wölfflin describes the transition from the Renaissance to the Baroque period in terms almost identical to the contrast between Good Design and French Orientalism described in Chapter 1, although with a significant emphasis on their transpersonal aspects. In his approach to art history, Wölfflin argued that understanding the transitions between stylistic periods of art and architecture involved looking at the 'super-individual' forces that govern such changes. In his view, 'It is self-evident that a style can only be born when there is a strong receptivity for a certain kind of corporeal presence' (Wölfflin 1968, p. 78). As Murray points out, Wölfflin viewed the work of art as a product of something much larger than itself. As opposed to a personal creative act, the work of art for Wölfflin, as for Jung and Deleuze, was the 'expression of an inescapable, super-individual force' (Murray 1968, p. 5).

Ultimately, Wölfflin does not specify the engine of such change, except to say that the Baroque's effacing of the defined forms characteristic of 'good' (classical renaissance) style (p. 86) seemed to correspond to an emphasis on 'atmosphere' – a feeling of 'overwhelmingness and unfathomableness' (p. 86). Whatever caused this transition, in his view the Baroque was the antithesis of the classical forms of the Renaissance. If the aesthetic sensibility of the Renaissance can be described in terms almost identical to the Good Design discourse as '[m]oderation and form, simplicity and noble line' (Justi quoted in Wölfflin, p. 88), the Baroque sensibility can be characterized as the opposite of each of these terms. In words that parallel Jung's description of the dispersed nature of perception characterized by the feminine *Luna*, Wölfflin argues that in contrast to the clean lines of the classical Renaissance, the Baroque sensibility 'could not be satisfied by the simple, well-defined and easily comprehended form. Our half-closed eyes no longer see the beauties of a line, we demand vaguer effects' (p. 87).

Above all, one gets a sense of movement and a release of emotion in Wölfflin's description of the Baroque; to use a term coined by Williams (1977), it is as if there has been a change in the 'structure of feeling'. Its effects are at once heavy, ponderous, and emotionally rapturous, 'plunging with ecstasy into the abyss of infinity' in the manner of the religious fervour evident in Jesuit religious practice or the hermetic ecstasies of Giordano Bruno (Wölfflin 1968, p. 86). In the Baroque's heavy, earthbound buildings characterized by half-formed piers and pilasters, and cut off corners, one gets 'the impression of an unceasing, restless struggle for liberty' (p. 52). This struggle for liberty drives the sense of movement inherent to the Baroque. For Wölfflin, the Baroque never offers perfection or fulfilment or the static calm of 'being' characteristic of the classic (p. 62). As in the runs and trills of Baroque music, one gets a sense of constant movement or becoming, whose seriousness becomes transformed by Mozart's time in the second half of the 18th century to a sort of skipping lightness, precisely the way Wölfflin describes the Rococo (p. 36).

Described in these terms, it is easy to imagine the Baroque, or the 'Ewig-weibliche', as a becoming or breaking through of archetypal feminine energies in an 'unceasing, restless struggle for liberty' – an earthbound feeling of movement, of the sensation of the vaguer effects of the in-between inherent to *Luna*, and the symbolic, containing curves and sense of transformation inherent to *Eros*. Note, however, that this sense of movement appears to be both central to the aesthetic of the Baroque itself, and derived from a sense of difference. The sense of 'a restless struggle for liberty' is vital to this feminine energy – the sense of breaking free that Wölfflin noted.

Art historians were not the only commentators to identify such an energy; as I will describe in Chapter 6, decades later Sombart (1967) described a wave of *Eros* that spread across Europe between the 13th and 17th centuries. This hedonistic, aesthetic celebration of women and love from the 13th century on, he argued, was reflected first in the songs of the troubadours, then in Botticelli's art and ultimately the Rococo artists Fragonard, Boucher, and Greuze. He linked this *Eros* to the rise of women in royal courts and to luxury spending, viewing it as the engine of early capitalism.

By the late 17th century, the energy of the Baroque was transforming into something higher and lighter, evident in the Rococo aesthetic, particularly as it appeared in France and southern Germany. By higher, I do not necessarily mean more evolved; this lightness could be a sign of the dispersion of its energy, or its ungroundness. Regardless, the aesthetic is by then firmly associated with the feminine. Beginning with the now well-rehearsed gender association, Lambert notes Starobinski's reference to Rococo's 'exaggeration of tendencies' found in the Baroque, concluding that the element of beauty in it must be gendered as feminine and 'thereby, given motion and sinuosity' (Lambert 2004, p. 43). For Hogarth as well, Lambert points out, Rococo's 'S' shape was gendered. In Hogarth's words, 'The grace and dignity of the undulation suggest the swaying movement of a dancing form and so reveal its feminine essence' (quoted in Lambert, p. 44).

But for Hogarth, the 'S' shape also functioned as a 'lure' to the eye that held the composition of the swarming elements of the Rococo surface. This tracing of the feminine curve was not just decorative, but suggested a new organization of space that is not organized in terms of surface/depth. In contrast to the implied depth of the grandeur of the High Baroque, for Rococo the swirling surfaces are gathered together or contained by the 'wandering eye of the spectator' as he/she searches for the arabesque holding things together, bringing them onto the same plane of consistency – a process more akin to the flickering of a flame that links all elements together into spectacle (p. 44).

This 'flickering' metaphor is striking in its similarity to Jung's analysis of *anima* as 'twinkling' soul. He says:

> *Anima* means soul and should designate something very wonderful and immortal. Yet this was not always so. We should not forget that this kind of soul is a dogmatic conception whose purpose it is to pin down and capture something cannily alive and active. The German word *Seele* is closely related, via the Gothic form *saiwalô*, to the Greek word αἰόλος, which means 'quick-moving,' 'changeful of hue,' twinkling,' something like a butterfly . . . which reels drunkenly from flower to flower and lives on honey and love.
>
> (Jung quoted in Hillman 1985, p. 24)

This image of a flickering, Dionysian butterfly suggests the attention to surface and spectacle that commentators such as Jameson and Harvey have linked with Postmodern culture, hence Lambert's allusion that the Postmodern might be compared to the Baroque. Lambert relates this preoccupation with surface and adornment to the development of early capitalism and the commodity form. The symbolic content that previously bound the cultural work to a specific, aristocratic class and location explodes, leaving it 'unbounded' (Lambert 2004, p. 45).

Yet according to Jung, the flickering surface of *anima/butterfly* is not necessarily unbounded. It is itself a symbol that has been disciplined, perhaps devalued is a better word, by a dogma that pinned it down by demanding a morality and 'depth' that is then contrasted with a supposedly superficial focus on surface. And since this 'molecular' *anima*/butterfly is symbolically feminine, its devaluation is projected onto its 'molar' likeness, woman. Viewed from this perspective, the *anima*/butterfly is an alternative way of being in the world, paralleling his idea of *Luna* perception as seeing the interval between the points. In addition to attention to surface, it involves a curvilinear form of perception different from the distinctions and judgments demanded by rationality, and an 'erotic' way of being in the world that exists by gathering points together and containing them, not by distinguishing them.

Deleuze saw the curve as the very nature of the soul. Invoking an image similar to Bergson's (2007, p. 2) understanding of *duration* as linking points on a line, he cites Leibniz:

> The division of the continuous must not be taken as of sand dividing into grains, but as that of a sheet of paper of a tunic in folds, in such a way that an infinite number of folds can be produced . . . but without the body ever dissolving into points or minima.
>
> (Leibniz quoted in Deleuze 1993, p. 6)

And a fold, Deleuze argued, was always folded within a fold, forming a sort of labyrinthine notion of the soul that was very different from Cartesian conceptions. In a description of the soul that resonates with Jung's description of *anima*/butterfly as soul he says,

> If Descartes did not know how to get through the labyrinth, it was because he sought its secret of continuity in rectilinear tracks, and the secret of liberty in a rectitude of the soul. He knew the inclension of the soul as little as he did the curvature of matter.
>
> (p. 3)

Although I agree with Jung's and Deleuze's contentions that the attention to surface in the Baroque and Rococo does not preclude profundity, I think it is possible that by the late 18th century, *anima's* flickering energy had become unbounded – 'uncontained' in the sense that I described it in Chapter 4. The princely 'dream of happiness' and the *fêtes galantes* have an ungrounded feeling to them epitomized in Fragonard's *Swing* (Figure 5.1) – a denial of the dark side of the feminine and, as we will see, an ominous swinging back and forth between masculine forces. In Jungian terms, there is also

Figure 5.1 Jean Honoré Fragonard, *The Swing*, 1767
Photo Credit: The Wallace Collection, London

a repression of the shadow here, a steadfast attempt to ignore the violent energies brewing. By this time, the mounting Baroque energy had brought with it not just a feminization of aesthetics, but of the social and political realms as well. In other words, along with this psychic change came material transformation. This Baroque energy both filtered through political conditions and transformed them.

By the end of the 18th century, another transition had begun, this time to a more masculine energy, with the violent consequences I will describe below. Repressed but not forgotten, however, the feminine re-emerges during the Goncourts' time, approximately 100 years after the demise of the

Rococo. Like a repressed memory, it filtered its way back into the late 19th and early 20th century European consciousness in the form of *Art Nouveau* and the Orientalist, decorative aesthetic evident in the fashion and stage designs of Poiret and Bakst and the art of Matisse described in Chapter 1 (Wollen 1993).

Unquestionably, explaining the collective transition from the sensibility of avowedly unadorned, masculine lines of the Renaissance to the feminine movement of the Baroque, where lines are 'banished' and all corners rounded into curves (Wölfflin 1968, p. 35) requires a considerable act of imagination. This transition was clearly unconscious, exhibiting the pattern of Jung's conception of the *enantiodromia* – a reversal of psychic energies where one energy peaks, then its opposite emerges with equal power. A sense of movement ensues – the sense of an energy struggling to be free. It succeeds, diffusing its particles over a period of century, reaching its point of transition in the Rococo. By this time, it is high and light, an energy losing the momentum of its release, preparing once again for transition. In the case of the French Revolution, this transition occurred with explosive violence and massive material consequences for anyone associated with this feminine energy – including women and the aristocracy. Perhaps grounding this *enantiodromia* in the specific history of the revolutionary and pre-revolutionary periods will clarify this imagery.

Anatomy of an *enantiodromia*

In a way, the Goncourts' attachment to the Rococo took courage, given that for most of the preceding half century, Rococo was synonymous with *mauvais goût* (bad taste) in France. In the context of the discourses of design taste, this is to be expected, given its frankly feminine and erotic nature. As Gutwirth notes, the Rococo always had a whiff of 'whorehouse elegance' about it (Gutwirth 1992, p. 6), and after its demise it was associated with the sort of kitschy ornamentation appreciated by those of weak character and/or questionable morals. The erotic nature of the Rococo was obvious and intentional. It was frankly sensual. In art, this meant a focus on the back, the leg, the foot – or even a rapturous gaze up a lady's skirt, as in Fragonard's *Swing*.

Rococo was about more than just erotic sensuality, however. As Saisselin argues, it was as much dreamy poetry as it was painting: an unreal quest for pleasure without pain. Indeed, he notes that the Rococo is better described as a dream than a stylistic development, 'a dream of happiness possible of realization only in and through art. It was short-lived' (Saisselin 1960, p. 151). Although it was aristocratic, he maintains, it was more about an aristocracy of spirit than class, characterized by 'a nature simple and beautiful, appeased passions, and love called tenderness' (Saisselin 1960, p. 146). It renounced the sublime, *grand goût*, ambition, power, heroism, and tragedy. It was explicitly and purposefully 'petit'. Rococo was about grace, charm, playfulness, intimacy, finesse, and pleasure. Hyde describes the central elements of Rococo painting as a tendency toward natural forms in which 'C', 'S', and spiral shapes dominate, the use of asymmetry, the rejection of linear perspective, and a sparkling palette of light colours such as pinks, pale blues, and greens. Surfaces were opulently filled and have the appearance of great painterly ease (Hyde 2006, p. 11). Dragons, cupids, and other mythological figures were also prominently placed (Figure 5.2). Sylvan scenes of well-dressed aristocrats engaged in (often illicit) amorous affairs, known as *fêtes galantes*, were also popular.

Figure 5.2 Dragon detail from a chest of drawers designed by Antoine-Robert Gaudreaus, 1739

Photo Credit: The Wallace Collection, London

In architecture, it meant a retreat from the monumental. In fact, Scott argues that it was originally a sign of aristocratic resistance to absolutism, as the courtly nobility fled the *grand goût* of Versailles after Louis XIV's death and set themselves up in Parisian apartments decorated in the *petit goût* of the intimate and ornamental *style modern* (Scott, K. 1996). Staircases were moved from the centre to the extremities of the building, since they were no longer concerned with show of royal descent. Interiors were more comfortable – constructed for "men", not "bureaucrats". New rooms appeared; the boudoir replaced the bedroom, and hostesses no longer received guests in bed. French cuisine was also perfected at this time, and intimate private dining rooms also become important. The *salon* became increasingly important for receiving guests (Saisselin 1960).

The word *salon* becomes capitalized as it moves from a purely spatial configuration into an institution: a meeting place where the cultural, intellectual, and political elite could meet and engage in conversation (or *commerce*, in the 18th-century idiom). The 'New Woman' reigned over the *Salon*. She was pretty, mischievous, intelligent, witty, gracious, and an excellent hostess. Like the Goncourts, Saisselin asserts that in this period 'women taught men how to live' (p. 151).

Rococo furniture had feminine names: *la bergère* (the shepherdess), *la chiffonnière* (the dresser), *la marquise brisée* (the divided marquise). Especially important was *la toilette* – both a dressing table and the process by which women decorated themselves for display. 'Furniture spoke in the eighteenth century,' Mantz claimed. 'Hearts were imprisoned as captives in the amorous curves of sofas the color of rose . . . Eroticism in ornament reigned . . . in all the luxury arts. The ideal had become feminized.' (Quoted in Silverman 1992, p. 125) Both men and women dressed in a highly decorated fashion featuring powdered hair, whitened skin coloured with heavy rouge or *fard*, beauty spots, and layers of lace and silk.

Says Saisselin:

> It may seem that I have overstressed this feminine element, the playfulness and the frivolity of the Rococo. But this I have done because I see it the essence of this princely dream of happiness, a dream which may take the form of a yearning for a quiet life in the country, exemplified in a pastoral scene, or the love of conversation and society, but also, a dream of love as removed from reality as would be platonic love.
>
> (Saisselin 1960, p. 151)

The Goncourts' idea of the pre-revolutionary aesthetic of the Rococo aligned with a sensibility summarized by the word *volupté*: voluptuousness, or sensual pleasure. Until the death of Louis XIV, they wrote, love in France was about chivalry and gallantry – a heroic and noble ideal. By the time of Louis XV, however, love had become *volupté*:

> the word of the eighteenth century; it is its secret, its charm, its soul. It breathes *volupté*, it emits it . . . it flies over the earth, possesses it, it is its fairy, its muse, the character of all of its fashion, the style of all its arts.
> (de Goncourt and de Goncourt 1929, p. 158)

Women dressed with *volupté*; houses were 'saturated' with it. The entire century appears to pulsate with sensual desire – to say 'I love you' in the 18th century, they wrote, meant 'I desire you' (p. 170).

The Goncourts' understanding of *volupté* evokes a collective, transpersonal energy similar to Williams' idea of the 'structure of feeling' of an era, or Wollstonecraft's sensibility. If interpreted in light of the Jungian/Deleuzean conception of desire – that is to say, not purely sexually, but as symbolic intensities, these allusions to a feminine energy permeating an entire century suggest an association with Jung's conception of the archetypal feminine, indicating that what may be happening is both an individual and collective re-negotiation of identity. Or, from the perspective of Deleuze and Guattari's schizoanalysis, it is as if a nostalgic wave of becoming-woman is permeating the collective body-without-organs of this time period, a line of transversal energy providing an escape from the increasingly stratified nature of the late 16th century *assemblage* of the Renaissance, or in the Goncourts' time, the industrial revolution.

Many art historians have contested the idea that the erotic force of the Rococo had anything to do with the power of women themselves. In response to the Goncourts' claim that 'women reigned' at this time, Starobinski countered that they were made to *think* that they reigned (quoted in Gutwirth 1992, p. 4). As Gutwirth notes, other art historians have also wondered whether paintings of 'seductive little goddesses of love set in splendidly stylized natural bowers be read as evidence of a time of woman regnant?' (Gutwirth, p. 5). The Goncourt brothers' titillating interaction with their Rococo objects appears to support this perspective. Their ideal woman corresponded only to the sensual, elegant, witty devotée of the Rococo aesthetic; in their eyes, the fearsome modern woman was a mannish figure bearing little resemblance to the manifestation of the feminine they sought to channel.

By contemporary standards, there is no question that women's power was severely constrained in both the 18th century Rococo period and the Goncourts' period of the late 19th century, and that men's projections of the growing feminine energy of this period were stereotypical in nature. Nonetheless, the public presence of women in both the intellectual and political realms increased markedly prior to the Revolution, a trend that continued into the early years of tumult post-1789. Although women's political rights were still greatly limited in the early 18th century, relatively speaking, women's power in the Royal Court (particularly the potent and influential mistress of Louis XV, Madame de Pompadour) (Figure 5.3) was evident enough to cause considerable criticism. Additionally, the intellectual importance of Paris's influential 18th century *Salonnières* such as Madame Geoffrin, Madame du Deffand, Julie de Lespinasse, Suzanne Necker, or Germaine de Staël cannot be denied, nor can women's articulate claims that the rights

Figure 5.3 François Boucher, *Madame de Pompadour*, 1759

Photo Credit: The Wallace Collection, London

and liberties discussed in the Enlightenment texts they read should also be applied to them (Scott J. 1996).

It is true that although these women were brilliant and talented, they knew their place. Pompadour prodigiously avoided any impression of interfering in political affairs, although everyone knew her overwhelming influence on her royal lover when it came to political matters. Similarly, although well read and highly intellectual, the ladies of the salons were often regarded as frivolous by the men who attended their gatherings and were tolerated mostly because of the financial support they provided to their followers. Relative to women's presence in the public sphere before and after this period, however, these changes were significant.

Not only did this time period witness a significant increase in women's participation in the public realm, this feminization of culture appeared to transfer into men's self-representations as well, augmenting the perception of feminine power. In addition to the tight breeches and volumes of lace and silk, men wore wigs made of women's hair, and covered their shaven cheeks in pink *fard* or rouge (Gutwirth 1992, p. 16). Hyde notes that the Rococo painter Boucher used a single facial type and the same poses for male and female figures in his paintings, and that cross-dressing and androgyny for both men and women were evident in both theatre and opera (Hyde 2006, p. 192). As I will argue further in Chapter 6, these trends were accompanied by a broader cultural emphasis in *mondaine* society on men adopting more gentle, effeminate manners that could be encouraged by interaction with women. Hirschman (1977) argued that Montesquieu's insistence on a movement away from the heroic, warmongering passions of the aristocracy toward the more gentle *moeurs douces* of commerce was part of larger movement toward an appreciation of the gentle manners of women in the 17th and 18th centuries. In the earlier years of this time period, calling a man effeminate was considered a compliment, not an insult. In this light, this contra-sexual exploration of identity can be considered what Hardt and Negri would call a biopolitical exploration of alternative subjectivities, and it was having real, material effects.

This feminization, however, had a class basis and Hyde emphasizes that the men and women of the aristocratic classes who embraced the delicacy and fineness of the Rococo aesthetic had more in common with each other than they did with their gender peers in lower classes (Hyde, p. 148). This overlapping of class and the feminized aesthetic of the Rococo highlights that what is being referred to as 'feminine' here is not something that is coincident with women's bodies, but rather is an energy that flows across bodies regardless of their gender identification. Within both the individual and collective psyche, it must be negotiated relative to complexes revolving around class, race, and ethnicity. But this overlapping of a feminine energy

146 Genealogies

that was soon to be despised, with a privileged class that was already bitterly resented, resulted in an explosion of unconscious energies.

It is not clear whether it was this cross-gendered infiltration of the Rococo's feminine energy or its overlapping with the aristocratic class that made it so repulsive to those who so virulently opposed it, but a sustained, highly gendered attack on the aesthetic and women followed its peak in the mid-18th century. As Lajer-Burcharth (1999, p. 14) notes, Rococo's 'democracy' of sexuality soon came to symbolize women's unprecedented and unauthorized presence in politics and society, a provocation that was at once gendered and class based. For the non-Rococo public, the androgyny of the Rococo indicated that aristocratic men had (ironically) lost their heads, abdicating their separateness and political agency. Thus it is not surprising that the aesthetic that opposed the Rococo was a stratified, sexually segregated, and hierarchical conception of art that reverted to the classical emphasis on the 'male body representing a specific, heroic-stoic ideal: an image of autonomous, impermeable, emotionally restrained manliness, controlled even in death' (Lajer-Burcharth 1999, p. 2). Exemplified by the neo-classicism of Jacques-Louis David, this became the aesthetic of the Jacobin Republic.

If one loosely associates the Rococo style with the reign of Louis XV (1710–1774), by 1750 the decadence of the Rococo was increasingly denounced in favour of heroic paintings of history or portraits. Exemplified by the work of David, the new art was moral, admonishing its viewers to become better citizens. Describing Boucher, Diderot wrote in 1761:

> His elegance, his affected winsomeness, his novelistic gallantry, his coquetry, his taste, his facility, variety, brilliancy, his made-up complexions, his debauchery, necessarily captivate fops, little women, young men, society people, the crowd of those who are strangers to real taste, to the truth, to just ideas, and to the seriousness of art; how could they resist the ostentation, the libertinage, the brilliancy, the pompons, the bosoms and bottoms, Boucher's licentious epigrams.
>
> (Diderot quoted in Hyde 2006, p. 3)

Women and their involvement in Rococo painting also came under attack, although as Hyde points out, almost all Rococo artists and architects were men, and painters like Boucher sold mostly to male customers. Since the 1740s, reformist critics such as La Font had criticized women, with a particular focus on Pompadour, for the immoral and degenerate state of the arts in France. According to La Font, 'It is chiefly the ladies one should blame if our productions so often descend to the level of trifles and trinkets. To please them, our greatest painters will one day be forced to transform everything into pygmies and marionettes' (quoted in Hyde, p. 63). In

Channelling the feminine: Rococo 147

Figure 5.4 Jacques Louis David, *The Oath of the Horatii*, 1789, Musée du Louvre, Paris
Photo Credit: Erich Lessing/Art Resource, NY

1773, Mercier complained 'Women are consulted too much, their taste is sufficiently refined, but not extensive enough. Since they have been guiding the arts, the arts have been degenerating' (p. 45). In an age when social and political critique was dangerous, attacks on the Crown were frequently made in the guise of attacks on women – the powerful Pompadour bearing the brunt of criticisms that were intended for her royal protector and the politically and financially powerful in general (p. 62).

In place of the erotic curves, the frilly lace, the asymmetry the ever-present pink of the Rococo, and the flirtatious *fêtes galantes*, David and his followers called for a return of the heroic, of rationality and morality, of history painting (Figure 5.4). According to Mantz, with post-Revolutionary art came the 19th century masculine 'triumph of the empire and boredom':

> The cult of the straight line, the pseudoantique tendencies; this was the beginning of the end, the transition that prepared the cruel triumph of

the empire and of boredom. Already the painter of Horaces [David] introduced menacing furnishings in his canvases, and already an arbitrary and simulated Egypt set facile sphinxes in every angle. Gone was the smile set in form, and gone was the warmth! By the fatal door opened by David, one felt the arrival of an icy wind. The time had come when, in the face of the frozen ideal, the chilled historian must request his coat.

(Mantz quoted in Silverman 1992, p. 125)

Mantz's reference to the chilly winds of David's classicism bears a striking resemblance to the emphasis on coldness in Deleuze's analysis of *Venus in Furs* and Bachofen's description of the decline of matriarchal influence, as discussed in Chapter 4.

According to Saisselin, it was the triumph of the pen over the brush. Art was no longer about happiness and pleasure. Instead, in terms identical to the discourse of Good Design discussed in Chapter 1, it must 'improve' men by moving them to social action and inspire conviction. In place of the New Woman comes the New Man: not a gentleman, but a virtuous and useful citizen. 'At this point', Saisselin maintains, 'it is no longer possible to talk of the Rococo'. *Logos* had triumphed over *Eros*, a step that moves France closer to its bloody revolution. As Saisselin (1960, p. 151) concludes: 'so it is that happiness taken seriously will turn from a dream into a nightmare'.

As Duncan (1976) and Hyde (2006) both note, in painting, Rococo taste never completely died, and numerous artists who painted in the Rococo remained popular into the Romantic period of the mid-19th century. Nonetheless, in official critical circles, and in the world of interior decor, the cult of classical Greece and Rome, the straight line, and the heroic re-emerged as the dominant aesthetic discourse in Revolutionary France. A significant body of historical analysis of the French Revolution confirms Saisselin's view, connecting gender- and body-related factors to the political and aesthetic issues of the time and the almost hysterical masculinization of culture and politics immediately prior to and during the Revolution (Crow 1995; Gutwirth 1992; Hyde 2006; Lajer-Burcharth 1999; Potts 1990; Solomon-Godeau 1997).

This hysterical repression of the feminine was accompanied by a significant loss in women's political power. Women were banished from the political realm as they were from Revolutionary painting. French women, inspired by Wollstonecraft's publication of *The Vindication of the Rights of Women* in 1792 and led by the outspoken Olympe de Gouges, originally gained political rights, but by 1804 those rights had been mostly revoked. Between 1792 and 1794, the Jacobin Republic gave women the right to witness public documents and contracts and legalized divorce. By 1793, however, their growing political power and apparent unruliness led to a gradual withdrawal of these rights.

In the year 1793, the Society of Revolutionary Republican Women was created, and there were food riots by women in the streets of Paris. In May of that year, Charlotte Corday assassinated Jean-Paul Marat, one of the most significant Jacobin leaders. All of this was used as evidence of the growing threat of women's power. In reaction to women's growing presence in the public sphere, the Jacobins began to withdraw the rights women had been given by the Convention. By October of 1793, not only had the execution of Marie-Antoinette taken place amid charges of incest, lesbianism, and promiscuity (Louis the XVI had been charged with treason), the Convention declared all women's clubs illegal (including the Society of Revolutionary Women) and executed de Gouges. After further riots by women in response to these moves in 1794, women were banned from the Convention galleries. By 1796, the principle of marital equality was struck from the Civil Code and the principle of paternal authority was affirmed, with women's right to divorce once again extremely restricted (Solomon-Godeau 1997, p. 15). Small wonder that the French Revolution has been considered the 'world-historic defeat of women' (p. 213). This swift repression of both feminine aesthetics and women's political rights belies Ranicère's emphasis on the progressive political impact of aesthetics at this time, as outlined in Chapter 3. From the perspective of sexual difference, Rancière's Aesthetic regime marks a new regressive politics for women.

From a materialist political-economy perspective, all of this can be viewed purely in terms of power politics. Women were gaining political power and were increasingly willing to use violence to achieve their ends. In the face of such a challenge to their hegemonic dominance, men used their control over the political and military apparatus to quash this threat. While not denying this interpretation, I question whether it can answer some of the broader issues I am raising here. Purely materialist accounts, for example, cannot explain some of the 'flip-flopping' between masculine and feminine symbolic politics that becomes particularly clear during the Terror, and they ignore some obvious contra-sexual negotiation of both individual and collective identity that appears to be occurring during the Revolution as well. Finally, such approaches throw little light on what it was that made men originally open to the growing predominance of something they referred to as 'feminine' in society in the first place, a force that was quite violently and suddenly expelled. I will address these points in turn.

The hysterical repression of the feminine becomes most evident in the symbolic politics of the Revolution. This argument appears to be belied by the fact that the most obvious symbol of the Revolution was a woman – Marianne. Feminist historians have dismissed the importance of Marianne as a symbol of women's power, arguing that she could be used as an emblem of the revolution only because women were excluded from public affairs. Beginning in 1793, however, the Jacobins even tried to replace Marianne as the symbol of the Revolution with a male figure – that of Hercules. David was charged with this task, and he set about organizing a ceremonial parade where a giant sculpture of Hercules would be paraded through the streets (Gutwirth 1992, p. 275; Solomon-Godeau 1997, p. 203).

As political chaos and civil war became increasingly prevalent within France and foreign enemies threatened from without, however, the Jacobins inexplicably reconsidered the Hercules approach. As if to atone for this repression of the feminine, they announced that a ceremony would be held in Notre Dame to celebrate the 'Goddess of Reason' (Gutwirth 1992, p. 276). This apparent concession to the sacred feminine, albeit a feminine enthroned as Reason and not *Eros*, was greeted with considerable derision by many Jacobins. This move to resurrect the symbolic feminine was quickly quashed, and many of the women who had volunteered to participate in it were later guillotined in the White Terror associated with the Directoire. In the terrible symbolism invoked by Payan, it was viewed as 'a mythology more absurd than that of the Ancients . . . goddesses more vile than those of Fable, were about to reign in France. The Convention saw these conspirators . . . They are no more' (Payan quoted in Gutwirth, p. 252).

This flip-flopping back and forth between the symbolic masculine and feminine is symptomatic of the chaotic state of the collective complex, a situation where reason had fled and the unconscious had taken over. In Jung's view, this episode was evidence of the shadow of primitive man still evident in this supposedly 'civilized' culture that claimed to base its political stance, ironically, entirely on reason. When a society abandons religion entirely (as the Jacobins did), he argued, it effectively becomes disembedded or unbounded and there is nothing but earthly authority to guide it, which is manifestly unprepared to handle these unconscious energies. Referring to this particular incident, he remarked, 'Even when Reason triumphed at the beginning of the French Revolution it was quickly turned into a goddess and enthroned in Notre-Dame' (Jung 1977, pp. 253–4).

Equally interesting are some fairly clear examples that provide evidence of a contra-sexual negotiation of identity in the collective psyche, and the psychic effects that arise when one of these energies is denied. The hysterical masculine monism (Potts 1990) of the neo-classical style that replaced Rococo taste was in part related to the exclusion of women from public life, but it also had the effect of greatly stratifying and restricting sexual and gender identities. A self-possessed heroic, ethical, masculine body emerges in contrast to a marginalized female body that is either eroticized in a manner characterized by the Goncourts' 'luxe, calme et volupté' (p. 17), or a de-eroticized maternal body characteristic of the gentle mother. The only figure that can be both ethical and physically desirable at the same time is male (p. 11).

Despite the extreme repression of the feminine body in neo-classical style, however, feminine energies resurface in some fascinating ways. Solomon-Godeau argues, for example, that this banishment of the female body was not sustainable, and in its place, a highly feminized male body once again emerges to counter the virile warrior evident in paintings such as David's *Oath of the Horatii* (Figure 4.4). The feminized young man or *ephebe*, characterized in David's painting *The Death of Young Bara* appears to stand in for feminine bodies. She notes,

> It is as though in violently 'expelling' the frivolity, decadence, and corruption of the *ancien regime* and its courtly culture, and linking these to a malign femininity (or a perverse and depraved masculinity), republican culture required a stand-in for an eroticized femininity deemed inimical to republican and civic values.
>
> (Solomon-Godeau 1997, p. 11)

Although they can be repressed, neither aspect of the energies of sexual difference can disappear. They continue to push forward, 'canalized' or redirected, in this case, onto the male form in light of the prohibition of female bodies.

Lajer-Burcharth provides another fascinating example of the apparent inability to fully repress feminine energies in her analysis of David's art in the post-Thermidor period following the coup against Robespierre in 1794. She argues that Thermidor, marking the overthrow of the Jacobins that resulted in Robespierre's execution and David's imprisonment, cast doubt on the heroic male ideal of subjectivity dominant in the Jacobin period. A reconsideration of this heroic-stoic ideal of manliness is particularly apparent in the work of David, she claims, who appears to have undergone a critical renegotiation of identity while imprisoned by the Directoire for his association with Robespierre.

In contrast to his extreme focus on manly figures in the early Revolutionary period, a new concern with femininity reappears in his post-Thermidor period. Woman returns, after her banishment as a 'repressed signifier' during the Jacobin period. In an argument with clear parallels to Jung's conception of the contra-sexual psychic role of the feminine and Deleuze and Guattari's emphasis on the destabilizing impact of becoming-woman, Lajer-Burcharth notes that woman appears to act as an 'agent of internal disorganization' in David's art, 'a signifier that unsettles the coherence of the male body from within'(Lajer-Burcharth 1999, p. 3). The feminine figure haunts David's Directoire period art; he no longer speaks in the 'visual language of clear gender opposites' apparent in paintings such as *The Oath of the Horatii*, but selectively paints certain male bodies in distinctively feminine poses (pp. 3–4), including what she argues (and I agree) is effectively an emotional self-portrait in which David portrays himself as a grieving female Psyche abandoned by *Eros*.

Lajer-Burcharth uses Lacan to argue that such a refusal to articulate sexual difference is a sign of hysteria and 'the hysteric's refusal to enter the world of sexual difference linked to "unspeakable desires" that cannot be properly articulated by the subject's own body' (p. 62). From a Jungian or Deleuzean perspective, however, David's *Psyche* can be considered more positively as a consideration of, and negotiation with, the feminine aspects of his psyche. As his hysterical repression of this feminine aspect of his identity releases during this contemplative time in prison, he is able to admit to a fuller understanding of his identity. David's example shows the repression and release of the feminine within his individual psyche, but what was happening 'within' was in large part a reflection of what was happening 'without'. The hysterical rejection of the feminine, followed by a gradual re-opening to it, was a collective phenomenon that unquestionably parallels Jung's concept of the collective complex. The violence that accompanied this unconscious transition indicates why Jung and Freud regarded these collective phenomena with such misapprehension.

But the story, as we know, does not end here. Repressed and disciplined, but never destroyed, the feminine re-emerges in the Goncourts' time period with an explicit revival of the Rococo and a collective, trans-European attraction to *japonaiserie* and *Art Nouveau* or *Jugendstil*. The Goncourts' Rococo collection was complemented by a variety of Japanese and *Art Nouveau* objects, paintings, and sculpture mostly acquired from the decorative arts entrepreneur Siegfried Bing. In addition to being one of the first major importers of Japanese works of art into France, Bing's gallery, named *L'Art Nouveau*, was the a central meeting place and repository for the works of artists of the *Art Nouveau* movement (Troy 1991). Although primarily intended to revitalize the French craft tradition that many felt had deteriorated since the abolishment of the guilds in the French revolution, *Art Nouveau* was deeply influenced by the organic sensuousness of the Rococo. In a contemporary world of increasing international threats to France's position as the pre-eminent design centre in Europe, *Art Nouveau* paid homage to the Rococo with a style that, although definitely modern in its approach, owed its distinctiveness to the Rococo legacy of feminine curvaceousness.

By 1900, the aesthetic predominance of Art Nouveau and its Rococo ancestry had solidified, its popularity obvious in the Paris Exhibition of that year. In contrast to the industrial aesthetic of the 1889 exposition, characterized most notably by the Tour Eiffel, visitors to the 1900 exhibition entered through a monumental gateway known as the Porte Binet, after its creator Réné Binet. This giant, womb-like structure was both feminine and Orientalist. Covered with jewels and mosaics, the archway was flanked by two minarets and topped with a sculpture of a female figure known as *La Parisienne*. Two curving walls joined the minarets to the archway, engraved with figures of artisans and workers inspired by *La Parisienne's* role both as an objet d'art, and the inspiration of the craftsman's work. This structure can be seen in the background of Figure 5.5, and is admired in this cover from the exhibition catalogue by an oriental woman and her entourage. The woman dressed in white at the top of the picture is *La Parisienne*. The aesthetic energies of the feminine had returned.

The attraction to such feminine aesthetics was accompanied by a greater focus on women's craftwork by men, who often appeared to be making this effort in spite of their own better judgement. During the Rococo period, there was a similar emphasis on women's handcraft, and (aristocratic women, at least) painted, embroidered, wove, and participated in the decorative art of *découpage*. This emphasis on women's art revived in the late 19th century. For example, the organizational body designed to revitalize French arts and crafts, the Central Union of the Decorative Arts, organized two Exhibitions of the Arts of Woman in 1892 and 1895, and established a woman's committee to encourage women's involvement in the decorative arts. This included primarily educating women as consumers of the decorative arts, but also encouraged those women who wished to follow in the footsteps of their aristocratic predecessors and become producers themselves.

Although barely concealing their disdain for the 'new woman' who wished to take over the tasks previously assigned to men, the leaders of the Central Union recognized that although women may not be fit for the 'high arts', their nimble fingers made them particularly suitable for the decorative arts. There was no contesting the important role women had always played in inspiring men's production of art, however, since their 'better and more refined taste' and their 'instinct for elegance' made them natural muses for male artisans. In this respect, the Central Union's support for women was unrestrained. 'Let women take over the direction of the movement, let us ask them for their help . . .' proclaimed an article in the *Revue des arts décoratifs* (Silverman 1992, p. 202).

The fashion designer Paul Poiret, who figured prominently in Wollen's story of early modern France in Chapter 1, opened a studio for the

Figure 5.5 Encyclopedie du Siècle: L'Exposition de Paris, 1900
Photo Credit: SSPL/Science Museum, Art Resource, NY

decorative arts named after his daughter, *Atelier Martine*. In a strikingly literal parallel to Deleuze and Guattari's emphasis on the transformative aspects of becoming-woman as the Girl, the atelier was a school for girls ages 13–17, where they were encouraged, under the supervision of a teacher, to make spontaneous drawings directly from their imaginations, with no intervention from adults. Poiret then took these designs and manufactured a series of wallpapers, textiles, and carpets based on them (Troy 1991, p. 118).

This time period, of course, also marked the beginning of the suffragist movement, further evidence that a relaxation of the repression of feminine energies during this period was having significant material effects. This is clear even if, paradoxically, the horrible 'mannish' suffragists the Goncourts so disparaged were 'channelling' the masculine aspects of their imaginations in order to find the psychic resources to fight this battle. As is generally recognized, the early feminist movement focused primarily on acquiring a political identity for women using contractualist, liberal notions of equality, arguing that men and women were fundamentally the same and, therefore, both equally deserving of political rights. As in the Rococo period, there is a contra-sexual exploration of identity occurring here, expressed in the willingness of men to explore the repressed feminine other of their psyches, and matched by women exploring the developing masculine aspects of their own subjectivity.

This biopolitical exploration was short-lived, however. By the time of the next Parisian exhibition of the decorative arts in 1925, the feminine aesthetic had been eclipsed. Le Corbusier's 'Pavillon de L'Esprit Nouveau' with its minimalist aesthetic of the straight line was considered by the critics to be the only really 'modern' architecture in the exposition. In Le Corbusier's own words, the Pavillon constituted 'a rejection of decorative art as such' (cited in Troy, p. 193). With it, came a rejection of the feminine as a guiding force in both modern art and architecture. In his radical adherence to the controlling discourses of Good Design, Le Corbusier once again banishes 'the ladies' from their aesthetic meddling:

> So young ladies became crazy about decorative art . . . Girls' boarding schools made room for periods of applied Art and the History in their timetables . . . At one point it looked as if decorative art would founder among young ladies, had not the exponents of the decorative ensemble wished to show, in making their name and establishing their profession, that male abilities were indispensable in this field: considerations of ensemble, organization, sense of unity, balance proportion, harmony.
>
> (Le Corbusier quoted in Sparke 1995, p. 111)

Although the curving lines of Art Nouveau would make a modified reappearance in Art Deco and still retain appeal today, in architecture and decoration the heroic modern obsession with the right angle and straight line would dominate for the next 50 years. Wollen's 'great masculine renunciation' had begun. Or perhaps I should say, returned.

This reading of the flow of aesthetic discourses and their relations to the unconscious supports Rancière's arguments outlined in Chapter 3 regarding the *a priori* nature of aesthetic forces and their integration into politics. It also confirms his claims about the role of aesthetics in the distribution of the sensible and decisions about what is considered inside or outside of art and politics, including how these things should be portrayed, and what can be said about them. During the Rococo period, the acceptance of this avowedly feminine aesthetic corresponded to a greater openness to or empathy with the role of women in society. Looking at this phenomenon from the perspective of sexual difference greatly changes Rancière's timeline, however. Looked at this way, the real revolution began in the Baroque/Rococo period of the 17th and early 18th centuries, and, paradoxically, the time period that Rancière characterizes as the most important in terms of the distribution of the sensible in my reading becomes a decisively regressive time when women are banished from painting. These changes highlight my arguments about the importance of imagining things from the perspective of sexual difference, and the key changes in our understanding of politics that such a point of view can bring.

Conclusion

I believe there is important evidence that a biopolitical event fuelled by the energies of sexual difference took place in the Rococo period. In Rococo's swarming curves, both men and women engaged in a contra-sexual exploration that blurred the lines of gender identity and led to significant political change. Perhaps it was the Baroque sensibility of the fold that allowed this opening. The curvature of matter emphasized by Deleuze (1993) evokes a notion of an infinite mystery that cannot be explored if one ignores these curves, focusing on the point on the line. Both the point and the curve are indispensible, but in a situation where the curve is devalued, the mystery is not there.

There is no question that the French Revolution ultimately led to a dramatic erosion of any rights women may have gained during that century. As Germaine de Staël lamented, 'since the Revolution men had found it politically and morally useful to reduce women to the most absurd mediocrity' (quoted in Gutwirth 1992, p. xvi). Joan Scott (1996) points out that elite women, at least, actually had more power during the Rococo period than they did in the post-Revolutionary period. Despite this defeat, however, she argues that one of the most significant legacies of the French Revolution was the irreversible imprint of the forces of sexual difference onto the language of liberal claims for political recognition and rights. In the Jungian language of alchemy, a new *coniunctio* had been achieved, and there was no turning back.

This biopolitical openness created a space not unlike the interval of *Eros* I described in my analysis of Demeter and Persephone in Chapter 4. What went on in the swarming curves of the labyrinthine Rococo was not necessarily 'deep', for a labyrinth is horizontal, but it is no less profound for being so. A more comprehensive intuition of a combination of the masculine points of *logos* and the joining, feminine curves of *Eros* hints at a labyrinthine journey where the heroic Theseus is guided by the wisp of Ariadne's thread. In fact, the labyrinth might be the most appropriate metaphor for Rococo's swarming curves. To borrow from Latour's (2004, p. 213) description of the *multiverse*, one might also characterize it as multiple articulations between points that disrupt the flow of parallel lines, producing turbulent eddies: an apt, Deleuzean-inspired insight that describes the unique biopolitical moments of the Rococo and *Art Nouveau* periods. I will pursue this politics of surface further in my analysis of the Postmodern in Chapter 7.

I have provided numerous references in this chapter that evoke a sense of a transpersonal, libidinal energy 'ripped from historical narratives' and layered by sexual difference. Regardless of the time period, although the words 'effeminate' and 'feminine' are often used disparagingly and in a sexist and essentialist manner, this energy is clearly transformative. Whether one is discussing political economy or aesthetics, it is associated with some of the most revolutionary changes in history, including the years of the Enlightenment preceding the French Revolution and the late 19th century struggles of the suffragists. What remains to be seen is how it might be more directly implicated in the development of capitalist markets, a question that will be examined in the next chapter.

Bibliography

Bergson, H. (2007) *Creative Evolution*, Palgrave Macmillan, New York.
Conley, T. (1993) 'Translator's Foreword: A Plea for Leibniz', in *The Fold: Leibniz and the Baroque*, ed. G. Deleuze, University of Minnesota Press, Minneapolis, MN, pp. ix–xx.

Crow, T. (1995) *Emulation: Making Artists for Revolutionary France*, Yale University Press, New Haven, CT.

Deleuze, G. (1993) *The Fold: Leibniz and the Baroque*, University of Minnesota Press, Minneapolis, MN.

Duncan, C. (1976) *The Pursuit of Pleasure: The Rococo Revival in French Romantic Art*, Garland Publishing, New York and London.

de Goncourt, E. and de Goncourt, J. (1929/1862) *La femme au dix-huitième siècle*, Flammarion, Paris.

Gutwirth, M. (1992) *Twilight of the Goddesses: Women and Representation in the French Revolutionary Era*, Rutgers University Press, New Brunswick, NJ.

Hardt, M. and Negri, A. (2009) *Commonwealth*, Belnap Press of the Harvard University Press, Cambridge, MA.

Hillman, J. (1985) *Anima*, Spring Publications, Dallas, TX.

Hirschman, A. (1977) *The Passions and the Interests*, Princeton University Press, Princeton, NJ.

Hyde, M. (2006) *Making Up the Rococo: François Boucher and His Critics*, Getty Research Institute, Los Angeles, CA.

Jung, C. G. (1977) *Collected Works*, vol. 14, trans. R. F. C. Hull, Bollingen Series, Princeton University Press, Princeton, NJ.

Lajer-Burcharth, E. (1999) *Necklines: The Art of Jacques-Louis David after the Terror*, Yale University Press, New Haven, CT.

Lambert, G. (2004) *The Return of the Baroque in Modern Culture*, Continuum, New York and London.

Latour, B. (2004) 'How to Talk About the Body? The Normative Dimension of Science Studies', *Body and Society*, vol. 10, nos. 2–3, pp. 205–229.

Marx, K. (1949) *Capital*, vol. 1, George Allen & Unwin Ltd, London.

Murray, P. (1968) 'Introduction', in *Renaissance and Baroque*, trans. Kathrin Simon, Cornell University Press, Ithaca, NY, pp. 1–12.

Potts, A. (1990) 'Beautiful Bodies and Dying Heroes: Images of Ideal Manhood in the French Revolution', *History Workshop Journal*, vol. 30, no. 1, pp. 1–21.

Rancière, J. (2004) *The Politics of Aesthetics: The Distribution of the Sensible*, trans. Gabriel Rockhill, Continuum, London and New York.

Saisselin, R. (1960) 'The Rococo as a Dream of Happiness', *The Journal of Aesthetics and Art Criticism*, vol. 19, no. 2, pp. 145–152.

Scott, J. (1996) *Only Paradoxes to Offer: French Feminists and the Rights of Man*, Harvard University Press, Cambridge, MA.

Scott, K. (1996) *The Rococo Interior*, Yale University Press, New Haven, CT.

Silverman, D. (1992) *Art Nouveau in Fin-de-Siècle France*, University of California Press, Berkeley, CA.

Solomon-Godeau, A. (1997) *Male Trouble: A Crisis in Representation*, Thames and Hudson, London.

Sombart, W. (1967) *Luxury and Capitalism*, University of Michigan Press, Ann Arbor, MI.

Sparke, P. (1995) *As Long as It's Pink*, Pandora Press, London.

Troy, N. (1991) *Modernism and the Decorative Arts in France: Art Nouveau to Le Corbusier*, Yale University Press, New Haven, CT.

Williams, R. (1977) *Marxism and Literature*, Oxford University Press, Oxford.

Wölfflin, H. (1968) *Renaissance and Baroque*, Cornell University Press, Ithaca, NY.

Wollen, P. (1993) 'Out of the Past: Fashion/Orientalism/the Body', in *Raiding the Icebox: Reflections on Twentieth Century Culture*, Indiana University Press, Bloomington and Indianapolis, pp. 1–34.

Wollstonecraft, M. G. (1972) *Posthumous Works of Mary Wollstonecraft Godwin*, vol. III, Augustus M. Kelley Publishers, Clifton, NJ.

Zizek, S. (1989) *The Sublime Object of Ideology*, Verso, London and New York.

Chapter 6

Erotic economics

Ever since capitalism became defined as such, a plethora of psychologists and social commentators have linked it to mental illness. Early socio-political commentaries linked capitalism to neurasthenia (Beard), hysteria (Charcot), and anomie (Durkheim). More recently, it has been associated with schizophrenia (Deleuze and Guattari (1983 & 1987), Harvey (1990), and Jameson (1995)), bipolar disorder (Martin 2007), depression (Berardi 2009a & 2009b) and post-traumatic stress disorder (Väliaho 2012). Despite a great variety of explanations and interpretations, the common link in these analyses is a connection (or better said, a *dis-connection*) between the material, or economic, basis of our lives and the individual and collective psyche. What is the cause of this disconnection?

Freud regarded many of these ailments as neuroses caused by repression of the pleasure principle by the reality principle. A central tenet of his thought is that 'animal man' possessed primitive drives that had to be repressed for civilization to progress. These unconscious drives lead people to focus on attaining pleasure and avoiding those tasks (such as work) that may be unpleasant. One of these essential drives, he argued, is the life instinct comprising sexual urges, or *Eros*. Freud's conception of *Eros*, of course, differed significantly from that of Jung and Deleuze, who conceived of desire much more broadly to include non-sexual manifestations that may erupt in the form of cultural production, from art to work.

In contrast to Freud's account, the libidinal economy literature (Deleuze and Guattari 1983 & 1987; Lyotard 1993) argues there is an economically productive element of erotic desire. Less, discussed, however, is the fact that the economic discourses surrounding these libidinal forces are frequently gendered. Indeed, going back to some of the most influential political economy of the 17th and 18th centuries, one finds reference to a passionate, erotic force that appears to be integrally related to the development of capitalist markets. Often portrayed as feminine and described in negative terms as hysterical, emotional, and irrational, this erotic aspect of the market was regarded as something that had to be disciplined and controlled.

Over time, we have gradually adapted the role of this erotic aspect of the market, although not, as many have noted, in a way that relieves the psychological discomfort associated with its repression. Addressing this mental distress more directly, therefore, involves a metaphorical reclining of the capitalist market on the psychoanalytical couch. Doing this effectively means going beyond the relatively narrow understanding of *Eros* emphasized in Freud's work.

Eros

Freud described the repression of *Eros,* or the pleasure principle, most concisely in his *Civilization and Its Discontents.* He saw *Eros* as one of the primary ways humans find happiness and pleasure. In an uncivilized state, that of the 'primal horde', humans might instinctively follow their desire for sexual pleasure without limitation (Freud (1961, p. 54). There are problems with this, however, the principal one being economic scarcity. If humans are to survive, they must be willing to forgo pleasure and work in order to support themselves with food and shelter. Since this is antithetical to the instincts, the 'reality principle' forces humans to deal with the conditions of economic scarcity. In Freud's view, this repression may be psychically painful, but it allows us to live together as a society and to achieve the control of nature that enhances our survival. Marcuse (1966, p. 12) summarizes Freud's conception of the transition in values from the pleasure principle to the reality principle necessary for civilization to develop:

From:	*To:*
immediate satisfaction	delayed satisfaction
pleasure	restraint of pleasure
joy (play)	toil (work)
receptiveness	productiveness
absence of repression	security

Marcuse expanded on Freud's ideas by offering an adaptation of the reality principle he believed was more appropriate to modern capitalism, called the *performance principle.* Under the performance principle, society is stratified according to competitive economic performance and the domination of social labour increases due to strict standards of rationalization and efficiency. Controlled as such, work becomes even further alienated from pleasure, since 'Men do not live their own lives but perform pre-established functions' (p. 45).

The libidinal economy literature, associated primarily with the work of Deleuze and Guattari (1983 & 1987), but also with Lyotard (1993), critiques both Freud's approach and the ways in which capitalism repressed and distorted this desire. As opposed to the Freudian/Lacanian view of desire as 'lack' or the craving for something or someone that one does not possess, libidinal economics views desire more positively as a productive force that can have a direct impact on economic or social production. In this respect, as I have shown, Deleuze and Guattari's understanding of desire and concepts such as becoming-woman, or becoming-animal, have more affinity with the Jungian/Bergsonian legacy of vital energy than with the Freudian understanding of libido.

For Deleuze, (as for Jung) these libidinal energies can be 'canalized' or redirected to manifest themselves directly in economic practices, without any sort of mediation or transformation (Cooper and Murphy 2005). But economic events and institutions are not just manifestations of unconscious desires; they are also represented in libidinal terms. Hence debates regarding economic crisis are frequently shaped by attempts to repress or reform these desires. Cameron et al (2011), for example, show how debates surrounding the financial crisis of 2007–2009 were expressed in libidinal terms, portraying the actions of financial actors as libidinal excesses that needed to be repressed or reformed by more moral institutions.

As liberating as Deleuze and Guattari's conceptions of the body and desire are, they present an individual-centred representation of the economy that closely mimics libertarian and neo-liberal conceptions of the market (Cameron et al 2011, Gammon and Palan 2006). Although desiring-machines intersect and combine, the ultimate reference point for all of these flows is individual subjectivity. I want to interject a collective element of sexual difference into this discussion by examining discourses of political economy from the 17th century to the present. This exercise will show not only an emphasis on the *Logos* of capitalism emphasized by Polanyi (1944) in Chapter 3, but on its *Eros* as well. Importantly, these erotic aspects of capitalist markets are frequently gendered feminine, albeit in a negative way.

Since the 17th century, capitalist markets have been described in gendered terms, with luxury spending and credit described as feminine and linked to all manner of sin and irrationality. Desire for material goods and consumption are frequently described as feminine, as if we seek to fulfil some primal feminine desire through the acquisition of sensual, material things. Thus, it is not surprising that we find the feminine and consumption linked in economic theory as part of a broader western discourse that associates an instinctive, irrational consumer with the feminine (Slater 1997, Chapter 2). Luxury consumption, in particular, is associated not just with women, but with 'foreignness' (Berg and Eger 2003). The irrational other is then contrasted to the rational, masculine saviour of 'civilization' and must be controlled or repressed. *Eros* must be restrained by *Logos* for civilization to exist.

Jung's ideas regarding the contra-sexual nature of the psyche are interesting in the context of political economy discourse because when commentators referred to the market or market actors as feminine, they were frequently referring to men, not women. Thus, they criticized the market for making society or individual men 'effeminate'. It is as if they were referring to a fearful feminine energy that not only lurks in the shadows of men's psyches, but pervades society as a whole. There have been analysts, such as Montesquieu, Mandeville, and Sombart, who have recognized the feminine aspects of commerce in a positive sense. Subsequently, however, these feminine aspects have been devalued by a discourse that portrays them as inferior and other, and then tossed across a boundary (to borrow a metaphor from Kristeva) that separates them from all that is rational, moral and good.

It is possible to remain agnostic on the issue of whether *Eros* actually *is* a feminine force, and still accept the argument that it is denigrated and repressed in contemporary political economy. Although I acknowledge the problems inherent in such essentialism, I believe that there is merit in consciously recognizing a feminine erotic aspect (in the Jungian sense) to the market. As Spivak has suggested, this emphasis on the feminine essence of *Eros* can be used strategically in a manner that disrupts and exposes the masculine values hegemonic in economic discourse (Best 2011; Spivak 1993, p. 5). In this case, I wonder if we might pull the energy of *Eros* away from the bodies of women to bring it into Deleuze's *intermezzo*, or Jung's subtle body to show how an emphasis on the energies of *Eros* have shaped, and might be used to transform, economic practices. Examining the gendered representations of libidinal energies affords different interpretations and new insights into the discomforts and crises of capitalism, as well as solutions for our dis-ease.

Eros versus *Logos*

It is possible to trace the lines of a profound distinction between a conception of a disciplined, masculine, moral aspect of the market, and pleasure (characterized as a feminine, hedonistic *Eros*) in economic debates dating back to the 17th century. Drawing on the work of Pocock, Martin points out that by the 19th century the market and its actors were considered masculine. In the 17th and 18th centuries, however, the capitalist market and the blossoming legion of entrepreneurs that fuelled its expansion were frequently referred to as 'effeminate' and associated with mental instability (Martin 2007). In this time period, the word effeminate referred both to a

164 Genealogies

condition of instability and to men who became more like women because of their excessive devotion to them (Laqueur 1990, p. 123).

Pocock argues that in the 17th and 18th centuries, property, including mobile forms of property such as commodities, was considered 'both an extension and a prerequisite of personality' (Pocock 1985, p. 103). In ancient Greek thought, property in the form of *oikos*, or the household, was considered essential to being a moral citizen and leading the good life. It was not considered appropriate to trade or exchange this property for profit, however, because these activities were regarded as incompatible with citizenship. Commercial activity was considered ignoble and inappropriate for aristocrats and members of the privileged landholding classes. Ironically, as Pocock points out, this aristocratic disdain for commercial activity remains a central aspect of leftist political economy. He places Marx in the company of a long line of Western moralists who mistrusted money and the process of exchange, and warned against the perils of being drawn into a wholly commodified lifestyle at odds with the natural and divine order outlined by the Greeks.

By the 18th century the 'virtue' of the heroic 'patriot' such as the landed gentleman was contrasted with the 'corruption' of the traders (Pocock, p. 109). Especially as the creation of government bonds and a system of credit grew, the person who made their livelihood by trade was portrayed as

> a feminised, even an effeminate being, still wrestling with his own passions and hysterias and with interior and exterior forces let loose by his fantasies and appetites, and symbolized by such archetypically female goddesses of disorder as Fortune, Luxury, and more recently Credit herself ... Therefore, in the eighteenth-century debate over the new relations of polity to economy, production and exchange are regularly equated with the ascendancy of the [erotic] passions and the female principle.
>
> (p. 114)

Building on Pocock's argument, Ingrassia argues that this gendering of the new commerce was partly due to the tendency to label anything that is devalued as feminine. It also reflected, however, the growing presence and involvement of women in the markets. Between 1690 and 1753, women comprised 20 percent of investors in major stock and bank funds (Ingrassia 1998, p. 20). In some senses, therefore, the fear of a rising tide of feminine energy was based in material reality, making it all the more terrifying and challenging to the status quo.

Even at the time, however, there were thinkers who saw an advantage to this rising tide of feminine energy. Hirschman argued in his exegesis of

Montesquieu's *doux commerce* principle, for example, that there was a propensity in late 17th-century thought to perceive the gentleness of the market as capable of harnessing the violence of the heroic patriots so revered in the classical approach, who had a tendency to go to war to defend the 'good life'. As Hirschman noted, the French word *doux* is difficult to translate. He defined it variously as 'sweetness, softness, calm, and gentleness and is the antonym of violence' (Hirschman 1977, p. 59). The word *commerce* is also worth examining because in the 17th and 18th centuries it had meaning apart from the notion of business or trade that we associate with it today. At the time, in both English and French the word *commerce* also referred to conversation, often between two persons of the opposite sex (p. 61). Today, the *Oxford English Dictionary* still lists 'intercourse' as a possible meaning for commerce.

According to Hirschman, a perspective emerged in the 17th century that the heroic passions of the aristocracy, which everywhere had caused war and destruction, could be balanced by the more mundane interests of commerce. In *Esprit des lois,* Montesquieu made the argument that 'it is almost a general rule that wherever the ways of man are gentle (*moeurs douces*) there is commerce, and wherever there is commerce, there the ways of men are gentle' (quoted in Hirschman, p. 60). As noted in Chapter 5, this application of the term *moeurs douces* to the market arose in the context of a broader tendency in 18th-century French polite society that praised the impact of the sensibilities and gentle manners of women on men and diminished the differences between the sexes (Hyde 2006, p. 148). Hence, although it was still considered a passion, moneymaking was considered a 'calm passion', provided it was held in check.

This clash between moralism and the feminine sensibilities of women is also inherent to two early 20th century accounts of the development of capitalism: those of Max Weber and his colleague, Werner Sombart. Weber's well-known account of the role of the protestant work ethic in the development of capitalism emphasized that capitalist trading had existed for several centuries prior to the full-blown appearance of industrial revolution in the 19th century. For Weber, however, the key distinction between previous capitalisms, both oriental and occidental, was the rationalization of profit making on a consistent, ongoing basis, as opposed to usurping large amounts of capital in a fell swoop in a series of individual events (like extremely preferential trading deals). He thus dated the emergence of Western capitalism in the 18th century, although the sources of this revolution obviously pre-date it.

Given the centrality of religion in European feudal society, he argued, it was logical to look to the church and organized religion as a central differentiating factor in occidental, as opposed to oriental capitalism. Specifically, he argued that the Calvinist quest for moral perfection and piety resulted in a more rationalized system of profit making that contrasted with previous mentalities of profit making. The spiritual preconditions for this began in the religious values of charity and thrift of the Catholic Church, which demanded that monks and nuns live ascetic lifestyles similar to those of later Puritan communities. In Catholicism, however, sinners who did not live up to these standards could be forgiven through confession, relieving them of the religious motivation to live their lives consistently according to these values. Only monks and nuns lived their lives according to ascetic values on a daily basis, which meant that the preconditions for rational profit making were restricted to these groups.

Following the Reformation, the abolition of monasteries and the constant quest for moral perfection demanded first by Luther, and then deepened by Calvin, spread the values of piety and asceticism more broadly through society. Calvinism demanded that everyday citizens live in a manner previously restricted to monks and nuns, motivated by the fear of burning in eternal hell if they failed to do so. Ironically, living by the values exemplified by Ben Franklin's adage 'a penny saved is a penny earned', which in turn was inspired by the Calvinist distaste for the accumulation of earthly goods, the Puritans began to get rich. Admonitions against wasting time, excessive sleep, excessive sexual intercourse (which was only for reproduction purposes and never to occur outside of marriage), and too much leisure and enjoyment also added to productivity.

Equally important, the Calvinist notion that each man had a 'calling' commanded by God encouraged the development of a division of labour (Weber 2003, pp. 158–61). Making money by pursuing this calling was acceptable, provided that one lived by the ascetic values outlined above. Over time, the demanding religious values of the Puritans were watered down and faded. By this time, however, the implications of the work ethic inspired by the Puritans had spread more broadly into society, accepted as the model not only for the moneymaking bourgeoisie, but for the workers they employed as well. According to Weber, this explained why the United States, with its Puritan origins, had more capitalists than any other country at the time he wrote his thesis.

Weber's association of the beginnings of capitalism with an ascetic, moral, and rather heroic discourse of hard work and denial was countered by Sombart's (1967) distinctly anti-heroic account in *Luxury and Capitalism*, which has more affinity with Montesquieu and Mandeveille's ideas discussed below. Sombart refuted Weber's claim that the Calvinist quest for moral perfection and piety was the source of capitalist development. In his early writings, Sombart had already countered Weber's claims regarding Protestant ethics by arguing that it was actually Judaism, not Puritanism, which originally set the stage for the ascetic values necessary for sustained capitalist production. In Judaism, he argued, one already finds many of the key elements Weber identified as unique to Protestantism: the idea of divine rewards and punishments, asceticism, a close relationship between religion and business, and the rationalization of life. Thus, Sombart proclaimed, 'Puritanism *is* Judaism' (cited in Siegelman 1967, p. xiii).

More relevant to my argument, however, are the ideas set up in his later tract *Luxury and Capitalism*. In this book, Sombart identifies the secularization of love, the growing prominence of women in royal courts, and the consequent demand for luxury items as the key drivers behind the rise of capitalism. As opposed to Weber's view that capitalism began in the 18th century, Sombart dates the origins of capitalism to the 13th and 14th centuries, with the rise of great Italian fortunes that were not based on the feudal economy. Instead, these fortunes were derived from trade and usurious money lending. The appearance of similar family fortunes occurred in Germany in the 15th and 16th centuries, and then in Holland, France, and England in the 17th century. What really incited the trend to more intensive as opposed to extensive forms of capital production, however, was the increase in demand for luxury items. This demand for excessive luxury, in turn, was due to 'the extent which women, especially women as objects of illicit love, have influenced the life pattern of our age' (Sombart 1967, p. 63).

Sombart is unequivocal in his emphasis on a process he refers to as the secularization of love in transforming society. 'I know of no event of greater importance for the formation of medieval and modern society,' he claimed, 'than the transformation in the relations between the sexes which occurred during the Middle Ages and through the eighteenth century' (p. 42). While the love life of the burgher may have been based on the sermons of Calvin and Knox, he argued, that of the courts, nobility and their sycophants evolved quite differently. It was these social contrasts that eventually led to the birth of the capitalist entrepreneur.

During the Middle Ages, according to Sombart, love was subordinated to the service of God. All unsanctioned and un-institutionalized love was considered a sin. The heavily veiled and covered woman of the early Middle Ages was 'estranged from the joyous spirit of living' and men took more interest in their dogs and hunting than love affairs. Changing attitudes toward love were reflected in paintings in the 15th century, however, when one begins to see the portrayal of a nude Adam and Eve, eventually followed by the celebration of the female body evident in works such as Botticelli's *Birth of Venus*. From this time on, poets, sculptors, and painters alike were united in their celebration of love and beauty, a process that culminated in the work of the Rococo artists Fragonard, Boucher, and Greuze, followed by Tintoretto, Rabelais, Aristo, and Rubens (pp. 46–47).

The hedonistic, aesthetic conception of woman and love that emerged during this period stood in sharp contrast to the religious restraints on love of the preceding period, to the point where love and marriage became differentiated. Although he had the greatest respect for marriage, for example, Montaigne maintained that love was related to pleasure, whereas marriage was a social institution with noble aims based more on friendship. As Rabelais and others further argued, love finds its highest justification not just outside of marriage, but outside of all institutions created for social or moral purposes. This not-so-subtle justification for extra-marital love affairs, Sombart argued, became the source of a wellspring of demand for luxury goods as enraptured kings and other nobility drowned their beloved mistresses in floods of jewellery, silk, luxury homes, and other forms of conspicuous consumption. At this time, women also began to dominate the Courts, beginning with the court of Francis I and reaching a peak of influence in the Court of Louis XIV. They became the tastemakers of their time, as women such as Louise de la Vallière, Madame de Pompadour, Madame Du Barry, and the grandest *cocotte* of all, Marie Antoinette, spent lavish amounts of money on clothing, carriages, and decorating their homes.

The impact of this massive spending was significant in itself, but it became more so when anyone connected with the court began to copy the consumption patterns of these trend-setting women. Monarchies in other countries patterned themselves after the extravagant French courts, with the Stuarts using the French courts as a model at the zenith of English royal spending, and similar patterns taking place in Germany, Spain, and elsewhere. As for the *nouveaux riches* bourgeoisie in Europe, which lacked the social capital of the aristocracy, the only way to communicate their wealth was to spend massive sums of money on lavish living. The result was the creation of highly efficient industries designed to meet the demand for luxury goods. One of the earliest industries to mechanize, for example, was the silk trade. Cities also sprung up in areas where there was concentrated luxury spending, as the more industrious burghers moved to locations of high demand.

In sum, sensuous pleasure is Sombart's version of the 'invisible hand' that led to the rationalization and improvement of productivity that characterized capitalism. 'In the last analysis', he argued, 'it is our sexual life that lies at the root of the desire to refine and multiply the means of stimulating our senses, for sensuous pleasure and erotic pleasure are essentially the same' (pp. 60–61). Sombart accepted Veblen's argument that conspicuous consumption is the result of an attempt to outdo others in their quest for social distinction (an argument with parallels to Smith's). He argued that Veblen's point presupposes the existence of luxury spenders that others are trying to 'outdo', however. If one looks to the ultimate wellspring of the most basic lust for personal, materialistic luxury, 'it must be predicated on an awakened sensuousness and, above all, on a mode of life which has been influenced decisively by eroticism' (p. 61).

Siegelman (1967, p. xx) argues that there are parallels to Freud in this reading, given Sombart's emphasis on sexual gratification. Reading Sombart from a Jungian perspective, however, one gets the impression that rather than critiquing Weber or providing a comprehensive explanation for the birth of capitalism, he is trying to point to another way. He offers an explanation for the development of capitalism that perhaps does not explain everything, but is plausible, possibly complementary, yet hidden underneath the dusky taint of otherness. The orientalism of the Jew, the sexuality and femininity of the mistress, the prominent role of love, the immorality of luxury spending – how could these possibly be the foundation for an economy, a global trading and financial system? Given that Sombart was a critic of capitalism, his emphasis on the feminine sources of its development can be interpreted as misogynistic. Also, given the periodic presence of extended witch hunts and other anti-feminine political movements up to the mid-17th century (Federici 2004), his timeline is somewhat sweeping, ignoring some of the changes in the energies of sexual difference outlined in the previous chapter. From a Jungian/Deleuzean perspective, however, Sombart's explanation supports the possibility of an important feminine, but perhaps morally and politically unacceptable, aspect of capitalist markets that is regarded as decadent and irrational by those with more puritanical, heroic views of capitalism.

This puritanism reigned in early political economy as well. In order to be taken seriously, whether in the patriarchal worlds of Montesquieu's Enlightenment or Sombart's 20th-century capitalism, desire had to be portrayed as more moral and rational, and ultimately, masculine. By the end of the 18th century, Montesquieu's gently erotic tribute to the benefits of feminine *commerce* had been transformed into a reforming discourse that contrasted the undisciplined aspects of the market with moral, masculine ones. In my view, this was a consequence of two factors, the first being a targeted effort to legitimate and reform luxury consumption and *laissez-faire* by transforming them into masculine, as opposed to feminine forces, the second deriving from a concept of efficiency that developed out of Locke's concept of 'improvement'.

The first trend is especially evident in the work of Joseph Addison in his early 18th-century newspaper *The Spectator*. Although it advocated commercial values, *The Spectator* also made clear that there were moral and aesthetic values so important to the social fibre that they must not be compromised by the pursuit of wealth. This quest for a moral code of taste had a gendered tone, as aesthetic values mixed with political ones and the consumption of 'effeminate' goods from France and the Orient came under attack. Addison compared women's fascination with china from the Orient to a young man's weakness for prostitution. French food was rejected in favour of more traditional British fare. It was not the idea of consumption he was challenging, nor the amount. It was the *way* in which the money was spent that should be a reflection of virtue and morality (Lubbock 1995). This also required respect for the masculine aesthetic referred to as Good Design and appropriately moral ways of spending (Jenkins 2006).

Of course, there were voices that exposed this moralization, such as Mandeville, who published his first edition of the *Fable of the Bees* shortly after the founding of *The Spectator*. He abhorred the moral highness of *The Spectator*, referring to Addison as a 'parson in a tye-wig' and arguing that although it was almost always immoral, the desire for luxury was highly productive (Mandeville 1957). Scoffing at the claims of the wealthy that massive spending on their homes or luxury goods was somehow their public duty, as well as the moral highness of *The Spectator*, he sought to expose the hypocrisy of these protestations by arguing that such expenditures could only be a reflection of self-interest and greed. Mandeville, nonetheless, championed such spending in recognition of the fact that it was a driving force of the economy, albeit not for the reasons claimed by luxury consumers. As he notes in the preface to *Fable*:

> For the main Design of the Fable . . . is to shew the Impossibility of enjoying all the most elegant Comforts of Life that are to be met with in an industrious, wealthy and powerful Nation, and at the same time be bless'd with all the Virtue and Innocence that can be wished for in a Golden Age; from thence to expose the Unreasonableness and Folly of those, that desirous of being opulent and flourishing People, and wonderfully greedy after all the Benefits they can receive as such, are yet always murmuring at and exclaiming against those Vices and Inconveniences.
>
> (p. 7)

In his view, even the most virtuous producers who practise the strictest frugality in their lives are dependent on the excesses of others; the merchant who trades cloth abroad in order to purchase wines and brandies is dependent on lavishness and drunkenness, just as the druggist is dependent on poisoning or the swordcutler to bloodshed (p. 85). Society would be best to abandon such moral pretence and openly embrace luxury spending, Mandeville argued. To charges that excessive spending on luxuries was 'enervating', he replied that

> Clean Linen weakens a Man no more than Flannel; Tapistry, fine Painting or good Wainscot are no more unwholesome than bare Walls; and a rich Couch, or a gilt Chariot are no more enervating than the cold Floor or a Country Cart.
>
> (p. 119)

With regard to charges that luxury spending was 'effeminate' and would lead to military weakness, he argued that the military might of a nation could not be compromised by spending on luxuries, so long as their soldiers were disciplined and well-paid (p. 123).

Mandeville's work caused a minor scandal at the time, so overt was it in its opposition not just to Whig political and moral principles, but also to Puritan religious ones. Despite its many florid references to lewd women and dissolute sailors, however, the *Fable* was of pivotal importance to British political economy. It served not only as a foil for the writing of the *Spectator* and other commentators (Frances Hutcheson in particular), but also provided one of the most detailed analyses at that time of the concepts of the division of labour and *laissez-faire*. It had a key influence on the ideas of Hutcheson's protégée, Adam Smith, despite the latter's objection to Mandeville's central argument regarding morality.

It was these two writers of the Scottish Enlightenment who brought Mandeville's colourful fable highlighting the immoral pleasures of luxury consumption into the moralist, rationalist fold. One of Smith's most important contributions was to moralize luxury consumption and make it more amenable to civilized society. Smith definitely had concerns about the feminine impact of consumption and commerce, noting that, 'By having their minds constantly employed on the arts of luxury, [men] grow effeminate and dastardly' (cited in Hirschman, p. 106). Nonetheless, in his support for the widespread benefits of *laissez-faire* he provides a moral rationale for the positive impact of both these economic forces.

Interestingly, this is first set out in a discussion of aesthetics. In his chapter on beauty and the utility of art, Smith begins by acknowledging that it is commonly assumed that harmony and utility are the central characteristics of a beautiful object or building. In the final analysis, however, Smith argued that it is not the actual features of a building that attract us, but the lifestyle that accompanies it. In our imagination, we see the ease and pleasure of the lives of those who inhabit such buildings and use such objects on a daily basis, which increases their desirability. Anyone accused of this would deny it as the most superficial and trifling of influences, yet it is this tendency which 'rouses and keeps in continual motion the industry of mankind' (Smith 1948, p. 214). In their quest for status through consumption, the wealthy are

> led by an invisible hand to make nearly the same distribution of the necessaries of life which would have been made had the earth been divided into equal portions among all its inhabitants; and thus, without intending it, without knowing it, advance the interest of the society, and afford means to the multiplication of the species.
>
> (p. 215)

As Hirschman noted, Smith effectively equated the heroic 'passion' for honour and respect in the eyes of others with the calmer 'interests' of the market. In doing so, he made the consumption of even luxury goods natural and moral, portraying it as an impetus to the hard work and striving so beloved to the puritan soul. Indeed, in the absence of the incentive to consume and to appear grander in the eyes of others, the desire to work hard appears irrational and unnecessary in Smith's eyes. In the process, he legitimated and made acceptable two major moral dilemmas: commerce and luxury consumption.

With regard to production, his emphasis on the efficiency of a rational division of labour contributed to the notion that developments in the world of commerce were actually improving society. The concept of 'improvement' appeared long before Smithian economics in the work of Locke and Petty, and essentially referred to the act of working on something (like land or raw materials) and deriving a profit from it (Wood 1992). Smith's contribution was to develop further the link between improvement and the division of labour, which he identified as one of the primary sources of increased economic productivity. In doing so, he provided a structure of discipline that set the stage for Marcuse's idea of the performance principle: the domination of both land and labour according to standards of rationalization and efficiency. He showed in a manner convincing to his 18th century readership that a commerce that appeared to be irrational, immoral and out of control was actually rational, moral, and improving. I agree with Wood's conclusion that this conception of improvement, derived from Locke, is the source of some of the most egregious travesties against nature and society inherent in capitalism – in other words, an anti-erotic force.

By the 19th century, the erotic and feminine nature of the market appears to be almost completely sublimated in economic discourse. The effeminate and irrational individual driven purely by desire is replaced by the completely rational *Homo oeconomicus* of neo-classical economics, the new hero of the day. Both the entrepreneur and consumption are made respectable, sanctified by the moralization of consumption and the concept of improvement. Mandeville's rejection of false morality and appreciation of the delectable (if scandalous) attractions of pleasure, as well as Montesquieu's *doux commerce*, are eclipsed by a moral and masculine model of the market.

As noted above, this moralistic view is replicated in Marx's political economy, where a productionist bias, an emphasis on the role of improving productivity, and the overwhelming importance of socioeconomic class difference in capitalist development tend to diminish the transformative aspects of the sensuous pleasures of consumption, relegating it to commodity fetishism. To be fair, Marx's description of the relations of production and the importance of capitalism in bringing workers together to see their common interests on the factory floor do emphasize the erotic (in the Jungian sense) aspects of capitalism. It was, after all, his call for the workers of the world to unite and lose their chains that created the First International. But the overall adversarial nature of the class relationship, combined with his emphasis on the implacable trajectory of the *Logos* of capitalism and the moralistic tone not just of his critique, but that of neo-Marxists as well, tends to overshadow this erotic element.

Sombart's work marked an exception to this moralistic view on capitalist markets that marked the overall tone of the political economy of the first half of the 20th century, but as Alexander notes, it was Keynes who had the greatest success in articulating the importance of pleasure and non-rational ways of being in a manner more acceptable to positivist, moral ears (Alexander 2011). It is important to remember that Keynes was a member of the Bloomsbury Group, whose overall approach to art, literature, and economics I described in Chapter 1 as 'anti-heroic' (Reed 2004). Whether they were painting domestic scenes, decorating houses (or university rooms in the case of Keynes), or writing about domestic life, the 'Bloomsberries' focused on the everyday as opposed to the morally heroic. Indeed, the *raison d'être* of this group was the rejection of the discourses of bourgeois morality and the embrace of eroticism and the pleasure principle. Their focus on decoration meant the celebration of the ornamental, as opposed to the purely functional. Paintings and décor frequently featured vibrant colour, and Bloomsbury artists made painted tables and chairs, light fixtures, and textiles that rejected the hegemonic minimalism of Modern design discourse.

In his economic writings, Keynes continually focused on the problems of attributing rationality to human nature, the importance of considering community in economic calculus, and invoked an aesthetic, as opposed to utilitarian, conception of 'fitness' or appropriateness of economic action (Maurer 2002). Maurer (2002) argues that Keynes's *Treatise on Probability* stresses a profoundly organic, anti-atomistic approach to probability that relies on this intuitive, aesthetic sense of 'fitness'. Individual factors interact and affect each other in varying and contingent combinations, carrying different weights of influence in different situations (pp. 108–9).

Keynes's probabilistic approach to both aesthetics and economics is ensconced, in Jungian terms, firmly in *Luna* – that misty interval between the points. In a statement that bears remarkable parallels to Jung's and Deleuze's emphasis on the decisive importance of unknown affective experience, he remarks in the *General Theory*,

> Most . . . of our decisions to do something positive . . . can only be taken as a result of animal spirits – of a spontaneous urge to action

rather than inaction, and not as the outcome of a weighted average of quantitative benefits multiplied by quantitative probabilities.

(Keynes quoted in Maurer, p. 117)

Instead of applying a Benthamite calculus of rationality to economics, which in his view had impoverished human nature as opposed to enriching it, Keynes argued that economic decisions had to be valued in the context of an 'aesthetics of fitness' that took into consideration 'valuable springs of feeling' (pp. 124–5). This approach characterized all of Keynes's work, whether he was discussing aesthetics, probabilities, or the new international clearing union he devised for post-war international trade.

Keynes, and the Bloomsbury world he lived in, can be viewed as a move away from the 19th century morality that characterized both British political economy and its aesthetics, where even critiques of *laissez-faire* capitalism took a nationalist and highly moral tone that often took the form of an attack on improper forms of consumption and taste. For example, Ruskin eloquently criticized the impact of the *Logos* of the division of labour on the soul of the worker:

It is not, truly speaking, the labour that is divided; but the men – divided into mere segments of men – broken into small fragments and crumbs of life; so that all the little pieces of intelligence that is left in a man is not enough to make a pin, or a nail, but exhausts itself in making the point of a pin, or the head of a nail.

(Ruskin 1852, p. 293)

But he still maintained a highly moralizing discourse regarding appropriate economic behaviour. Unconvinced by Smith's belief that improvement and productivity emerged from the quest for more and more commodities, Ruskin still adhered to a very principled stance where the real value of a nation's wealth was the moral sign attached to it. This highly moral approach to consumption and design was pervasive in 19th century commentary, with women taking the brunt of the blame for the 'bric-a-brac' deemed antithetical to good taste (Cohen 2006; Sparke 1995).

Although greatly influenced by Ruskin, Morris avoided the ascetic, religious overtones implicit in Ruskin's morality in favour of a connection with pleasure (Arata 2003, p. 25). He embraced the ostensibly feminine realm of home decoration, as well as traditional women's handicraft such as embroidery. The socialism he advocated was a dreamy, utopian one with an emphasis on taking pleasure in work that would re-emerge later in the ideas of Keynes. The interconnections between art, pleasure, and labour were essential to Morris's understanding of a just system of labour. Indeed, he defined art as pleasure in labour:

> That thing which I understand by real art is the expression by man of his pleasure in labour. I do not believe he can be happy in his labour without expressing that happiness; and especially this is so when he is at work at anything in which he specially excels . . . As to the bricklayer, the mason, and the like – these would be artists, and doing not only necessary, but beautiful, and therefore happy work, if art were anything like what it should be. No, it is not such labour as this which we need to do away with, but the toil which makes the thousand and one things which nobody wants, which are used merely as the counters for the competitive buying and selling, falsely called commerce.
>
> (Morris 1988, p. 207)

Despite his emphasis on pleasure, moralistic assumptions regarding appropriate consumption are still implicit in his ideas. After Morris's death, as Reed notes, the Arts and Crafts movement became representative of a more nationalist 'Ye Olde England' style that became associated with the establishment. As cheaper, machine-made imitations of Morris & Co. designs flooded the market, any association with medieval craftwork seem ludicrous. Morris & Co. designs soon became officially sanctioned by the government, representing modern design in the 'History of British Furniture' exhibit at the Franco-British Exhibition of 1908. (Reed 2004, p. 115). This reflected not only how popularized Morris's designs had become, but also the degree to which his socialist associations were diluted after his death.

Aesthetically, Bloomsbury can be seen as a 'shabby chic' evolution of the Arts and Crafts movement – one that rejected its nationalist and moralistic undertones. In this respect, it can be seen as closer to the socialist individualism of Wilde and other members of the Aesthetic movement than the more Marxist influenced socialism of Morris. Both Wilde and Whistler had criticized the heavy-handed morality of the Arts and Crafts movement and their influence on the Bloomsbury was clear. Virginia Woolf's sister the painter Vanessa Bell, for example, had artistic connections with Whistler, and Roger Fry had direct connections with both. The individualism of the Aesthetes was attractive to the 'Bloomsberries', many of whom, despite their privileged class positions, could be considered outcasts in terms of identity politics. As Reed notes, 'As homosexuals, feminists, pacifists, or members of religious minorities, Bloomsbury's members had reasons to distrust majority culture' (p. 14). Utopian ventures, such as the countryside guilds popular in the Arts and Crafts movement, provided an element of surveillance repugnant to those on the margins, who found more support in the principles of individual rights.

Bloomsbury did adopt Morris's emphasis on decoration, however, pushing it even further toward what Reed calls 'housekeeping' and embracing decoration as the equivalent of art, despite the denigration of this term in Modern art circles. In their focus on colour, decoration, and significant form, Bloomsbury emulated the values of the French Post-Impressionists, with whom Fry had intimate ties. Ultimately, however, their dedication to the production of the sort of art that the Modernist critic Clement Greenberg would classify as 'kitsch' meant that the members of Bloomsbury were marginalized in the story of Modern Art (pp. 2–3).

The fascination of Bloomsbury artists with painting murals, making mosaics, designing or decorating houses (or university rooms, in the case of Keynes), or in Woolf's case writing novels about domestic life, are testimony to the groups embracing of the anti-heroic 'everyday' as opposed to the heroic designs of their contemporary, Le Corbusier. Indeed, they rejected the discourse of Good Design in significant ways. Their focus on decoration meant the celebration of the ornamental, as opposed to the purely functional. Paintings and décor frequently featured vibrant colour, and Bloomsbury artists made painted tables and chairs, light fixtures, and textiles.

Wicke (1994) claims that this style, combined with the writing of Woolf and the economics of Keynes, contributed to a Modernist re-writing of the market focused on consumption. The Bloomsbury style that emanated from their Omega workshop and from the homes and domestic decoration of Bloomsbury members, she claims, was an example of coterie consumption. If consumption can be considered as the creative exercise of taste, Bloomsbury served as an example to atomized consumers by providing a 'concerted effort of knowledge, taste and power' offering an alternative lifestyle (p. 10). She argues that Keynes's openness to consumption, irrationality, and culture coincides with Virginia Woolf's portrayal of modern life. Whether it is Clarissa Dalloway shopping for a party, or airplanes skywriting advertisements for toffee, Woolf provides a 'fluid, soft, disoriented' description that writes consumption into the experience of modern life. In doing so, she mirrors Keynes's anti-classical, a-rational conception of the market. In the work of both Keynes and Woolf, Wicke argues, consumption is stripped of its stigma. The magic of the marketplace becomes:

> soft, fluid magic, feminized, anarchic, yet interconnected, playful at best . . . The lines of demarcation between and among consumption and production, use value and exchange value, art and commerce, male and female, gay and straight, are unsettled and whirled about by Bloomsbury. Debt, savings and spending are refigured, rewritten, and relived.
>
> (pp. 21–22)

In Woolf's disoriented, amorphous readings of modern consumption and the market, we see the roots of the Postmodern, but with a softer, more embedded sensibility. Mrs. Dalloway's day of spending is embedded in memory, as each purchase invokes recollections of the past, and forgotten love. Similarly, Bloomsbury paintings, houses, and furniture were embedded in the home – albeit a frankly bohemian interpretation of one.

I believe that Bloomsbury's aesthetics and Keynes's economics are the product of a unique 'biopolitical moment' similar to the one I described in the Rococo. The liberal sexual mores of Bloomsbury were legendary, as married couples cohabited with lovers and members of the group moved easily and without judgment between homosexual and heterosexual relationships. This fluidity of gender, family, and identity could be the source of Bloomsbury's focus on the home, as members sought to re-define domesticity in ways that suited their non-conformist ways and enabled them to feel 'at home'. They embraced a marginal, transient modernity with a sensibility that Maurer argues is encapsulated in the word 'queer'.

Without attempting to diminish the meaning of this word in terms of its importance for sexual identity, I want to pull the word queer away from its usual association with sexual identity and apply it more broadly to the fluidity inherent to the process of renegotiating identity and subjectivity necessary for political change. As Hardt and Negri (2009, pp. 62–3) note, 'The biopolitical event . . . is always a queer event, a subversive process of subjectivization that, shattering ruling identities and norms, reveals the link between power and freedom, and thereby inaugurates an alternative production of subjectivity'. The aesthetic-economic moment of Bloomsbury, I believe, was one such biopolitical moment, where the rejection of what Foucault called biopower or power over life, was temporarily suspended by the experimentation of a small, and admittedly privileged, group of people.

Yet just as the Bloomsbury aesthetic was eclipsed by that of Modern minimalism (Reed 2004), Keynesian economics, if not abandoned, have been seriously censured by neo-liberal approaches to 'market fundamentalism' (Somers 2008). Despite the apparent renaissance of Keynesian policies in response to recent economic crises, contemporary neo-conservatives are fighting hard to reign in the excessive spending of this period, which many perceive as sinful. As Alexander points out, in the conservative commentaries on Greece, Iceland, or Ireland, there is a constant reprise of the morality theme that those who spend must be chastened and punished for their profligate ways. In response to European requests for North American assistance to support the Euro in June 2012, for example, a Conservative Canadian member of parliament was adamant that Canadians should not be asked 'to bail out *sumptuous* euro welfare-state countries' (Curry 2012, A4, my emphasis). Austerity is the new reality principle – *Eros* must be repressed.

178 Genealogies

As Pocock noted, however, leftists participate in morality discourses as well. Leftist politics are often characterized by a moral superiority of the working class or 'lowly' that cultivates hatred toward the 'high and mighty' and a sense of victimhood, resentment, and reaction (Gibson-Graham 2006, p. 5). The issue is not that this morality discourse has no inherent value, but that it has become overwhelmingly hegemonic. Citing Arendt, Gibson-Graham call for leftist approaches that foster a 'love of the world', emphasizing friendliness, trust, and conviviality, and using tactics such as 'seducing, cajoling, enrolling, enticing, inviting [with] a greater role . . . for invention and playfulness, enchantment and exuberance' (p. 7).

Developing and accepting such erotic aspects of economic life involves accepting that *Eros* has an ethic of its own. *Eros* in its broadest sense provides its own transcendent morality through wisdom, pleasure, and the gentle or '*doux*'. This means accepting the pleasure of consumption and revelling in the connections the economic brings. The challenge is to accept and find balance in both ethics: the ascetic morality of Weber's Puritan and the erotic morality of Diotima/Socrates/Plato (2001). Marcuse referred to this as 'sensuous rationality' or the development of a '*rationality of gratification* in which reason and happiness converge. It creates its own division of labor, its own priorities, its own hierarchy' (Marcuse 1966, p. 224).

Keynes had important insights into how these priorities must change, describing this adjustment in terms that might be considered 'slow work'. To face this change, he maintained, would require an alteration in our code of morals. We will have to get rid of 'pseudo-moral principles' and economic practices affecting the distribution of wealth and economic rewards. Instead, we will have to learn to 'spread the bread thin on the butter', taking advantage of our wealth through measures such as shared work, three-hour work days and 15-hour work weeks. If we can achieve this, he said,

> We shall once more value ends above means and prefer the good to the useful. We shall honour those who can teach us how to pluck the hour and the day virtuously and well, the delightful people who are capable of taking direct enjoyment in things, the lilies of the field who toil not, neither do they spin.
>
> (Keynes 1931, p. 372)

Keynes's evocation of the gentle pleasures of capitalism is far from the capitalism we live in today. As I noted above, the moralization of the market means that *Eros* has been usurped by the stratified standards of the reality/performance principle, which now has become 'hyper'-reality. Our desire is expressed almost entirely in the stratified symbols of socioeconomic status and achievement, justified by the moral standards of 'hard' (read endless) work. Yet as analysts from Marx to Baudrillard have commented, this world of the reality/performance principle is not 'real' – and thus its rewards are hollow and do not satiate desire. Hence, it is not surprising that the same pattern repeats itself over and over in the form of a crisis: we endlessly look for ways to materialize our desire (whether in the form of houses financed by sub-prime mortgages, or new financial instruments that generate enormous profits) that ultimately do not satisfy. Unbounded and uncontained, we go too far. We might then be subjected to moral chastening, but we are not sated. Repressed but unfulfilled, the pattern is destined to repeat itself. This hyper-real political economy will be the focus of the next chapter.

Bibliography

Alexander, J. (2011) 'Market as Narrative and Character', *Journal of Cultural Economy*, vol. 4, no. 4, pp. 477–488.

Arata, S. ed. (2003) 'Introduction', in *News from Nowhere*, Broadview, Peterborough, ON, pp. 11–49.

Berardi, F. "Bifo". (2009a) *The Soul at Work: From Alienation to Autonomy*, Semiotext(e), Los Angeles, distributed by MIT Press, Cambridge, MA.

Berardi, F. "Bifo". (2009b) *Precarious Rhapsody*, Minor Compositions, London, distributed by Autonomedia, New York.

Berg, M. and Eger, E. (2003) *Luxury in the Eighteenth Century*, Palgrave/Macmillan, London.

Best, S. (2011) *Visualizing Feeling: Affect and the Feminine Avant-Garde*, I.B. Tauris, London and New York.

Cameron, A, Nesvetailova, A. and Palan, R. (2011) 'Wages of Sin?' *Journal of Cultural Economy*, vol. 4, no. 2, pp. 117–135.

Cohen, D. (2006) *Household Gods: The British and Their Possessions*, Yale University Press, New Haven, CT.

Cooper, B. and Murphy, M. (2005) ' "Libidinal Economics": Lyotard and Accounting for the Unaccountable', in *New Economic Criticism: Studies at the Intersection of Literature and Economics*, eds. Mark Osteen and Martha Woodmansee, Routledge, Florence, KY, pp. 196–207.

Curry, B. (2012) 'P.M.'s EU Stand Angers Germany', *The Globe and Mail*, Friday June 8, 2012.

Deleuze, G. and Guattari, F. (1983) *Anti-Oedipus: Capitalism and Schizophrenia*, trans. Robert Hurley, Mark Seem, and Helen R. Lane, University of Minnesota Press, Minneapolis.

Deleuze, G. and Guattari, F. (1987) *A Thousand Plateaus: Capitalism and Schizophrenia*, trans. Brian Massumi, University of Minnesota Press, Minneapolis.

Federici, S. (2004) *Caliban and the Witch: Women, the Body, and Primitive Accumulation*, Autonomedia, Brooklyn, NY.

Freud, S. (1961) *Civilization and Its Discontents*, W.W. Norton and Co., New York.

Gammon, E. and Palan, R. (2006) 'Libidinal International Political Economy', in *International Political Economy and Postructural Politics*, ed. Marieke de Goede, Palgrave Macmillan, New York, pp. 97–114.

Gibson-Graham, J. K. (2006) *Postcapitalist Politics*, University of Minnesota Press, Minneapolis.

Hardt, M. and Negri, A. (2009) *Commonwealth*, The Belknap Press of Harvard University Press, Cambridge, MA.

Harvey, David. (1990) *The Condition of Postmodernity*, Blackwell, Cambridge, MA.

Hirschman, A. (1977) *The Passions and the Interests*, Princeton University Press, Princeton, NJ.

Hyde, M. (2006) *Making Up the Rococo: François Boucher and His Critics*, Getty Research Institute, Los Angeles.

Ingrassia, I. (1998) *Authorship, Commerce, and Gender in Early Eighteenth-Century England*, Cambridge University Press, Cambridge, UK.

Jameson, F. (1995) *Postmodernism or, the Cultural Logic of Late Capitalism*, Duke University Press, Durham.

Jenkins, B. (2006) 'The Dialectics of Design', *Space and Culture*, vol. 9, no. 2, pp. 195–209.

Keynes, J. M. (1931) 'Economic Possibilities for Our Grandchildren', in *Essays in Persuasion*, Macmillan and Co, London, pp. 358–373.

Laqueur, T. (1990) *Making Sex: Body and Gender from the Greeks to Freud*, Harvard University Press, Cambridge, MA.

Lubbock, J. (1995) *The Tyranny of Taste: The Politics of Architecture and Design in Britain 1550–1960*, Yale University Press, New Haven, CT.

Lyotard, J.-F. (1993) *Libidinal Economy*, Indiana University Press, Bloomington and Indiana.

Mandeville, B. (1957) *The Fable of the Bees*, vol. I, Oxford/Clarendon Press, Oxford.

Marcuse, H. (1966) *Eros and Civilization: A Philosophical Inquiry into Freud*, Beacon Press, Boston.

Martin, E. (2007) *Bipolar Expeditions: Mania and Depression in American Culture*, Princeton University Press, Princeton.

Maurer, B. (2002) 'Redecorating the International Economy: Keynes, Grant, and the Queering of Bretton Woods', in *Queer Globalizations: Citizenship and the Afterlife of Colonialism*, eds. Arnaldo Cruz-Malavé and Martin Manalansan, New York University Press, New York, pp. 100–133.

Morris, W. (1988) 'The Art of the People', in *William Morris by Himself*, ed. G. Naylor, Macdonald Orbis, London and Sydney, pp. 207–208.

Plato. (2001) *Symposium*, trans. Seth Benardete, University of Chicago Press, Chicago.

Pocock, J. G. A. (1985) *Virtue, Commerce, and History*, Cambridge University Press, Cambridge, UK.

Polanyi, K. (1944) *The Great Transformation*, Beacon Press, Boston.

Reed, C. (2004) *Bloomsbury Rooms: Modernism, Subculture, and Domesticity*, Yale University Press, New Haven, CT.

Ruskin, J. (1852) 'The Nature of the Gothic', in *News from Nowhere*, ed. S. Arata, Broadview, Peterborough, ON, pp. 277–280

Siegelman, P. (1967) 'Introduction', in *Luxury and Capitalism,* ed. W. Sombart, University of Michigan Press, Ann Arbor, MI.

Slater, D. (1997) *Consumer Culture and Modernity,* Polity Press, Cambridge, UK.

Smith, A. (1948) 'Theory of Moral Sentiments', in *Adam Smith's Moral and Political Philosophy,* ed. H. Schneider, Harper and Row, New York, pp. 7–274.

Sombart, W. (1967 /1913) *Luxury and Capitalism,* University of Michigan Press, Ann Arbor, MI.

Somers, M. (2008) *Geneologies of Citizenship: Markets, Statelessness, and the Right to have Rights,* Cambridge University Press, Cambridge, UK.

Sparke, P. (1995) *As Long as It's Pink,* Pandora Press, London.

Spivak, G. (1993) *Outside in the Teaching Machine,* Routledge, London and New York.

Väliaho, P. (2012) 'Affectivity, Biopolitics and the Virtual Reality of War', *Theory Culture Society,* vol. 29, no. 2, pp. 63–83.

Weber, M. (2003) *The Protestant Ethic and the Spirit of Capitalism,* trans. Talcott Parsons, Dover Publications, Mineola, NY.

Wicke, J. (1994) ' "Mrs. Dalloway" Goes to Market: Woolf, Keynes, and Modern Markets', *NOVEL: A Forum on Fiction,* vol. 28, no. 1, pp. 5–23.

Wood, E. (1992) *The Pristine Culture of Capitalism,* Verso, London and New York.

Chapter 7

Life in the rhizome

When Carl Jung offered his reflective metaphor of life as a rhizome in 1963, he could not have anticipated that it would become one of the central tenets of contemporary radical political economy. This is largely due to Deleuze and Guattari's adoption of this term in *Anti-Oedipus* (1983) and *A Thousand Plateaus* (1987), whose focus on the immanent and nomadic power of desire greatly influenced Hardt and Negri's trilogy *Empire* (2000), *Multitude* (2005), and *Commonwealth* (2009). Aligned with those writing in the Italian autonomist tradition (Alliez and Osborne 2013; Berardi 2009a & 2009b; Lazzarato 2002 & 2009; Mitropoulos 2012a & 2012b; Patton 2010; Surin 2010), Hardt and Negri refer to the power relations of the networked rhizome of communication and capitalist power we live in as 'Empire'. In addition to describing the dispersed and overlapping nature of contemporary corporate power, the metaphor of the rhizome can also be applied to relations between people or 'singularities', who they refer to as the multitude.

In contrast to the Fordist methods of standardized manufacturing and unionized labour that characterized Keynes's time period, contemporary labour is dispersed, decentralized, and takes immaterial forms. As will become clearer in my discussion below, much of the production that takes place in contemporary capitalism involves creativity, knowledge, or provides services rather than manufacturing material products. When a software designer creates a new application, for example, the product is immaterial compared to more Fordist capitalist commodities such as automobiles or television sets. Even these latter products, however, now require the application of speciality knowledge such as design, branding and advertising strategies, or financing schemes involving workers who are generally considered to be professionals, and therefore are rarely unionized.

Often such forms of work can be provided on a contractual or consulting basis, which means that it is not necessary to hire these workers as full-time employees. Enabled by new communication technologies, they might work at home, or in an office setting thousands of miles away from their employer. Not only does this provide a serious challenge to organizing workers, it means that many of the jobs provided in the contemporary economy are what Hardt and Negri call 'precarious' or insecure. Contract workers do not know when or where their next job will come from, nor can they reasonably confine their work to an eight-hour day. When the work comes, it must be completed quickly for the worker to remain competitive relative to the many others seeking similar work.

As I noted in Chapter 3, although they are aware that such changes in the nature of labour and production call for new strategies for organizing labour, Hardt and Negri also believe they offer the opportunity for more immanent practices of power based on singularities, as opposed to hierarchical organizations such as trade unions or corporations. They are optimistic that a spontaneous coming together of the multitude via a biopolitical exploration of alternative subjectivities can bring new forms of interaction, governance, and production that will ultimately be more satisfying. In the previous two chapters, I have applied Hardt and Negri's concept of the 'queer' biopolitical event to describe the Rococo period as well as the aesthetics and politics of the Bloomsbury Group. Here, I will use it to analyze our contemporary Postmodern moment, but doing so involves a more aesthetic description of capitalism than Hardt and Negri provide. In what follows, I will draw heavily on neo-Marxist and post-structuralist accounts of contemporary capitalism, but eventually draw them back into my Jungian/ Deleuzean understanding of sexually differentiated desire. In the process, I will show the parallels between the aesthetics of political economy in the Baroque/Rococo period, and our contemporary situation. This involves a more in-depth understanding of the aesthetic sensibility of contemporary capitalism.

The Postmodern 'structure of feeling'

Some of the most important analyses of 20th century capitalism might be better described as cultural economy as opposed to political economy. Jameson, for example, described Postmodern art and architecture as the 'cultural logic of late capitalism', arguing that its depthless reproduction of images reflected capitalist commodification (Jameson 1995). Similarly, Harvey (1990) maintained that the depthlessness of Postmodern art and its attention to immediacy and spectacle urged surrender to commodification and the commercialization of capitalist markets. For both Harvey and Jameson, however, culture does not simply manipulate consciousness. Instead, it presents an unconscious manifestation of the subjectivity inherent to capitalism, including experiences of space and time. Effectively, their argument is that one can read off attempts to express and resolve the feelings of alienation and fragmentation inherent to capitalism by examining cultural production.

Both authors consider architecture to be exemplary in this regard. The Modernist emphasis on clean, unadorned, and rationalized buildings, for example, is seen as both a reflection of the industrial *Logos* of Fordist assembly lines and an attempt to bring order to the chaotic changes and alienation people were experiencing in the first half of the 20th century. Postmodern architecture, on the other hand, reflects the simultaneity and decentredness inherent to post-Fordist methods of production. In contrast to the emphasis on economies of scale and the standardization of production inherent to Fordism, post-Fordist production is based on economics of scope that allow flexibility and rapid changes in product niches. The extensive globalization of production and consumption, where production is fragmented into discrete stages that are dispersed around the world and goods are superficially altered for consumption in different markets, results in a sensibility of simultaneity and bombardment by a flood of unrelated signifiers that attempt to brand these commodities.

Postmodern art and architecture, they agree, rejects the *Logos* of Modern aesthetics and foundationalist philosophy for an anti-foundationalist, almost schizophrenic 'structure of feeling' characterized by a preoccupation with surface; a sort of 'contrived depthlessness' that borrows aimlessly from various time periods and aesthetics. In architecture, this is reflected in the combination of various historical styles in a single building, the incorporation of pop cultural cues into building designs, or an emphasis on neo-traditional heritage intended to provide a much-needed sense of history and embeddedness in society. All of this is incorporated into a strategy of spectacle, however, where the images provided by such sites are key to their attraction.

This focus on depthlessness, surface, and spectacle is also evident in Baudrillard's descriptions of Postmodern aesthetics and economics, which he argues are organized around simulation, or the act of 'simulating' reality through the play of images and signs. Baudrillard (2004) called these signs simulacra, which might be described as a copy of an image where the original does not exist. In this sense, it is not a representation in the usual sense of a signifier indicating a signified, but has become detached from the signified to float around and find its meaning relative to other images and simulacra. His most famous example of this is Disneyland, where sites such as 'Main Street USA' evoke an idealized image of America that does not really exist. In fact, Baudrillard argued, these obviously unreal images are produced to make it seem that the world surrounding it is 'real', when in fact America itself is the ultimate simulacrum, or as Vidich (1991, p. 136) paraphrases Baudrillard, 'an insubstantial semblance definable only by its simulacra'.

From Baudrillard's perspective, identity is constructed by the appropriation of images or codes such as brands, which determine how individuals perceive themselves and others. Everything – economics, politics, social life, culture – is governed this way. The result is a 'hyperreality' where entertainment, information, and communication technologies provide experiences more intense than everyday life. Individuals flee the 'desert of the real for the ecstasies of the hyperreal' – computers, Disneyland, amusement parks, malls become more real than the real. As people choose this hyperreal spectacle over meaning, these images begin to control our thoughts and behaviour.

As Jameson describes it, this is a society where the economic is cultural and cultural economic, a claim reinforced by Lash and Urry's (1993) emphasis on the reflexivity of consumption. In a context where the design intensity of these objects makes their 'sign' value critical to their exchange value, consumers become more reflexive as they consider the impact of a product (from automobiles to tourist destinations) on their self-image and their social standing. The aesthetics of commodities, buildings, and humans becomes integral to the presentation of their identity. Cities, regions, and countries are no exception to this trend, as they compete for the 'creative class' workers who manipulate these images, as well as high technology investment and tourists via branding strategies extensively based on culture (Evans 2003, Florida 2002, Jenkins 2005).

Rather than viewing this as the commodification of culture, Baudrillard describes it as a sort of 'transaesthetics' characterized by:

> the aestheticization of the whole world . . . What we are witnessing, beyond the materialist rule of the commodity, is a semio-urgy of everything by means of advertising, the media, or images. No matter how marginal, or banal, or even obscene it may be, everything is subject to aestheticization, culturalization, museumification. Everything is said, everything is exposed, everything assumes the force, or the manner, of a sign.
>
> (Baudrillard 1990, p. 17)

Contemporary architectural trends can also be described in these terms, where the built environment appears either to embrace these transaesthetics, or as a compensatory attempt to re-embed identity (à la Polanyi) in local tradition, community, and neighbourhoods. A reflection of this latter impulse is New Urbanism – a form of urban planning that emphasizes community interaction, walkability, and a neo-traditional design aesthetic. Rejecting the Modernist grids and alienating auto-oriented roadways of many large urban areas, New Urbanism calls for the creation and integration of walkable neighbourhoods that downplay the car and encourage human interaction. In contrast to the integration of pop cultural themes and the combination of historical references common to many Postmodern designs, New Urbanism commonly makes use of heritage design traditions such as pitched roofs, picket fences, and front stoops or verandas in an attempt to develop a sense of familiarity and conviviality that encourages neighbours to feel an affinity with, and hence interact with, one another.

New Urbanism appears to have an avowedly 'erotic' approach in the sense that I have been using the term – an emphasis on relatedness, interaction, and connection. It appeals to our urge for containment – creating a *temenos* of sorts that offers boundaries and a sense of belonging in the face of the decentring, schizophrenic tendencies of Postmodern capitalism. It can perhaps be described as the aesthetic version of the affective labour I will describe below – it plays a compensatory role by attempting to provide comfort and containment in an increasingly alienating urban world of strangers.

This ostensible eroticism is overlaid with a heavy morality, however, that closely aligns with the discourse of Good Design outlined in Chapter 1 (Jenkins 2006). The explicit intent of much New Urban planning is to effectively control the behaviour of people in line with fairly narrow definitions of 'heritage' and interaction. Neighbourhoods are designed in a way that encourages surveillance of both self and others in line with acceptable modes of behaviour. Aesthetic designs are closely enforced by building codes, and in many cases neighbourhood organizations, that limit and restrict aberrations from traditional designs. Tradition, in turn, is defined narrowly in reference to a primarily European design heritage.

Overall, the effect can be an attempt to 'improve' the tastes, behaviour, and interactions of people in narrowly defined, highly moralistic ways. In practice, many New Urban developments are a parody of their supposedly erotic intentions, as they attempt to construct a feeling of belonging in a context that often ends up being expensive, racially segregated and re-absorbed into the economy of spectacle. Examples of this latter point are Seaside, Florida (which provided the setting for the film *The Truman Show*) and Disney's new urban development, Celebration, Florida (Ross 2000).

In contrast, Deconstructivist (Decon) architects embrace Baudrillard's transaesthetics by explicitly rejecting any sort of discourses in their designs, including those of morality, nationality, or any expectation of what a building is supposed to look like. The result is buildings that look 'unexpected' – stairways lead to nowhere; the 90 degree angle is frequently abandoned, resulting in sharp angles or curved walls; the aesthetics of surrounding buildings are often ignored so that Decon buildings stand out, rather than blend in with their surroundings.

This last element in particular has led to accusations that Decon is a kind of 'show dog' architecture designed purely to attract attention (Rybczynski 2002). This has resulted in a consistent clamour for such buildings around the world, as cities attempt to cultivate a sense of cultural dynamism and an avant-garde sensibility that has turned many Decon architects into global celebrities. The resulting 'star-chitecture' frequently turns buildings into branding devices regarded almost solely for their ability to attract tourists or to contribute to the municipal economy (Jenkins 2005). In their urgency to reject discursive expectations, the Decon version of freedom is suspiciously neo-liberal, confirming an iconoclastic individualism that celebrates market connections, consumption, and tourism, as opposed to the spontaneous grassroots interactions New Urbanism claims to encourage. The aesthetic aspired to in many of these buildings is often described as 'ecstatic' (Jencks 1999) or delirious (Koolhaus 1978), indicating an uncontained, collective unconsciousness.

The autonomist author Berardi (2009a & 2009b) argues, somewhat paradoxically, that this ecstasy and delirium often results in depression, as the gentle ways of *Eros* and pleasure celebrated in the Rococo or Bloomsbury aesthetics get absorbed into the constant bombardment of signs inherent to what he calls 'semiocapitalism'. Influenced by Baudrillard, Berardi defines semiocapitalism as the fusion of media and capitalism. Characterized by the semiotic manipulation of signs and the incessant compulsion to consume described in Baudrillard's concept of hyperreality, semiocapitalism 'thrusts us toward enjoyment'. It seems paradoxical that Berardi views the energy-drained state of depression as a manifestation of this psychosis. But the pleasure resulting from this indulgence, he argues, is hollow and the symptoms of our contemporary discomfort reveal this: alcoholism, bulimia, obesity, panic. We become depressed because the constant mobilization of nervous energy stimulated by the hyperreality of semiocapitalism overwhelms us. Faced with a barrage of 'signifying impulses' in highly mobile forms that we cannot possibility process in any meaningful way, we shut down (Berardi 2009b, pp. 109–15). Rather than being repressed, it is as if *Eros* becomes hyperreal.

The barrage of communication we face is overwhelming, he argues, magnified by the inability to escape or be incommunicado. Neoliberal capitalism is hyper-competitive; it runs 24 hours a day. Workers immerse themselves in their precarious jobs (de Peuter 2011; Ross 2008) in order to stay competitive, but the result is that they throw themselves, body and soul, into work. Martin argues, for example, that bipolar disorder used to be considered a mental illness that primarily affected women. Now, however, it has become a 'masculine' mental disorder and is regarded positively in the business press. The manic behaviours of hyper-consumption and functioning around

188 Genealogies

the clock with little sleep are considered bonuses in the context of contemporary capitalism (Martin 2007).

Berardi's emphasis on the human desire for relatedness bears far more affinities to the Jungian concept of *Eros* than to Freud's pleasure principle outlined in the previous chapter. In contrast to the Freudian model, for Jung relatedness does not occur because of the social repression of desire, but is an essential and original element of desire. *Eros* is relatedness and community, as opposed to Freud's notion that true community can only ensue when the erotic is repressed. Similarly, Berardi rejects the Freudian notion of repression as the source of the alienation many people feel in contemporary society. Instead, he argues that our current 'discontent' (which is more accurately translated in his work as 'discomfort') is the result of an explosion of expressivity, rather than repression. Instead of being a neurosis, which is the result of repressing something, it is a psychosis, or an excess of emotion or energy. As opposed to being forced to repress our basic instincts, as Freud argued, in contemporary capitalism we are urged to indulge them.

Responding to the competitive demands of the manic new work world, our soul's desire becomes our work. The result, according to Berardi, is a loss of *Eros:*

> It seems that ever less pleasure and reassurance can be found in human relations, in everyday life, in affectivity and communication. A consequence of this loss of *Eros* in everyday life is the investment of desire in one's work, understood as the only place providing narcissistic reinforcement to individuals used to perceiving the other according to rules of competition, that is to say as danger, impoverishment and limitation, rather than experience, pleasure and enrichment.
>
> (Berardi 2009a, p. 80)

The 'everywhereness' of semiocapitalism forms an elusive and canny foe. Individuals become what Deleuze called 'dividuals' – humans whose identity becomes endlessly divided into bits of information that are then algorithmically re-aggregated into a new 'virtual' form (Deleuze 1992). In the virtual web of the internet, for example, identity is algorithmically determined by surfing patterns – one might be 60 percent female and 40 percent male one day then different the next, depending on the gender attributions of the websites visited (Cheney-Lippold 2011).

Far from the queer biopolitics described by Hardt and Negri, this statistically allocated 'dividualized' identity – paradoxically both divided into data points and gathered together by probabilistic curves – is the new form of control. Deleuze described it as a serpent, contrasting the disciplinary societies analyzed in the work of Foucault with the societies of control we live in today. In the disciplinary societies, one moved through *enclosures* – moulds with distinct castings. But *controls* are modulating, continuously changing from one movement to another. If the spaces of enclosure were symbolized by the mole, the societies of control operate like a slithering and undulatory serpent, controlling more by means of a contingent modulation than containment within four walls. As Deleuze warned, the coils of the serpent are much more complex than the burrows of the mole (Deleuze 1992).

The spread of the serpent extends into the household and the affective or caring labour performed there. Mitropoulos refers to the contemporary political economic expansion into the household as oikonomics – her adaptation of the ancient Greek word for the household economy, or *oikos,* which the contemporary meaning of the word economics evolved from. Oikonomics involves 'the ways in which a politics of the household – domesticity and genealogy – are crucial to the organisation of intimate forms of self-management, but also the conflations of nation, race and sexuality with re-production' (Mitropoulos 2012b, p. 45). Mitropoulos applies a logic similar to Deleuze's endlessly divided dividual to the merging of the household and broader capitalist economy. Under current conditions of capitalist regulation, she argues, the apparently 'caring' relations within the household are characterized by a pervasive contractualization of human relations to the benefit of the oikonomy, where even apparently uncommodifiable types of affective labour such as caring for family members become integral to its maintenance.

Affective or caring labour is a vital aspect of the autonomist concept of immaterial labour. Autonomist authors have insisted that just as immaterial forms of production such as creativity and service labour have become central to contemporary capitalist production, the affective labour commonly provided by women in the form of caring for, or providing emotional support for others is necessary to the functioning of contemporary economics. Within the home, future workers and citizens are taught the norms and discipline of belonging to a capitalist workforce and the values inherent to national citizenship, not to mention racial, gender, and ethnic identities. Particularly with the expansion of precarious, contractual forms of work performed in the home, affective labour is made to seem as if it is freely given, but is in fact a compensatory aspect of the neo-contractualism Mitropoulos refers to. She argues that the caring aspects of such labour is compensatory in the sense that it emotionally supports and maintains workers who have effectively commodified their minds and bodies by contracting them out to their various employers. Ironically, this in turn contractualizes affective labour itself, drawing it into the oikonomy and its dehumanizing web.

The images painted by all of these fairly depressing scenarios is that of an uncontained hyper-sensationalism overlaid or usurped by a heavy *Logos,* or in Mitropoulos's terms a neo-contractualism. If the emphasis on surface and spectacle inherent to all of these accounts provides a sense of *déjà vu*, however, it is because in many ways contemporary aesthetics parallel the sensibilities of the Baroque/Rococo period described in Chapter 5. During the 18th century Rococo period, a similar focus on pleasure and surface was accompanied by the implacable and growing *Logos* of the Enlightenment. Not surprisingly, therefore, many have attributed a neo-Baroque sensibility to contemporary aesthetics.

Neo-Baroque

Calabrese (1993), Ndalianis (2004), and Wacker (2007) all make a connection between Baroque and Postmodern aesthetics, although not specifically in terms of a feminization or an aesthetic attachment to the curve as I have done. Instead, comparisons are made between the Baroque and Postmodern attention to surface, fluid boundaries, and sense of movement. The work of artists such as Jeff Koons, Lucien Freud, Jenny Saville, and the designs of architect Frank Gehry have all been described as neo-Baroque, not necessarily in terms of their visual components, but because of their sensibility to these factors (Wacker 2007).

Of particular interest for my purposes is Lambert's (2004, p. 23) examination of the return of the Baroque to contemporary culture. He describes the Baroque as marked by themes of 'novelty, variety and multiplicity' and the involvement of the spectator in the work via an emotional sense of participation that, in addition to creating a sense of wonder and enthusiasm, provides a feeling of dizziness or swooning. In light of the analyses of Harvey, Jameson, and Baudrillard above, it is not difficult to see why Lambert makes the connection between the Baroque and Postmodern periods. Like all of the political economists above, he draws a parallel between economic and political changes and this aesthetic sensibility, arguing that such 'forms of experience' could not have emerged without the 'new horizons' provided by early capitalism and the influx of new and diverse cultural products that flowed into Europe from the colonies (p. 42). One can extrapolate from this argument to view the Baroque period as a decisive and transformative aesthetic experience that, using d'Ors' terms is an 'eon' or 'type' ripped from history that returns or reappears, as I described it in Chapter 5.

Lambert's exegesis of the Baroque mentions many of the habitual discursive references to the feminine, particularly in his analysis of Hogarth and Starobinski (pp. 43–44). I would argue, however, that in all of the political economy analyses of the Postmodern noted above, the emphasis on the feminine is implicit in the emphasis on consumption, which as I argued in the previous chapter, is generally associated with the feminine. In a world dominated by mass consumption, where consumption is assumed to be feminine (Berg and Eger 2003; Slater 1997), our entire culture is metaphorically feminine.

Modleski (1991) argues that this assumption is explicit in Baudrillard's (2007) work, when he compares the passivity and obedience of the masses to Hegel's notion of the 'eternal irony of femininity' (p. 30). For Baudrillard (2007, p. 57), 'the masses' become so 'bombarded with stimuli, messages and tests' that they become an 'opaque, blind spectrum' silenced by the impossibility of expressing such a bombardment. In his view, however, their silence takes the same form of resistance as Hegel's ironic femininity: 'an ultimately impenetrable simulation of passivity and obedience . . . which annuls in return the law governing them'. Although Baudrillard's conception of these feminized masses allows for a sort of 'apolitical political' (for lack of a better term) Modleski (1991) justifiably wonders if comparing the feminine to what is effectively a giant black hole is really an empowering image. In any case, inherent to all of the political economy accounts I have described is a sense that the gentle, containing pleasures of *Eros* are either discounted as superficial, or absorbed (as in Berardi's and Mitropoulos's accounts) into the *Logos* of capitalism.

Yet the feminine is still there, often in its darkest forms. Deleuze's allusion to the serpent reveals what I will argue is the dark side of the neo-Rococo sensibility in the contemporary rhizome. In my analysis of the Rococo, I described Hogarth's emphasis on the serpentine 'S' shape, and his idea that we are instinctively attracted to the intricacies of the serpentine line of winding walks and rivers that lead the eye in 'a wanton kind of chace' (Hogarth 1973, p. 25). This is because we enjoy the challenge of not seeing what is ahead. What delight does a play or novel bring as the mind follows a well connected, serpentine plot that 'thickens, and ends most pleas'd, when that is most distinctly unravell'd?' (p. 24). The wafting lines of curved objects, ornamentations, or even a country dance gather disparate points and guide the eye to a pleasing drawing together of an otherwise swarming group of stimuli. Yet even Hogarth's feminine curve reveals its dark side as it becomes usurped into the *Logos* of algorithmic calculation.

For example, Amoore describes how Hogarth's Rococo sensibility of the curve has been adapted to suit the needs of profiling and surveillance inherent to contemporary security practices. In addition to his focus on the curve, Hogarth insisted upon the importance of looking at objects in profile to capture their 'out-lines' as opposed to viewing them full-face, a perspective that Amoore argues was integral to the emergence of the modern conception of the subject and object (Amoore 2013, pp. 135–9). She argues that his aesthetic logic of the curve prefigured the methods of statistical identification developed in the late 18th and early 19th centuries, such as biometry and bell curves. These methods, which focused on the retrieval of otherwise randomly scattered dots into statistical regularities generally visualized as curves, also became integral to economic analysis.

Amoore shows that Hogarth's aesthetic sense is central to contemporary methods of 'profiling' and risk management. Such methods, she argues, have effectively become new forms of governance, replacing traditional notions of sovereignty with the 'politics of possibility'. In place of an emphasis on probabilities based on past performance or norms, such methods attempt to project unknown events into the future. Rather than basing such projections on past behaviour, estimates are based on relations between individuals or groups, interactions between 'teeming singularities' that could result in the 'low probability, high consequence event' occurring. Such 'possibilistic' projections are based on decision trees and algorithms – an 'if this happens, then this happens' approach. In this more contingent context, it is the 'outliers' that count, not the norm.

Hogarth's 'S' curve remains operative in a slightly different sense in these methods. Allowing Hogarth's point that the curve of the outline or profile can bring order to even the most 'chaotic of vistas', new risk management software allows the design engineer to enter into the shape of mass quantities of data in order to determine which points lie outside of the norm (p. 139). Hogarth's 'aesthetic grammar' becomes integral to crowd control, for example, where apparently randomly distributed figures and objects can be converted into correlated points on a serpentine line. In the UK Home Office's 'crowded places technology', or the public vigilance programs initiated in New York, London, and Madrid, the emphasis is on that which feels 'out of place' from this line, where emerging movement is detected or outliers from the norm are intuited (pp. 140–1). Rather than generating the spontaneous collective that Hardt and Negri have characterized as the multitude, associations between singularities become algorithmically digitized into potential, possibilistic risks (pp. 137–8).

In Amoore's description of the new calculus of risk and security, one sees the erotic aspects of Hogarth's gentle, serpentine curve turned to more devouring, controlling images. More generally, erotic ways of being are obliterated, as in Berardi's semiocapitalism, where even the erotic impulse to pleasure appears to be usurped by the discipline of the reality/performance principle – manifested in its hyper form. Berardi argues that many of the essential 'containers' of the individual are highly compromised in semiocapitalism: the body, the mother, and relatedness to others. These erotic flesh-and-blood aspects of life are devalued in the context of the 'virtual' reality principle of semiocapitalism. Because of this, semiocapitalism has the effect of a collective and individual disembodiment. The excessive speed of electronic capitalism reduces empathy because there is no time for a sensorial meeting – to touch or smell. Mothers (and fathers) are separated from their children by the demands of the all-encompassing work world.

Interactions become *connections*, as opposed to *conjunctions*. Conjunction, according to Berardi, is an unrepeatable fusion of rounded, irregular forms. Connection is algorithmic and repeatable, the joining of straight lines and points that have been made compatible and standardized. The result is an impoverishment of affect, sensibility, and bodily interaction (Berardi 2009b, pp. 86–98). To recuperate *Eros*, he argues, we must renew our sensibility. This involves, he argues in terms almost identical to mine, a focus on the body, pleasure, sensuality, a 'sensitization to the curve', and to 'spheres of relationality' such as affectivity, eroticism, and deep comprehension (pp. 87–89).

As noted above, Berardi's work, with its focus on relatedness, the soul, and human interaction is closer to a Jungian than a Freudian view of *Eros* (although Berardi is not a Jungian himself). He does not relate *Eros* to the feminine, nor does he make any direct reference to Jung. Perhaps it is via the Deleuzean connection, therefore, that his terminology comes to bear some uncanny parallels with Jung's terminology. Specifically, his use of the term 'conjunction' (the English version of the alchemical Latin *coniunctio*), his reference to what I have labelled the feminine energy of containment, and his focus on the 'curve' make his work especially useful for my purposes. In what follows, I will attempt to redeem the transforming, containing aspects of the feminine energy being manifested in contemporary political economy by re-writing the supposed superficiality of the attention to surface and re-creating the sense of *Eros* evoked by Keynes, Hogarth, and Montesquieu. In doing so, perhaps we can bring the full alchemical sense of the hermaphroditic *coniunctio* back into play.

Re-visioning *Eros*

If we imagine, as I have been arguing throughout this book, that an important aspect of the Baroque/Rococo/Postmodern cultural economy is an archetypal feminine energy that has the potential to be transformative in its effects, this emphasis on spectacle, consumption, and surface need not be regarded in such a negative fashion. There is, as I have outlined in previous chapters, a positive side to this feminine energy inherent to a feeling of relatedness and sensual pleasure. Building on Berardi's argument, however, I will emphasize that although this sense of relational pleasure must be consciously acknowledged, it also needs to be somehow gently contained.

Deleuze, in his philosophy of surface, provides a possibility for re-imagining the supposedly superficial effects of the Baroque/Postmodern attention to surface. Using the example of Lewis Carroll's *Alice in*

Wonderland, Deleuze notes the constant use of paradox in this story. In this tale, Alice grows larger, but as she continues to grow, she is smaller now than she will be later. There is, Deleuze argues, a sense of the 'simultaneity of becoming' here. At the same moment that Alice becomes larger, she is simultaneously smaller than she will become. 'This is the simultaneity of becoming whose characteristic is to elude the present' he notes. 'It pertains to the essence of becoming to move and to pull in both directions at once: Alice does not grow without shrinking, and vice versa.' (Deleuze 1990, p. 1) In this moving in both directions at once, one is always in the past or in the future, never in the present. This capacity to elude the present, he argues, is the paradox of pure becoming and infinite identity. In these reversals and sliding back and forth in double directions, one loses fixed identities and 'false depth'. This is the adventure that Alice faces throughout the story.

At the beginning of *Alice,* there is much digging underground looking for secrets, Deleuze claims, but as the story continues, everything happens at the surface. The animals below ground are replaced by card figures that have no thickness. The digging and hiding in the story are replaced with a lateral sliding from left to right. 'One could say that the old depth having been spread out became width. The becoming unlimited is maintained entirely within this inverted width.' (p. 9) There is no need to look for something hidden behind a curtain; all is visible –

> all possible science is along the length of the curtain . . . It suffices to follow it far enough, precisely enough, and superficially enough, in order to reverse sides and to make the right side become left or vice versa.
>
> (p. 9)

Thus, Deleuze claims that the real adventure in *Alice* is her climb to the surface and her disavowal of false depth.

This attention to surface is continued in Carroll's *Through the Looking Glass,* he argues, where a focus on volumeless, 'pure events' ordered on a chessboard prevails. Things in this world happen not in the depths, but at the borders, where by skirting the surface one transforms from the bodily to the incorporeal. This emphasis on paradox and events at the surface is characteristic of Stoic philosophy, he argues, and presupposes a great deal of wisdom and an entirely new ethic. And yet it is a discovery made by the little girl, he notes in a reference that presages the emphasis on becoming-woman/ girl in his work with Guattari. She knows how to grow and diminish at the edges, to stay on the surface and avoid the depths. 'History teaches us that sound roads have no foundation, and geography that only a thin layer of the earth is fertile.' (p. 10)

Aesthetics, Deleuze believes, faces similar issues. On the one hand, there is the possibility of art as representation, as a copy of experience or a model as Plato would have it in his philosophy. On the other hand, there is the possibility of experimentation, of several different and divergent stories being told at the same time, an unformed chaos that comes together in the 'Great Work' such as Joyce's *Finnegan's Wake* (p. 260). The key to such chaotic experimentation is to have these heterogeneous stories affirm each other, creating an internal resonance that induces 'forced movement' (p. 261). This, he argues, is true of the simulacrum. As opposed to Baudrillard's focus on the emptiness of the simulacrum, Deleuze argues that when the simulacrum breaks its chains and rises to the surface, it affirms a repressed, phantasmic power.

Breaking from the rules of representation, where the world is an icon that images copy or represent, he argues for a view of the world as 'differences that resemble each other' and are not judged by their resemblances to some original model, but in their 'constitutive disparity' (p. 262). In doing so, one reverses Platonism to 'make the simulacra rise and . . . affirm their rights among icons and copies' (p. 262). This is a re-imagination of the world as 'nomadic distributions' where hierarchies and fixities of distribution are impossible.

This contrast between Baudrillard's more cynical view of the simulacrum and Deleuze's more positive one carries into their respective sexual politics. In contrast to Hardt and Negri's Deleuzean-inspired emphasis on biopolitics and the transformative possibilities of the queer event, or Jung's and Deleuze's celebration of the hermaphrodite, Baudrillard describes a 'transsexuality' that plays on indifference rather than difference. By this he does not literally mean transsexuality, but a sexuality based on artifice. Against the glacial aesthetic of Madonna, the customized curves of La Cicciolina or the 'Frankensteinian' androgyny of Michael Jackson he rails, 'All of them are mutants, transvestites, genetically baroque beings whose erotic look conceals their generic lack of specificity. They are all "gender-benders" – all turncoats of sex' (Baudrillard 1990, p. 23). Rather than a bursting forth of the erotic forces of the body, the sexual revolution has been reduced to a generic sexual identity where we are all transsexuals 'politically indifferent and undifferentiated beings, androgynous and hermaphroditic' left only wearing masks (p. 27).

I accept Baudrillard's point about the negative aspects of neutering the hermaphrodite. An emphasis on the energies of sexual difference is integral to my story here and 'generic sexuality' has nothing to do with this. All the same, the cynical despair of his critique is deadening – what is the way out of this all-encompassing, Disneyfied existence? Baudrillard's analysis may pertain to the transsexuality of spectacle inherent to the entertainment complex, but it does not apply to the greater openness and fluidity of sexual identity that is increasingly accepted in other contemporary politics and culture. In this 'queer' moment, parallel to similar events in the Rococo and Bloomsbury periods, there is potential for a biopolitics that includes, but goes far beyond, sexual identity.

In Hardt and Negri's biopolitics we see a politics of the rhizome stretched out along the surface based on openness and creation – *amor* as a subversive force based on the 'rationality and desire of singularities' (Negri 2013, p. 97). This definition resonates with Marcuse's concept of sensuous rationality – a 'rationality of gratification in which reason and happiness converge' (Marcuse 1966, p. 224). It also resembles the importance of *Eros* and *Logos*, *Luna* and *Sol* inherent to Jung's philosophy. How do we cultivate such a feeling?

I will attempt to answer this question by returning to Jung, who I believe also channelled serious Baroque/Rococo vibrations. Jung consistently found himself, consciously and unconsciously, dwelling in the 17th and 18th centuries. For example, in a dream that became key to his eventual break with Freud, Jung found himself on the upper story of a house decorated in the Rococo style with furniture made sometime between 1650 and 1750. Cambray (2005, p. 196) argues that the 'later 17th to early 18th century . . . furnishes the most immediate level of what is to become Jung's view of the collective unconscious'. Even more obviously, his fascination with alchemy, which reached its zenith in the 17th century, connects him to this period. His unconscious presaged this attraction in another dream where he ends up caught for years in a 17th-century manor house.

But Jung's fascination with the Baroque period is even more obvious in the elaboration of acausal connectedness evident in his concept of synchronicity. Collaborating with the Nobel laureate physicist Wolfgang Pauli on this concept, Jung drew primarily on 20th-century physics in developing this concept, but he also noted the inspiration of the Baroque philosopher Leibniz. In words that sound very much like Hardt and Negri's account of the spontaneous relations between singularities, or Deleuze's emphasis on the simultaneity of difference, Leibniz argued that there was an acausal connection between individual monads that brought them into a pre-established harmony. Although each monad has their own individual trajectory, they somehow remain in alignment with each other. This alignment or relation, according to Leibniz, is an accident that 'supervenes' from each monad. Cambray shows that in the tradition of 20th-century emergentist thought, supervenience is a concept describing the mind/body relationship where the mind is neither wholly independent from the body nor reduced to it. Rather, 'the mental world emerges from, or supervenes on the somatic' (p. 197). With reference to the accidental alignment of monads, Leibniz argues:

> Relation is an accident which is in multiple subjects; it is what results without any change made in the subjects but supervenes from them; it is the thinkability of objects together when we think of multiple things simultaneously.
>
> (quoted in Cambray 2005, p. 198)

Similar to Leibniz's attempt to explain the apparently unexplainable simultaneity of monads, Jung's concept of synchronicity was intended to explain meaningful coincidences in which two related events occur without any apparent relation of causation between them. He characterized such incidents as 'a falling together in time, a kind of simultaneity' (Jung quoted in Cambray 2002, p. 412). Although Jung predated Prigogine's work on complexity theory in the 1970s, Cambray points out that this work is also relevant to Jung's ideas on synchronicity. Focusing on the emergence of structures in far-from-equilibrium phenomena, Prigogine showed how order can emerge on the edge of chaos. An important subset of this work on complex adaptive systems focuses specifically on 'emergent' patterns of macro-behaviour that appear to supervene from interactions between units in self-organizing systems, without being inherent to individual units themselves. In other words, units interacting on a lower level start manifesting behaviour at a second, 'emergent', higher level without any particular explanation for this (p. 415). Not surprisingly, Jungians have found many parallels between complexity theory and synchronicity, as well as the emergence of the archetypes.

I want to combine Jung with Deleuze by pointing out that this idea of 'order in chaos' is yet another paradox, another aspect of Deleuze's philosophy of surface. This finding of order on the edges of chaos is precisely how Deleuze (1990, p. 10) describes the girl 'who grows and diminishes only from the edges', not to mention his emphasis on the forced movement that comes from the chaotic experimentation with divergent stories. There is something inherent not just to the curve, but the attention to surface, that is also an aspect of feminine energy. The swarming surfaces of the Rococo or the simultaneity of the Postmodern simulacra, far from being superficial, may herald an alternative understanding of order out of chaos linked to the feminine. Recall Jung's conception of *anima* as butterfly outlined in Chapter 2, 'which reels drunkenly from flower to flower and lives on honey and love' (Jung quoted in Hillman 1985, p. 24), skimming the surface of the field. Or perhaps, as I mused in Chapter 4, it is not feminine in itself, but a form of rationality that comes from an appreciation of the feminine, of *anima*/becoming-woman/the girl, that when combined with *Logos* forms a new kind of rationality, a novel combination of rationality and desire (*amor*), of sensuous rationality, that allows one to see or feel in this way.

Amoore's ominous portrayal of Hogarth's aesthetics emphasizes the potentially dark aspects of this approach. But she also argues that there is another way of approaching the serpentine line, a way of dwelling between the data points of algorithmic projections of the possible. Embracing uncertainty, it sees different ways to connect and associate that cannot be pre-programmed and allows for a more imaginative response to the organization of chaos (Amoore 2013, p. 176). In her view, a critical response to the possibilism of algorithmic judgment "would invoke an associationism that can never be known, a life of associating with other things and people that is not amenable to calculation. It would not, as Foucault reminds us, 'hand down sentences', but it would imagine the forks in the road, the potentialities as yet unrealized" (p. 175).

Her image evokes a sense of Maurer's description of Keynes's use of probability described in Chapter 5 – a misty, contingent, constantly morphing sense of being between the lines inherent to *Luna*, and a Bergsonian sense of residing in the interval between the data points (Gardner and Jenkins 2016). Life in this interval, the space that Bergson referred to as *duration*, is an affective, felt experience where past, present, and future mingle. One could never dwell permanently here, without the points that demarcate its amorphous existence. To use Deleuze and Guattari's terms, one can never completely 'de-stratify'. But attention to this interval, to this misty luna-like aspect of existence, is a necessary antidote to the algorithmic logic that dominates contemporary life.

Attaining this goal involves developing a notion of *Eros* capable of containing our modulating, serpent-like control economy. Or, to invoke a more Jungian vocabulary, some sort of *temenos* is necessary. Deleuze's serpent analogy is ominous, eliciting biblical images of deceit, evil, and sinful temptation. In polytheistic traditions, however, the serpent (sometimes portrayed as a dragon) is a chthonic symbol that has both positive and negative connotations. *Eros* was in his original, primordial form a chthonic snake. In Hindu, Egyptian, and Aztec mythology the serpent is considered one of the most elemental of all creatures, appearing in myths of both creation and destruction. Only in the monotheism of Judeo-Christianity is this 'doubleness' of the serpent lost and it is portrayed solely as a symbol of evil. But the serpentine movement of the snake reveals its essential doubleness. Slithering first in one direction, then the other, it manifests the potential for holding contradiction, balancing in its serpentine path the extremes of opposites (Mogenson 2003).

It is difficult to image maintaining a balanced, slithering movement in the vast, dispersed, electronic universe of semiocapitalism. Perhaps that is why Hogarth, in his tribute to the serpentine line, emphasized that its beauty was most truly manifest when it was contained within the geometric form of the triangle or pyramid. Hogarth believed that combined with two other principles, the serpentine line provided a wholeness and unity of form that provided endless pleasure. One of these principles is the triangle or pyramid; in his view the triangle and serpentine line constitute 'the two most expressive figures that can be thought of to signify not only beauty and grace, but the whole *order of form*' (p. xvii, his emphasis). Contained within the pyramidal arrangements used frequently not only by the ancient Greeks, but the great Renaissance artists such as Leonardo or Michelangelo, the twists of the serpentine line provide movement and interest.

This is especially true when the serpentine is combined with another principal: infinite variety. Hogarth, like Deleuze, believed that variety had more interest than uniformity, hence the frequent use in nature of odd numbers (in combinations of leaves and blossoms, for example) rather than even, and the greater beauty of the oval over the circle – especially in the form of the egg. The frontispiece for his book *The Analysis of Beauty* (Hogarth 1973) featured a serpentine line, contained in a glass triangle, with 'VARIETY' at its base.

If Berardi is correct that semiocapitalism is a psychotic release of excess emotion or energy, could it be that part of the insatiability of our desire is that it is unbounded and not contained, as Hogarth's serpents are? If so, how do we contain our desires without smothering or moralizing them? How do we skim the surface, create order at the edges of chaos, without succumbing to the sensation of chaos itself? These are questions that require experimentation, testing various lines of flight – constantly changing and adapting to new contingencies and circumstances. For this kind of experimentation, a triangle (perhaps emblematic of the Oedipal triangle?) is too constraining. Perhaps the container is not a shape, but a process, an intra-action. Imagining this intra-action will be the focus of my final chapter.

Bibliography

Alliez, E. and Osborne, P. (2013) *Spheres of Action: Art and Politics*, MIT Press, Cambridge, MA.

Amoore, L. (2013) *The Politics of Possibility: Risk and Security beyond Probability*, Duke University Press, Durham, NC.

200 Genealogies

Baudrillard, J. (1990) *The Transparency of Evil: Essays on Extreme Phenomena*, Verso, London and New York.

Baudrillard, J. (2004) *Simulacra and Simulation*, trans. Sheila Faria Glaser, The University of Michigan Press, Ann Arbor.

Baudrillard, J. (2007) *In the Shadow of the Silent Majorities or the End of the Social*, trans. P. Foss, J. Johnston, P. Patton, and A. Barardini, Semiotext(e), Los Angeles.

Berardi, F. "Bifo". (2009a) *The Soul at Work: From Alienation to Autonomy*, Semiotext(e), Los Angeles, distributed by MIT Press, Cambridge, MA.

Berardi, F. "Bifo". (2009b) *Precarious Rhapsody*, Minor Compositions, London, distributed by Autonomedia, New York.

Berg, M. and Eger, E. (2003) *Luxury in the Eighteenth Century*, Palgrave/Macmillan, London.

Calabrese, O. (1993) *Neo-Baroque: A Sign of the Times*, trans. C. Lambert, Princeton University Press, Princeton, NJ.

Cambray, J. (2002) 'Synchronicity and Emergence', *American Imago*, vol. 59, no. 4, pp. 409–434.

Cambray, J. (2005) 'The Place of the 17th Century in Jung's Encounter with China', *Journal of Analytical Psychology*, vol. 50, pp. 195–207.

Cheney-Lippold, J. (2011) 'A New Algorithmic Identity: Soft Biopolitics and the Modulation of Control', *Theory, Culture and Society*, vol. 28, no. 6, pp. 164–181.

Deleuze, G. (1990) *The Logic of Sense*, trans. Mark Lester, Columbia University Press, New York.

Deleuze, G. (1992) 'Postscript on the Societies of Control', *October*, vol. 59, Winter, pp. 3–7.

Deleuze, G. and Guattari, F. (1983) *Anti-Oedipus: Capitalism and Schizophrenia*, University of Minnesota Press, Minneapolis.

Deleuze, G. and Guattari, F. (1987) *A Thousand Plateaus: Capitalism and Schizophrenia*, University of Minnesota Press, Minneapolis and London.

Evans, G. (2003) 'Hard-Branding the Cultural City: From Prado to Prada', *International Journal of Urban Research*, vol. 27, no. 2, pp. 417–440.

Florida, R. (2002) *The Rise of the Creative Class*, Basic Books, New York.

Gardner P. and Jenkins B. (2016) 'Bodily Intra-actions with Biometric Devices', *Body and Society*, vol. 22, no. 1, pp. 3–30.

Hardt, M. and Negri, A. (2000) *Empire*, Harvard University Press, Cambridge, MA.

Hardt, M. and Negri, A. (2005) *Multitude: War and Democracy in the Age of Empire*, Penguin Books, New York.

Hardt, M. and Negri, A. (2009) *Commonwealth*, The Belknap Press of Harvard University Press, Cambridge, MA.

Harvey, D. (1990) *The Condition of Postmodernity*, Blackwell, Cambridge, MA and Oxford.

Hillman, J. (1985) *Anima*, Spring Publications, Dallas, TX.

Hogarth, W. (1973) *The Analysis of Beauty*, Garland Publishing, Inc., New York, NY.

Jameson, F. (1995) *Postmodernism: Or, the Cultural Logic of Late Capitalism*, Duke University Press, Durham, NC.

Jencks, C. (1999) *Ecstatic Architecture*, Academy Editions, London.

Jenkins, B. (2005) 'Toronto's Cultural Renaissance', *Canadian Journal of Communication*, vol. 30, pp. 169–186.

Jenkins, B. (2006) 'The Dialectics of Design', *Space and Culture*, vol. 9, no. 2, pp. 195–209.

Koolhaus, R. (1978) *Delirious New York: A Retroactive Manifesto of Manhattan*, Office for Metropolitan Architecture, Rotterdam.

Lambert, G. (2004) *The Return of the Baroque in Modern Culture*, Continuum, New York.

Lash, S. and Urry, J. (1993) *Economies of Signs and Space*, Sage Publications, London.

Lazzarato, M. (2002) 'From Biopower to Biopolitics', *Pli*, vol. 13, no. 2002, pp. 99–113.

Lazzarato, M. (2009) 'Neoliberalism in Action: Inequality, Insecurity and the Reconstitution of the Social', *Theory, Culture and Society*, vol. 26, no. 6, pp. 109–133.

Marcuse, H. (1966) *Eros and Civilization: A Philosophical Inquiry into Freud*, Beacon Press, Boston.

Martin, E. (2007) *Bipolar Expeditions: Mania and Depression in American Culture*, Princeton University Press, Princeton.

Mitropoulos, A. (2012a) 'The Time of the Contract: Insurance, Contingency, and the Arrangement of Risk', *South Atlantic Quarterly*, vol. 111, no. 4, pp. 763–781.

Mitropoulos, A. (2012b) *Contract and Contagion: From Biopolitics to Oikonomia*, Minor Compositions, Wivenhoe, New York, Port Watson.

Modleski, T. (1991) *Feminism without Women*, Routledge, New York.

Mogenson, G. (2003) 'The Serpent's Prayer: The Psychology of an Image', published on the C.G. Jung webpage www.cgjungpage.org/index.php?option=com_content&task=view&id=277&Itemid=40.

Ndalianis, A. (2004) *Neo-Baroque Aesthetics and Contemporary Entertainment*, MIT Press, Cambridge, MA and London.

Negri, A. (2013) *Spinoza for our Time: Politics and Postmodernity*, Columbia University Press, New York.

Patton, P. (2010) 'Activism, Philosophy and Actuality in Deleuze and Foucault', *Deleuze Studies*, vol. 10, supplement, pp. 84–103.

de Peuter, G. (2011) 'Creative Economy and Labor Precarity: A Contested Convergence', *Journal of Communications Inquiry*, vol. 35, no. 4, pp. 417–425.

Ross, A. (2000) *The Celebration Chronicles: Life, Liberty and the Pursuit of Property Value in Disney's New Town*, Verso, New York and London.

Ross, A. (2008) 'The New Geography of Work: Power to the Precarious?' *Theory, Culture and Society*, vol. 25, nos. 7–9, pp. 31–49.

Rybczynski, W. (2002) 'Bilbo Effect: Public Competitions for Architectural Commissions Don't Necessarily Produce the Best Buildings', *Atlantic Monthly*, vol. 290, no. 2, pp. 138–142.

Slater, D. (1997) *Consumer Culture and Modernity*, Polity Press, Cambridge, UK.

Surin, K. (2010) 'On Producing (the Concept of) Solidarity', *Rethinking Marxism*, vol. 22, no. 3, pp. 446–457.

Vidich, A. (1991) 'Baudrillard's America: Lost in the Ultimate Simulacrum', *Theory, Culture and Society*, vol. 8, pp. 135–144.

Wacker, K. ed. (2007) *Baroque Tendencies in Contemporary Art*, Cambridge Scholars Publishing, Newcastle, UK.

Chapter 8

Finding Ariadne

Who knows apart from me what Ariadne is! . . . To all such riddles no one has yet had the solution; I doubt anyone has ever even seen riddles here. – At one point Zarathustra strictly specifies his task – it is mine, too – so that no one can be mistaken about its sense: he is yessaying to the point of justifying, of redeeming even all that is past. I walk among human beings as among fragments of the future: that future which I envisage.
Friedrich Nietzsche (2007, p. 75)

Ariadne, the mythical woman who symbolized *anima* not just for Nietzsche, but also Deleuze, is generally recognized for helping the heroic Theseus escape the Minotaur's labyrinth by providing him with a long piece of thread to help him find his way back. Less emphasized is that she eventually paired up with Dionysus, who found her grieving on an island after the ungrateful Theseus abandoned her there. Both Nietzsche and Deleuze were fascinated by this coupling, as was Jung. For all three men, there was something in the Ariadne/Dionysus relation that held a secret. I suppose you could say the secret of her thread also guides my argument here; she haunts these pages, in the swarming curves of the Rococo, in the pleasures of capitalist markets, in the politics of surface of the simulacrum.

My analysis of the energies of sexual difference has primarily been dedicated to understanding her, for the exploits of Dionysus and Theseus are generally well known. I have been describing her in terms that Jung attributed to the archetypal energies he called feminine: *Eros* (relatedness), or the misty space of *Luna* (the probabilistic in-between), or the interval formed by the negotiation of the energies of sexual difference manifested in the myth of Demeter/Kore/Persephone. In the previous chapter, I read these energies of the interval into the politics of surface – to *anima* as butterfly for Jung, or the girl Alice for Deleuze, who brings false depths to the surface and finds order on the edge of chaos. I have also argued that feminine forces are containing/

204 Genealogies

transformative energies – an apparent paradox that only seems so in the context of assumptions that feminine symbols of containment indicate passivity or entrapment. Ariadne/Demeter/Persephone/Alice somehow seems to be key to piecing together the fragments of our future – her thread of *Eros* draws these pieces together like Hogarth's serpentine curves.

This love or *Eros*, I have argued, is key to a biopolitics of transformation. But if democracy is an act of love, as Negri claims, what constitutes love as a political act? I have portrayed it as an intra-action – a process of negotiation between the forces of sexual difference. These energies flow across and through us, but we also emit them – absorbing their particles into the molar spaces of our bodies, then transforming and projecting them into the realm of representation. In this respect, the communication of these energies is by proxy – by means of the images that come closest to presenting their meaning. This communication comes to us in many ways: through art and aesthetic discourse, but also via politics and economics. In this respect, the love that Negri invokes is a complex process of negotiation that, when successful, creates an interval – a plateauing of eddying energies that both affirms sexual difference by bringing it to the surface, and enacts an interval allowing a subtle transformation of power.

Once pulled away from bodies and held in that in-between space that Jung called the subtle body and Deleuze called the *intermezzo,* the forces of sexual difference become relevant not only in terms of sexual identity, but as the basis of a new politics of the rhizome. This highly political model of love presumes that everyone standing in the circle belongs there. Its political manifesto is not a series of proclamations and rules, but the exegesis of a process outlining the psychological and political travail necessary to encourage effective participation in the circle. This travail, in Rancière's words, affects the 'distribution of the sensible' – who counts or does not count as an aesthetic-political subject.

A conscious recognition and assimilation of this primal dance between the energies of sexual difference, and the arduous negotiations necessary for a peaceful resolution that preserves this difference, can form the basis of a new social 'contract', a new form of political agreement based on the conciliation of immanent energies. By this, I mean a respect for *Eros* as a political principle equal to *Logos,* and which *Logos* is not allowed to dominate. It represents a plateauing or eddying of these energies in which they become both mutually constitutive and simultaneously contained in each other. In this respect, it provides an alternative approach to the heteronomous delegation of power inherent to the classical liberal social contract.

Jung presents the forces of sexual difference in terms that appear to confirm a stark binary between them, but especially when viewed from a

Deleuzean perspective, these dualisms become joined in a politics of paradox. In his philosophy of surface, Deleuze perceived the potential for paradox in such apparent binaries – a sliding back and forth where one can be simultaneously one *and* the other. This simultaneity of binaries, where one can be both getting larger and be smaller than you will be, means it is also possible to slide sideways between masculine and feminine, *Luna* and *Sol*. In this context the *coniunctio* is not a 50/50 split, it is not a bifurcated hermaphrodite as the illustrations suggest (because this is, after all, a symbol, not a signifier). It is wherever the sliding stops, however briefly, in the gentle eddy of the plateau that the *coniunctio* occurs. This is the space or interval of love.

This interval of love is a highly contested place. It is the space between parent and child, men and women as political collectivities, partners in a relationship, the energies of sexual difference within the psyche and the energies of sexual difference within a collectivity. It is also symbolic of the overcoming of negative fusion, ensuring the coexistence of the energies of sexual difference in a negotiated truce. As Caputo notes in his description of Derrida's understanding of love,

> to love the other on this model requires always to respect that distance, which means that love is not the desire to have the other for oneself or to get something back from the other in return, but the unconditional affirmation of the other, which is what Levinas is calling 'desire'.
>
> (Caputo 2004, p. 41)

This gap or distance, in Derrida's view, is not an obstacle but a *condition* of love. This, in essence, is what love as democracy means. It also involves a Baroque understanding of politics in the sense that it softens the sharp edges of reason with gentle curves; in contrast to the stasis inherent to the social contract, it assumes a sense of movement by acknowledging the power of the in-between. It does not reject rationality but transforms it into a process that is both felt and reasoned – contingently, intuitively, with flexibility and a willingness to change.

Much of what I am saying has already been outlined by those who advocate an 'ethic of care'. In response to the neo-contractualism described by Mitropoulos (2012), feminist political theorists have proposed an alternative to the autonomous, individual-centred model of rights that is the cornerstone of most contemporary legal and moral theory. While early versions of this argument (Chodorow 1978; Gilligan 1982; Held 1993; Ruddick 1980) argued that this ethic grew out of the practices of mothering and managing a family, more recent versions (Robinson 2011; Tronto 2011) have taken an approach that effectively uses a model of care based on 'feminine' interactions and abstracts it onto non-family issues such as economic welfare, refugee issues, migration, security, or trade. Robinson argues that an ethic of care should not be considered either morally superior to more contractual approaches, nor inherently 'feminine', but rather as a more contingent approach to moral principles emphasizing the relations between people, rather than the separations between them.

Ultimately, I will differentiate my argument from the ethic of care approach; nonetheless, there are broad similarities between our views. This perspective eschews deontological, rule-based ideas of rights and obligations based on distance and objectivity in favour of an approach based on a relational ontology where selves exist only through 'complex, constitutive webs or relations with others' (Robinson 2011, p. 131). Robinson argues that the predominant moral paradigm emphasizing self-reliant, moral selves in effect marginalizes those who are more likely to define themselves in the context of the family, such as women, the elderly, or the chronically ill. Instead of focusing on impartiality or distance as a measure of fairness, it focuses on responsibilities toward others and a commitment to context. This latter feature involves an emphasis on situatedness in specific circumstances, a sharp contrast to deontological approaches that attempt to formulate universal rules that apply to all situations.

In the ethic of care approach, differences in ability, race, gender, sexuality, religion, culture, and geography must all be considered in individual circumstances to form an appropriate solution to the issues involved (p. 133). The result is a potentially critical approach to world political issues that, according to Walker, is capable of challenging 'principled' moral stances in situations 'where these are surrogates for, or defenses against, responsiveness in actual relationships' (Walker quoted in Robinson 2011, p. 134). Rather than being a set of moral guidelines, it is a practice of contingent and negotiated 'love' not unlike that suggested by Negri or outlined in my interpretation of the Demeter/Kore/Persephone myth in Chapter 4.

I like the contingent, adaptive strategies inherent to this way of thinking, but have three central objections to this approach. First, although I appreciate the attention to the caring relations of affective labour in the home, greater sensitivity is required to the ambiguous relation between containment and transformation. If Derrida is correct that mother *is* origin, and given that the mother/child relation appears to be central to understanding all subsequent individual transformation, it makes sense that the *Eros* inherent to this mother/child relation be abstracted into an equally important political economic principle, as the ethic of care approach has done. Political theorists such as Robinson (2011) and Tronto (2011) attempt to recreate the responsibilities and contingencies inherent to this relation and pull it away from the mother/child relation to show its relevance as a political principle. In light of the potential for negative political reactions explained in my analysis of the collective complex in Chapter 3, however, a highly calibrated approach to containment is necessary.

This proviso explicitly recognizes the need for care and containment, while simultaneously acknowledging its negative aspects. There is a tendency in the ethic of care tradition to a) regard caring relations as always positive and b) ignore the possibilities for what Hardt and Negri refer to as love that has gone 'bad'. On the one hand, attention to the basic human need for containment, and affirming containment as integral to transformation and becoming, can avoid the kind of internecine politics that Polanyi described as 'protectionist' or Hardt and Negri characterize as 'love gone bad' (2009, p. 195). Identitarian forms of love such as racism, sexism, or nationalism are in effect ways for unmoored, frightened people to form a protective container around themselves. Ultimately, however, they devour us, as they devour others. Thus, another aspect of this ethic of caring has to be a conscious consideration of safeguards against such excessive forms of 'care'. Indeed, this is precisely where the *Logos* of reason can play a strategic role, a proviso that is entirely compatible with their approach, but merits greater emphasis. Part of the contingent approach to 'care', therefore, has to be a focus on both mitigating this disembeddedness through caring relations, and ensuring that this *Eros* is a gentle one, based on Montesquieu's *moeurs douces*, or Leonardo's gentle image of containment in his painting of St. Anne (Figure 4.1).

This painting also visually symbolizes the sensuous pleasure inherent to such a relation, pointing to a second difference between what I am advocating here and the ethic of care approach. I am uncomfortable with labelling what I am describing here as an 'ethic', which to me suggests a didactic approach designed to show people 'the way'. Although it is clearly not the intent of such approaches, there is a danger that this focus on morality and ethics can become heavy handed and exclusionary, as morality discourses historically are wont to do. I am much more inclined to apply Gibson-Graham's (2006) principles of enticing, cajoling, or seducing people to work together, as opposed to convincing them it is their moral imperative. A focus on pleasure (as opposed to asceticism), on spontaneity (as opposed to rules), and the productive nature of desire (in contrast to its moral condemnation) are, in my view, all central to a thriving, democratic political economy.

Finally, the biopolitics I have been advocating throughout this book apply to the intra-action between the unconscious and the realm of representation, in contrast to the more policy-oriented application of the interval advocated by the ethic of care approach, which resides firmly in the realm of representation/signification. Working on the phenomenology of politics in the realm of representation will have an impact on the ontology of becoming, but it is not enough. The biopolitics I have been discussing constitute a process, an intra-action between *Eros* and *Logos* that is metaphorically parallel to the method Robinson and Tronto describe, but is more a subjective process of becoming than a purely material process based on an ethic.

In the intra-action between the realm of representation and the unconscious I discussed in Chapter 3, I accepted the idea that such material practices can have an impact on the unconscious. In this respect, I agree with Hardt and Negri's idea that the production of love, in terms of the production of affective networks, cooperative schemes, and new subjectivities, is a material economic power that can be planned and have real effects. It is not 'spontaneous or passive. It does not simply happen to us, as if it were an event that mystically arrives from elsewhere. Instead it is an action, a biopolitical event, planned and realized in common' (Hardt and Negri, p. 180). Insofar as it creates new subjectivities, this process is also productive of being, an ontological 'event' that 'marks a rupture with what exists and the creation of the new . . . To say that love is ontologically constitutive, then, simply means that it produces the common' (p. 181).

But this phenomenology is incomplete without a consideration of unconscious energies, which also intra-act in the form of the embodiment or working through of Jung's unconscious knowledge or Deleuze's virtual Ideas. The constitutive nature of Spinoza's *conatus,* or Jung's libido, or Deleuze's desire also needs to be attended to for a full understanding of the intra-active nature of this relation. This involves a careful individual and collective attention to the intricate relations of sexual difference within the psyche – a process of labyrinthine experimentation. What I mean by this can be abstracted from Nietzsche's and Jung's description of the relation between Dionysus and Ariadne. Upon finding a grieving Ariadne, distraught over Theseus's abandoning her on the island of Naxos, Dionysus takes her by the ear and says:

> Be clever, Ariadne! . . .
> You have little ears, you have my ears:
> Put a clever word into them!—
> Must one not first hate oneself, in order to love oneself? . . .
> *I am your labyrinth.*
> (Nietzsche quoted in Jung 1988, p. 189)

In his epic exegesis of Nietzsche's *Zarathustra,* Jung draws on these lines to reinforce a point about understanding personal truth. He tells the story of a wise old man who lived in the forest and invented the first mandala. After a dream that portrayed the world as a circle around him, he made a circle, put a point in it, then filled it with pictures of the world. Young people came upon him in the forest one day and were impressed with his circular wisdom. They began to make such circular mandalas themselves and stared at them in an attempt to find the wise man's truth. They did not realize, Jung argued, that in doing so they had actually stepped out of the truth. 'They omitted one thing, the great rhinoceros of the alchemistic process: namely, that *they* are the truth, not the circle. The old man made the circle out of himself: *he* is the truth' (pp. 188–9).

Metaphorically, Jung's story describes the need to walk the labyrinth in terms of an intra-action between the world and the psyche, rather than simply materializing them in the realm of representation. Adding the Dionysus/Ariadne relation to this story of the labyrinth injects the importance of a negotiation of the energies of sexual difference. In telling Ariadne that he is her labyrinth, her mandala, Dionysus is making this point, but Ariadne and her thread are also integral to this labyrinthine journey. Unlike the contrast between Dionysus and Apollo in his earlier work (Nietzsche 1956), Nietzsche moves to a more affirming relation in the coupling of Dionysus and his fiancée Ariadne. Dionysus needs a woman, a fiancée to affirm him. Deleuze also highlighted the Ariadne/Dionysus coupling in Nietzsche's work. In the Apollo/Dionysus binary, he claimed, Dionysus was the affirming god, but to 'become', he himself needs another affirmation. 'Ariadne is this second affirmation,' notes Deleuze. 'Ariadne is the fiancée, the loving feminine power', for in the labyrinth (represented here by the ear) 'only Anima is capable of reconciling us with the unconscious, or giving us a guiding *thread* for its exploration (Deleuze 2006, p. 188, his emphasis). The labyrinth, as Deleuze points out, is circular; it designates the eternal return. But as long as Ariadne was with the heroic Theseus, the labyrinth opened the wrong way – upward, toward higher values, and the thread was the *moral* thread (my emphasis). In this respect, the Ariadne/Dionysus dyad is more analogous to my idea of the plateauing of the energies of sexual difference than the Adriadne/Theseus relation, more likely to produce the interval of love I have been arguing for here.

I invoked this idea of the interval as circle in my discussion of the negotiation of individual and collective identities inherent to the Demeter/Kore/Persephone myth. But this conception of the horizontal labyrinth also appeared in my discussion of the Rococo. In the labyrinthine, swarming curves of the Rococo, not just the frères de Goncourt, but many other men and women found their way through the maze of this aesthetic becoming. Although the biopolitical changes of this time period were brought to an abrupt halt by the heroic politics of the French Revolution, the affirmation had taken place and could not be fully reversed. The sensuous pleasure of

210 Genealogies

Eros re-emerged in the late-19th-century Art Nouveau period in France, and also in the period of French Orientalism of the early 20th century.

Anima as *Eros/Luna* also makes a brief appearance in the aesthetics, politics, and economic theory of Bloomsbury. In Keynes's emphasis on the contingent and probabilistic, or in Woolf's summation of 'a life' subsumed in one day of a woman's shopping for a party, the misty, sensuous pleasure of the feminine pushes the *homo oeconomicus* of neo-classical economics to a new plateau from which, like the Rococo period, there is no return. I made the case that these moments of *Anima* affirmation had a profound effect on sexual politics, as the overall acceptance of feminine aesthetics and politics in these time periods resulted in new perspectives on the role of women in society.

In my analysis of the Postmodern period I reviewed political economy and art history approaches that portrayed a return of the Baroque/Rococo *Eros,* uncontained and unmoored in the hyperreality of this period. If Baudrillard's conception of the superficial floating of the unmoored simulacrum paints a picture of the superficial nature of the Postmodern politico-aesthetic, however, Deleuze's philosophy of surface provides a different interpretation. In his view, the simulacrum need not be attached to a signified to have meaning; on the contrary, this 'false depth' can be transformed into multiple becomings through the affirmation of heterogeneous stories.

This focus on surface brings me back to the interval, the circle created by the negotiation of the forces of sexual difference, where the depth of life contained in the centre of the plateau moves to the top as the eddying energies of the plateau pull the contents into a swirling, parallel labyrinth that is no less complex for its horizontal nature. Energies in this plateau are implicitly contained. This is not a repression of an unrestrained *Eros* by *Logos,* nor the devouring of a cold, implacable *Logos* by a suffocating *Eros.* They slide sideways across one another, retaining their identities but emerging in different configurations in multiple, contingent ways. The interval is hermaphroditic, but not divided through the middle as the alchemical images show. It is multiple; as Deleuze and Guattari showed us, there are many intervals, thousands of plateaus spinning in their own unique labyrinthine eddies.

In the compensatory, symbolic unconscious conveyed to us by Jung and Deleuze, the potentially affirming energies of sexual difference emerge as a new site of biopolitical becoming. Affirming the interval as a joining force in democratic politics is a way to avoid the *enantiodromia* of the collective complex feared not just by Jung, but also by Freud and Benjamin. Developing this consciousness can come in many ways. A conscious aesthetics of sexual difference need not be feared as the 'aestheticization of politics' that Benjamin warned of. By highlighting the necessity of relatedness and sensuous pleasure, aesthetics can be integral to conveying the feeling of 'gentle' containment I have been advocating. Like many of the political economic commentaries on aesthetics I have reviewed, I believe that architecture and urban planning hold particular promise in this respect. As the spaces where we come together to work, play, and enact community, the forms of our built environment are uniquely placed to affect our feelings of both containment and transformation.

A politics and economics acknowledging *Eros* can do the same, although doing so will involve some major changes to the current neo-liberal economic discourses of morality and fear. Innovations are already evolving in new forms of economic cooperation, novel approaches to finance and banking, new types of currency, and experimentation with new approaches to rights and justice, all of which allow for a more erotic approach to politics and economics than the contemporary univocal approach of the contract. In celebrating the sensibility of Marcuse's 'sensuous rationality' or Negri's insistence on the convergence of rationality and desire, we work toward a more conscious, affirmative coexistence of the energies of sexual difference.

Bibliography

Caputo, J. (2004) 'Love Among the Deconstructibles: A Response to Gregg Lambert', *Journal for Cultural and Religious Theory*, vol. 5, no. 2, pp. 37–57.

Chodorow, N. (1978) *The Reproduction of Mothering*, University of California Press, Berkeley.

Deleuze, G. (2006) *Nietzsche and Philosophy*, Columbia University Press, New York.

Gibson-Graham, J. K. (2006) *Postcapitalist Politics*, University of Minnesota Press, Minneapolis.

Gilligan, C. (1982) *In a Different Voice*, Harvard University Press, Cambridge, MA.

Hardt, M. and Negri, A. (2009) *Commonwealth*, The Belknap Press of Harvard University Press, Cambridge, MA.

Held, V. (1993) *Feminist Morality: Transforming Culture, Society and Politics*, University of Chicago Press, Chicago.

Jung, C. G. (1988) *Nietzsche's Zarathustra*, vol. 1, ed. J. Jarrett, Bollingen Series, Princeton University Press, Princeton, NJ.

Mitropoulos, A. (2012) *Contract and Contagion: From Biopolitics to Oikonomia*, Minor Compositions, Wivenhoe, New York, Port Watson.

Nietzsche, F. (1956) *The Birth of Tragedy*, trans. F. Golffing, Doubleday Anchor, New York.

Nietzsche, F. (2007) *Ecce Homo: How to Become What You Are*, trans. D. Large, Oxford University Press, Oxford and New York.

Robinson, F. (2011) 'Care Ethics and the Transnationalization of Care: Reflections on Autonomy, Hegemonic Masculinities, and Globalization', in *Feminist Ethics and Social Policy: Towards a New Global Political Economy of Care,* eds. R. Mahon and F. Robinson, UBC Press, Vancouver, pp. 127–144.

Ruddick, S. (1980) *Maternal Thinking: Toward a Politics of Peace,* Beacon Press, Boston.

Tronto, J. (2011) 'A Feminist Democratic Ethics of Care and Global Care Workers: Citizenship and Responsibility', in *Feminist Ethics and Social Policy: Towards a New Global Political Economy of Care,* eds. R. Mahon and F. Robinson, UBC Press, Vancouver, pp. 162–177.

Index

Note: Numbers in italics indicate figures.

Addison, Joseph 169–70
aestheticization of politics 79
aesthetics and sexual differences
  10–21, *11*
alchemy/alchemical knowledge 34–5
Alexandrian hermeticism 34
Alice in Wonderland (Carroll) 193–4
amor concept 93–4, 103
The Analysis of Beauty (Hogarth) 199
anima (becoming-woman): Ariadne
  myth 203–11; as butterfly 123, 137–8;
  introduction 8, 25; negotiating
  identity 61–2
Anti-Oedipus (Deleuze, Guattari) 45,
  182
anti-Semitism 82
anumus (becoming-man) 61–2
a priori feminine forces 123
archetypes: as collective 39–41;
  coniunctio process and 43–4;
  feminine/masculine 5–6, 17;
  symbols and psyche 41–2; virgin
  archetype 114–15; *see also* feminine
  archetypes; masculine archetypes
architecture during Rococo 142
Ariadne myth 203–11
Art Nouveau period: channeling the
  feminine 132, 134; curving lines
  of 156; *Eros* in 210; European
  consciousness and 140; genealogy
  of 63; introduction 14; masculine
  renunciation 86
Arts and Crafts movement 175
assimilation/plateauing 115

austerity principle 177
autonomism 89
awareness and the self 32

Bakst, Léon 10, *11*
Baroque period: channeling the
  feminine 135–40, *139*; introduction
  14; Neo-Baroque 190–3
Baudrillard, J. 191, *195*
Beard, George Miller 133
beaux arts 78
belles lettres 78
Benjamin, W. 18–19, 79–80
Bergson, Henri 26, 198
Bernheim, Hippolyte 133
Binet, Réné 153
biological difference 58
biopower 91
bipolar disorder 160, 187
bipolitics 24, 132, 188, 207–8
bisexual psyche 44–5, 49
Bloomsbury Group 12, 173, 175–7
Bodies without Organs (BwOs) 25–6
the body as open materiality 56
body schemas 99–100
Boucher, François *144*
Butler, Judith 50–2, 75, 111

Calvinism 166
capitalism: commodity fetishism
  3–4, 134; contemporary capitalism
  182–3, 188–9; cultural *vs.* political
  economy 183; laissez-faire capitalism
  85, 171; libidinal economy literature

162; *Logos* of 103; performance principle 161; political economy of 72; semiocapitalism 187, 188, 192–3; sensuous pleasure and 168–9; services *vs.* manufacturing 182; sexual differences and 19

Carroll, Lewis 193–4

castration symbolized 110, 124

Catholicism 166

Central Union of the Decorative Arts 153

Charcot, Jean-Martin 132–4

chymical marriage 35–6

collective archetypes 39–41

collective complexes 80–95

commerce, defined 165, 169

commodity fetishism 3, 134

Commonwealth (Hardt, Negri) 182

communism 81–2

conatus phenomenon 90, 93–4, 103

coniunctio process: archetypal knowledge and 43–4; Ariadne myth 205; chymical marriage and 35–6; hermaphrodite and 116; immanent power and 90

containment/transformation: *anima* and 108–9; containment 98–103; Demeter/Kore/Persephone myth 110–24, *122*; inadequate containment 104–8; introduction 97–8

contemporary architectural trends 185–6

contemporary capitalism 182–3, 188–9

Corday, Charlotte 149

cult of consciousness 83

cultural *vs.* political economy 183

cupidas: introduction 8, 25; negotiating identity 61–2; notion of transformation 54–5; projection of 45–6

Darwin, Charles 58–60, 102

David, Jacques-Louis 146–7, *147*, 150–2

da Vinci, Leonardo 121–2, *122*

Deconstructivist (Decon) architects 186–7

Deleuze, Gilles: *anima* conception 8, 108–9, 119–20; conception of ontological difference 42–3;

dualism concept 16–17; inadequate containment 103–7; *intermezzo* space 163; intra-action concept 75–6; labyrinth notion of the soul 138; masculine/feminine archetypes 24–5; masochism 107; 'S' curve/serpent analogy 191–2, 198–9; sensibility of surface 48, 193–4; the unconscious 25–31

Demeter/Kore/Persephone myth 110–24, *122*

democracy 81–2, 93, 146

depression 160, 187

Derrida, J. 97, 206

'dividualized' identity 188

double-sided sublime 109

doux commerce principle 165

dream interpretation 28

dream-symbols 40–1

dualism concept 16–17

duration space 198

elemental symbols 48–9

Eleusinian Mysteries 119

embodied experiential 108

Empire (Hardt, Negri) 182

enantiodromia phenomenon: anatomy of 140–56, *141*, *144*, *147*, *154*; biopolitics and 210; channeling the feminine 121, 140, 150; defined 84–5; fascination with feminine 88; overview 49, 121

enlightened state 34

Enlightenment period 88

Eros (Luna): Ariadne myth 204; of capitalism 162–3; conscious assimilation of 94; creation of 122–3; erotic economics 161–3; as essence/essential 20; ethic of care approach 102; feminine/masculine archetypes 8, 46–7; Freud's conception of 160, 161; imposed on by *Logos* 93; as interval 110–24, *122*; Jungian definitions of 17, 75, 188–9; *Logos vs.* 163–79; as uncontained 108

erotic economics: *Eros* and 161–3; *Eros vs. Logos* 163–79; introduction 160–1

esotericism 33–61, *36*

'eternally unique' symbology 113
European consciousness 140
'everywhereness' of semiocapitalism 188
experimentation process 34–5

fascism 70–1
the feminine, channeling: anatomy of
enantiodromia 140–56, *141, 144,
147, 154*; Baroque/Rococo periods
135–40, *139*; as compensatory
aesthetic force 132–4; conclusion
156–7; introduction 131–2
feminine archetypes: cultural economy
of 193; *Eros* 8, 46–7; Jung, Carl
5–6, 17–18; sexual difference and
24–5; virgin archetype 114–15
feminine energy: channeling of 57,
132; conception of desire 143;
conscious recognition of 63–4;
as containment/transformation
references 49, 98, 119, 193;
contra-sexual nature of the psyche
163; as *Eros* 102, 104; introduction
7–8, 11–14, 19, 21; material
consequences with 140; 'order
in chaos' and 197; repression of
88; rising tide 143, 164–5; sexual
differences and 24; struggle for
liberty' 136; transformative feminine
117–19; unconscious energies 146
feminine subjectivity 4, 116–17
feminization of culture 145–6
Finnegan's Wake (Joyce) 195
Fordism 184
Foucault, Michel 15, 91
4EA (embodied-embedded-extended-
enactive-affective) approach 100
Fragonard, Jean Honoré 138–9, *139*
Frankfurt School 71
French feminism 6
French Orientalism 210
French Revolution 140, 149, 156–7
Freud, Sigmund: containment/
transformation 105–6; libidinal
energy 25–7; pleasure principles
188; repression of pleasure 160;
the unconscious 28

Gallé, Emile 133
Gatens, M. 56–7

de Goncourt, Edmond 131–4, 142–3,
151–2
Good Design aesthetic 12, 135–6, 148,
155
Great Mother 118, 120
The Great Mother (Neumann) 48
Greenberg, Clement 10, 176
Grosz, E. 56–60
Guattari, F. 8, 25, 108–9, 119–20

Hannah, Barbara 41
Hardt, M. 182–3, 188
hermaphrodite 35–8, *36*, 116, 195
Heroism 13
hierosgamos concept 52
Hirschman, A. 164–5, 172
Hogarth, W. 137, 191–3, 198–9
Homo oeconomicus 172
homosexual relationships 38
horizontal labyrinth conception 209
hyperreality 185
hyper-sensationalism 189–90
hysteria 160

idea notion 29–30
identity creation 185
imaginary bodies 56–7
immanent power *(potentia)* 90
individual-centred model of rights
205
individuation 31–3
intermezzo space 8, 109, 163, 204
intra-action concept 75–6
Irigaray, L. 116–17, 119

Judaism 166–7, 169
Judeo-Christian patriarchy 105, 198
Jung, Carl: archetypal feminine/
masculine 5–6, 17–18; Ariadne myth
204–5, 208–9; collective archetypes
39–41; Demeter/Kore/Persephone
myth 110–24, *122*; *enantiodromia*
84–5; individuation 31–3; intra-
action concept 75–6; Oriental
wisdom 63; sensibility of surface
48; subtle body 8; *temenos* concept
120–1; the unconscious 25–31;
unconscious regressions 106; vital
energy concept 162; *see also* life as
a rhizome

Index

Kantian definition of aesthetics 77
Kerényi, Karl 119, 120
Keynesian economics 20, 173–4, 177–8
Knox, Jean 19, 98, 121

labyrinth notion of the soul 138
Lacan, Jacques 40–1, 59, 64n1, 80–3, 110–14
Lacanian perspective of ideology 6, 80–2
Lacanian Real 30, 81–2
Lacanian Symbolic 81
laissez-faire capitalism 85, 171
Lajer-Burcharth, E. 151–2
Lambert, G. 137
Law of the Father 112, 114
libidinal energy (libido): conclusion 64; erotic desire and 160; esotericism 33–61, 36; individuation 31–3; introduction 24–5; negotiating identity 61–4; the unconscious 25–31
life as a rhizome, metaphor: introduction 182–3; neo-Baroque 190–3; postmodern structure of feeling 183–90; re-visioning *Eros* 193–9
Logos (Sol): as archetypal masculine 8; Ariadne myth 204; of capitalism 162–3; conscious assimilation of 94; *Eros vs.* 163–79; ethic of care approach 102; hyper-sensationalism 189–90; imposing on *Eros* 93; Jungian definitions of 17, 75

Mandeville, B. 170–1
Mantz, Paul 147–8
Marat, Jean-Paul 149
Marcuse, H. 161, 172, 196
Marx, Karl 3–4, 172–3, 175
masculine archetypes: *Eros (Luna)* 8, 46–7; Jung, Carl 5–6, 17–18; renunciation and 11, 86; sexual difference and 24–5
masochism 104–5, 107
materialist political-economy perspective 149
Matisse, Henri 10
mauvais goût (bad taste) 140–1

microfemininity concept 26
minoritarian status of woman 54
Mitropoulos, A. 189–90
mob behaviour *see* collective complexes
Modernism (Modern aesthetic) 12–14, 177
moeurs douces (gentle manners) 63, 165
moralism 165, 173, 178, 186
Morris, W. 174–6
mother/child relationship 97–8
Multitude (Hardt, Negri) 182

National Socialism in Germany 84
negotiating identity 61–4
Negri, A. 90–4, 123, 182–3, 188
neo-Baroque 190–3
neo-classicism 146, 172
neo-Marxism 71
Neumann, Erich 48, 98, 119
neurasthenia 160
neuronal networks 99
New Man 148
New Urbanism 185–7
New Woman 148
nomadic nature of desire 90
Nordau, Max 133–4
noumena, defined 74

Oedipal myth 52, 106, 110, 112
Orientalism 10–11, 63, 169
othering process 63

Pankhurst, Emmeline 69–71, 73
participation mystique 116
Pauli, Wolfgang 42, 196
penis envy 4
performance principle 161
phallic symbols 41, 110–12
phenomena, defined 74
physical mirroring 98–9
pleasure principle 173
Pocock, J.G.A. 163–4
point de capiton concept 40, 81–3, 87
Poiret, Paul 10–11, 153
Polanyi, Karl 85–6, 93, 103, 207
political economy of unconscious: aesthetics and sexual difference 10–21, 11; capitalism and 72;

introduction 3–9; materialist political-economy perspective 149; Venus idea 80–95
polysemy process 100
postmodern architecture 183–4
Postmodernism 14
postmodern structure of feeling 183–90
post-traumatic stress disorder 160
power/domination in society 91–2, 103
primal matter 35
psyche: archetypal symbols and 41–2; bisexual psyche 44–5, 49; contra-sexual nature of 163
'psychoid' functions 28–9
puritanism 166–7, 169, 171

'quasi-transcendental' status 111

Rancière, J. 18–19, 77
religious restraints on love 168
repression of pleasure 160
re-visioning *Eros* 193–9
Richardson, Mary 'Slasher' 69–71, 73, 74, 80
Rococo period: channeling the feminine during 131, 134; genealogy of 63; horizontal labyrinth conception 209; introduction 12, 14–15, 19–20; as *mauvais goût* (bad taste) 140–1
Rodin, Auguste 133
Rosarium Philosophorum (1550) 37
Ruskin, J. 174

Sacher-Masoch, L. 103–7
Saisselin, R. 140–2, 148
satori goal 29, 31
schizoanalysis 8, 25
schizophrenia 160
Schwartz-Salant, N. 116
'S' curve/serpent analogy 191–2, 198–9
self agency 98–101
semiocapitalism 187, 188, 192–3
sensuous pleasure and capitalism 168–9, 196
sensus communis 69, 77–9, 87

sexual differences: aesthetics and 10–21, *11*; masculine/feminine archetypes 24–5; negotiating identity 61–4; phallic symbols 41, 110–11; *a priori* understanding of 61, 73–4; during the Terror 132
Siegelman, P. 169
simulacra 184
'slaying the dragon' 116
Smith, Adam 171–2
socialism 175
Sombart, Werner 165–9, 173
The Spectator newspaper 169–70
sublime world 108–9
subtle body 8, 37
symbolic feminine 51, 73, 76

Taoism 63, 84, 86
temenos concept 120–1
A Thousand Plateaus (Deleuze, Guattari) 182
Through the Looking Glass (Carroll) 194
transformative feminine 117–19

the unconscious 80–95, 207

Velázquez, Diego 69–73, *70*, 74, 104
Venus 69–80, *70*, 80–95
Venus in Furs (Sacher-Masoch) 103–6, 148
Venus with the Mirror (Titian) 104
virgin archetype 114–15
vital energy concept 162
volupté (sensual pleasure) 63, 142–3

Weber, Max 165–7, 178
Wicke, J. 176
Wölfflin, P. 135
Wollen, P. 10–11
Wollstonecraft, Mary 131–2, 143, 148
Woolf, Virginia 176–7

Young-Eisendrath, P. 62, 111–12

Zen Buddhism 86
Zizek, S. 6–7, 80–2, 87–8

Taylor & Francis eBooks

Helping you to choose the right eBooks for your Library

Add Routledge titles to your library's digital collection today. Taylor and Francis ebooks contains over 50,000 titles in the Humanities, Social Sciences, Behavioural Sciences, Built Environment and Law.

Choose from a range of subject packages or create your own!

Benefits for you
- Free MARC records
- COUNTER-compliant usage statistics
- Flexible purchase and pricing options
- All titles DRM-free.

Benefits for your user
- Off-site, anytime access via Athens or referring URL
- Print or copy pages or chapters
- Full content search
- Bookmark, highlight and annotate text
- Access to thousands of pages of quality research at the click of a button.

Free Trials Available
We offer free trials to qualifying academic, corporate and government customers.

eCollections – Choose from over 30 subject eCollections, including:

Archaeology	Language Learning
Architecture	Law
Asian Studies	Literature
Business & Management	Media & Communication
Classical Studies	Middle East Studies
Construction	Music
Creative & Media Arts	Philosophy
Criminology & Criminal Justice	Planning
Economics	Politics
Education	Psychology & Mental Health
Energy	Religion
Engineering	Security
English Language & Linguistics	Social Work
Environment & Sustainability	Sociology
Geography	Sport
Health Studies	Theatre & Performance
History	Tourism, Hospitality & Events

For more information, pricing enquiries or to order a free trial, please contact your local sales team: www.tandfebooks.com/page/sales

Routledge
Taylor & Francis Group

The home of Routledge books

www.tandfebooks.com